THE COMICS OF CHARLES SCHULZ

Critical Approaches to Comics Artists
David Ball, Series Editor

THE COMICS OF
CHARLES SCHULZ
The Good Grief of Modern Life

Edited by Jared Gardner and Ian Gordon

University Press of Mississippi • Jackson

www.upress.state.ms.us

Designed by Peter D. Halverson

The University Press of Mississippi is a member of the Association of
American University Presses.

First printing 2017

∞

Library of Congress Cataloging-in-Publication Data available

Cloth	978-1-4968-1289-6
Epub single	978-1-4968-1290-2
Epub institutional	978-1-4968-1291-9
PDF single	978-1-4968-1292-6
PDF institutional	978-1-4968-1293-3

British Library Cataloging-in-Publication Data available

This volume is dedicated to Jean Schulz, in profound gratitude for all she does for the preservation of her late husband's legacy and on behalf of comics.

CONTENTS

PEANUTS AND HISTORY

TRANSMEDIAL PEANUTS

THE COMICS OF CHARLES SCHULZ

INTRODUCTION

JARED GARDNER AND IAN GORDON

There is in the history of American comics no strip more beloved or more familiar. *Peanuts*, it seems, has always been there. This holds especially true for the baby boomer generation. Beginning in October 1950 and still appearing in reruns seventeen years after the death of its creator, the strip is a hallmark of the second half of the twentieth century. Indeed, it is impossible to imagine newspaper comics pages without *Peanuts*, and even as newspapers themselves face the prospect of demise, it is clear that Schulz's creation will persist—as it does already—in new media for generations to come. If anything, *Peanuts* seems to be going through a period of growth in the twenty-first century. For example, 2015 saw the release of *The Peanuts Movie*, with a new animated TV series debuting in 2016. And the Seattle firm Fantagraphics has recently completed its publication of the complete *Peanuts*, collecting the entire strip run for the first time—with the introduction to the final volume in the series written by none other than President Barack Obama. "Like millions of Americans, I grew up with *Peanuts*," Obama writes, "[b]ut I never outgrew it."[1]

As Garrison Keillor said: "[T]here is not much in *Peanuts* that is shallow or heedless."[2] Schulz famously wrote and drew the entire run of the strip himself without the aid of an assistant. For the best part of fifty years, after Schulz introduced a Sunday strip in 1952, he produced a comic strip every day. By contrast to this artisanal crafting of the strip, its impact grew to massive proportions, and at its height it appeared in 2,600 newspapers worldwide in an array of languages. Moreover, along with televised animated specials came a vast number of licensing and endorsement deals. While it might be tempting to see this state of affairs, with the disparity between the small scale of the strip's production and its massive commercialization, as contradictory, it may be better to see it as one of the last vestiges of the Horatio Alger type of classic American

3

success story. A hardworking midwesterner, the son of a hardworking barber, works diligently, retains his pride in work and his individuality throughout a long career, and enjoys spectacular success. Except, of course, Schulz's strip is so often about failure or thwarted desire, somehow having resisted ever becoming self-satisfied or complacent.

The strip has inspired countless acts of devotion over the decades. The director Wes Anderson, for example, includes allusions to Charlie Brown in all his films, and the series *Arrested Development* channeled the strip repeatedly in its first three seasons. Among the many cartoonists who cite *Peanuts* as a primary influence on their own careers are Bill Watterson, Gilbert Hernandez, Matt Groening, Paige Braddock, and Keith Knight. Indeed, the list could easily fill up an entire volume on its own, which is a major reason why it has always been easy to get cartoonists to write or talk about *Peanuts* for one of the many tribute volumes published over the decades, or for each of the twenty-five volumes of Fantagraphics' collected *Peanuts*, whose introductions are written by such comics luminaries as Lynn Johnston, Garry Trudeau, and Tom Tomorrow.

Given the impact of *Peanuts* and its unparalleled influence on the history of American cartooning over the past sixty-seven years, one might expect a treasure trove of academic scholarship on Schulz's creation. But the truth is in fact very different. Even as the comics form has belatedly entered academic discourse in the most recent generation with a growing number of essays and books devoted to the graphic novel and to the history and analysis of everything from the American superhero comic book to Japanese manga to Franco-Belgian *bande dessinée*, the number of peer-reviewed academic volumes and scholarly essays dedicated to *Peanuts* over the past twenty years can likely be counted on two hands.

There are several reasons for this, including the fact that newspaper comics more broadly have suffered considerable academic neglect in favor of the graphic novel and its cousins during this period. However, here a comparison to George Herriman's *Krazy Kat* is illuminating. As Michael Tisserand makes clear in his contribution to this volume, Herriman's strip was an important influence on Schulz's own, and while it never achieved the popularity of *Peanuts*, it was embraced as early as the 1920s as the prime example of the artistic potential of the comics form. Today, Herriman's strip is a frequent topic of academic analysis in papers and published essays, easily outpacing all rivals as the most analyzed newspaper strip in contemporary comics studies.

Part of the explanation for this disparity lies with Schulz himself and his unflagging refusal to be labeled an "artist." In large measure, in declining such labels, Schulz was doing no more than fellow comic strip creators had done since the origins of the form. After all, newspaper comic strips are a form of mass entertainment, designed for the whole family's appreciation, for people from every walk of life. Their survival depended in no small part on not offending readers and editors, and on speaking simultaneously to readers coming to the strip for different reasons. *Krazy Kat* and *Peanuts* both did this exceptionally well, and both Herriman and Schulz ignored the courtship of the intellectual classes who would read deeper meanings into their work.

But even as Herriman fluently talked the talk of the humble crafts-man, he was simultaneously traveling in the orbits of high modernism and the avant-garde such that his protestations always seemed to carry with them a wink for the "knowing" reader. When Herriman raised his hands in wonder, as he did with one fan in search of deeper meanings, at "your strange interest in my efforts," one sensed an aw-shucks perfor-mance that was intended to be dismissed *as* performance.[3] Not so with Charles Schulz. When he insisted that "it is important to me . . . to make certain that everyone knows that I do not regard what I am doing as Great Art," he meant it. He identified most strongly with craftspeople—people like his father, who ran a barbershop in Saint Paul for almost as long as the son would "run" his strip. Or like any one of the members of the adult world he saw coming into his father's shop:

> When I finish the last drawing of the day and drop the pencil in the tray, put down the pen and brush and put the top on the ink bottle, it always reminds me of the dentist when he puts his instruments down on the tray and reaches to turn off the light.[4]

For Schulz, there is nothing disingenuous in this self-identification, no wink that encourages the scholar to say for him what he could not say for himself.

And here we come to the heart of the problem—although it is, we suspect, a problem that lies with academic scholarship and not with the strip that scholars both adore and ignore in equal measure. The themes we read about in *Peanuts*—the profound existential concerns about loneliness, love, faith, and grief—are there for the taking. No advanced degree or theoretical apparatus is required. Where Herriman's *Krazy Kat* makes us work for much of what we take away beyond the perverse erotic triangle at its core, *Peanuts* seems to offer its riches *too* easily, too democratically for an academic scholarship built on the fetishization of "rigor" and intellectual priestcraft. A strip that offers its profundities so freely might well be art, but it is not the kind of art scholars often know what to do with. Making the situation all the more discouraging for the scholar, we have here an archive whose primary text alone is made up of almost eighteen thousand individual strips, and it is not hard to see why the self-contained and often "difficult" graphic novel has garnered the lion's share of critical attention in recent years.

This volume serves in part as a manifesto for some of the myriad things that we can do with *Peanuts*. We offer essays in four broad categories: philosophy and poetics, identity and performance, history, and transmedia. Casting Schulz as a philosopher might seem presumptuous, but the matters he dealt with in his strips readily fit philosophical domains like rationalism, phenomenology, hermeneutics, epistemology, metaphysics, ethics, aesthetics, ontology, and existentialism. Ben Saunders argues for Schulz as a philosopher of desire. He reminds us that Schulz visited the topic of human longing and resulting disappointment many times over. We need only to think of Lucy constantly sabotaging Charlie Brown's attempts to kick a football to conjure Schulz's dealings with the subject. Through a close reading of several episodes featuring Peppermint Patty unpacking her desires and frustrations, Saunders offers a queer reading of *Peanuts*. Anne McCarthy takes up the football gags and reveals them as moments of sublimity. She argues that these episodes show Charlie Brown's capacity to understand the limits of meaning and reason. Roy Cook reads the different nonstandard notational forms Schulz employed, for example nonstandard fonts for lettering and musical notes and scores, to render jokes in different fashions. In doing so, Schulz called attention to the formal conventions of comics even while transgressing those norms. Cook points to the multilayered readings Schulz's use of music allowed and argues that these pushed the strip beyond the mundane to the area of art, no matter how much Schulz himself downplayed his achievements.

Much of *Peanuts* is about sorting out, imagining, establishing, or performing an identity. Snoopy as the World War I fighter ace atop his doghouse, and as the big man on campus Joe Cool, are two exemplary moments of such imaginings. Lara Saguisag examines how *Peanuts* addressed changing conceptions of childhood after World War II. Saguisag places *Peanuts* at the center of a set of issues concerning the nature of childhood and social anxiety about the impact of a burgeoning consumer culture. Fears about the erosion of childhood, and with it the innocence

of children, went hand in hand with worries about the impact of afflu-
ence. She argues that while Schulz gave children some autonomy in his
strip, this was limited, and the implied presence of adults reigned in
worries about loss of authority. Importantly, *Peanuts* performed a reas-
suring version of childhood for the adult readers of comic strips. Leonie
Brialey discusses Schulz's handling of sincerity in *Peanuts*. As her essay
makes clear, the issues of sincerity and authenticity were very much in
play in American society from the 1950s to the 1970s, and indeed Lionel
Trilling devoted a book to just that subject. And *Peanuts*, the first episode
of which eloquently captured the issue of sincerity by moving in three
panels from "Good Ol' Charlie Brown . . . Yes Sir!" to "How I hate him,"
offered numerous opportunities to meditate on the issue of sincerity
and insincerity. From Lucy's ball snatching to Linus's belief in the Great
Pumpkin, the strip provoked thought on our need and hopes for sincerity
in others and the profound recognition of its absence and even the problems of its presence. Jeffrey Segrave observes that sports in *Peanuts* is a
locus for much of the strip's engagement with the seemingly mundane
aspects of life that so often reverberate for the individual at profound
levels. Segrave points out that *Peanuts* reverses the standard winning
narrative of sports stories and engages with what for most of us is the
far more familiar experience of losing. *Peanuts* does not just offer solace
to a sporting inept like Charlie Brown; it celebrates the joy of playing.

Michael Tisserand opens the section on history with an examination
of the influence of Herriman's *Krazy Kat* on *Peanuts*. At first glance, the
strips look and feel completely different from each other. *Krazy Kat* is
rendered with an expressive line, its action playing out against a dynamic
landscape of shadow and shimmering sun, while *Peanuts* is drawn with
a flowing clean line against a spare background dominated by negative
space and minimalist details. *Krazy* takes place in the surrealist desert
land of Coconino County, while *Peanuts* takes place in a suburban community that could be almost anywhere in America. Yet, as Tisserand demonstrates, from the iconic design on Charlie Brown's shirt to some of the
most important and long-running gags in the strip's history, Herriman's
influence on this understudied genealogy help us newly understand what
Schulz was after with *Peanuts*.

In his contribution, Joseph Darowski focuses on Schulz's commentaries—both direct and indirect—on the often tumultuous history of the
late 1960s through the character of Snoopy. While Snoopy's growing
prominence in the strip is sometimes cited by fans of the earlier strip as a

symptom of the strip's declining power, Darowski argues that Snoopy was a vital tool for Schulz to engage with current events. In Snoopy's imaginary journey to the moon, for example, Schulz commented obliquely on how even this triumphant moment of human achievement became mired in the provincial politics of the Cold War, just as in Snoopy's ongoing battles with the Red Baron Darowski identifies commentary on the futility and failures of the Vietnam War. Christopher Lehman's essay focuses on Franklin, the strip's first African American character, whom Schulz primarily utilized to help in the development of Charlie Brown's character and the integration of Peppermint Patty into the strip. Nonetheless, Franklin in the early 1970s briefly emerged as a central character in his own right both as a symbol of the ideal of integrationism and as a surrogate character through whom Schulz was able to meditate on his own experiences as a new grandfather.

The volume's final section, "Transmedial *Peanuts*," considers the life of Charlie Brown and the gang outside of the newspaper comic strip—in the animated specials, the marketplace for original art, and global franchising. Ben Novotny Owen argues that *Peanuts* provided the ideal content for early TV animation precisely because Schulz had already honed, within his strips, an expressive range within a graphically simple idiom that worked perfectly with the animation style director Bill Melendez had learned during his decade at United Productions of America (UPA). In addition to the flat, graphic style shared by *Peanuts* and the postwar UPA cartoons, the two also had thematic concerns in common, including the de-emphasis on violence, the use of recognizable human characters, and the interest in exploring issues of isolation and conformity that made the marriage between the two so successful and influential.

M. J. Clarke's contribution examines the secondary market for original art used in the production of *Peanuts*, arguing that the traffic in Schulz's work is demonstrative of a new and growing market for American art in which value is established through the iconicity of its subject matter, complicating current sociological theories of the business of art and the cultivation of taste. Ian Gordon presents a study of the franchising of *Peanuts* restaurants and theme park attractions in Asia, where Schulz's creation is perhaps best known through the animated specials and not the newspaper comics. Gordon examines the appeal of Charlie Brown and Snoopy in Asia with particular reference to the cafés and clientele they attract, utilizing observational studies at cafés in various cities as well as food blogs and restaurant reviews. Gordon argues that franchisees in

Asia have successfully made the characters available to audiences who would not necessarily connect to their American postwar aesthetic or themes by focusing on the qualities of *kawaii*—or "cuteness"—increasingly sought out in Asian popular culture. Finally, Gene Kannenberg concludes the volume with an analysis of the contemporary parodies Schulz's masterpiece has inspired.

As the broad interdisciplinary range of the contributions to this volume should make clear, *Peanuts* offers countless possibilities for study and analysis, and we hope that this volume serves as an invitation to a new generation of scholars and students. As *Peanuts* continues to speak to readers born after the strip ended its run and as its global influence continues to spread, there is a wealth of material in the strip that cries out for scholarly attention. It is reasonably safe to say that all the chapters in this volume could easily form the basis of a separate monograph and/or a whole volume of essays. At the very least, the impact of *Peanuts* on other artists begs for more critical study. Likewise, *Peanuts'* place in American culture demands further inquiry, as does its global reach. Much has been written about American soft power in a globalized world: is there any softer American figure than Snoopy? For many years, scholars who studied comics felt a need to justify their interest and pursuit. Without being too prescriptive, we feel that perhaps scholars might now need to justify their lack of attention to *Peanuts*, one of the quintessential comics experiences of twentieth-century American—and indeed global—culture.

NOTES

1. Barack Obama, introduction to *The Complete Peanuts: 1999–2000*, by Charles M. Schulz (Seattle: Fantagraphics, 2016), x.

2. Garrison Keillor, introduction to *The Complete Peanuts: 1950–1952*, by Charles M. Schulz (Seattle: Fantagraphics, 2004), xi.

3. Quoted in Patrick McDonnell, Karen O'Connell, and Georgia Riley de Havenon, *Krazy Kat: The Comic Art of George Herriman* (New York: Harry N. Abrams, 1986), 25. As Herriman continued: "[Y]es sir I can't add it up at all—It must be something *you* give to it."

4. Quoted in Charles M. Schulz, *My Life with Charlie Brown*, ed. M. Thomas Inge (Jackson: University Press of Mississippi, 2010), xiii.

PHILOSOPHY AND POETICS

PEPPERMINT PATTY'S DESIRE

Charles Schulz and the Queer Comics of Failure

BEN SAUNDERS

To describe Charles Schulz as a success in his profession is to court under-statement. It's therefore ironic that his most reliable source of inspiration over the course of his half-century-long career is failure: failure at sports, academic failure, romantic failure, even the experience of being failed by one's idols.[1] Despite this tendency to depict life as a parade of de-feats, however, Schulz was no simple depressive. Failure is an ontological given of his universe, but it is always experienced from within a complex economy of desire. Indeed, the relationship between the persistence of desire and the impossibility of satisfaction is as significant for Schulz as it is for Freud or Lacan (and the contemporary theorists who continue to wrestle with those thinkers). It is not merely that Schulz displays an acute sensitivity to the paradoxical notion that desire must be frustrated in order to be sustained—although he does, alongside an equal aware-ness of the related notion that a measure of misery is necessary for the concept of happiness to be meaningful. He is also profoundly aware that our desires are never fully available to us: they can be inchoate, deceptive, mysterious, and surprising. He grasps instinctively that desire is inextri-cably bound up in psychological structures of misrecognition, as well as social structures of division and exclusion, and he skillfully exploits these structures for their tragicomic potential. Consequently, while Schulz was not a philosopher in the recognized sense, many of his comics cry out to be read as witty meditations on the mutual interdependence of desire and disappointment. In this chapter, then, I explore the interconnections between desire, frustration, misrecognition, and exclusion as played out in Schulz's work. Rather than focusing on Schulz's most obvious arche-type of longing and losing, the existentialist everyman named Charlie

Brown, I approach Schulz's central question—the question of why we can't always (or maybe ever) get what we want—through the character of Peppermint Patty. In the process, I hope to show that Schulz's *Peanuts* is not only a brilliantly intelligent work of popular culture but also a less than fully appreciated site of antinormative impulses and genderqueer inclusivity: a counterhegemonic comic of ideas, in fact.[2]

Like Charlie Brown, Peppermint Patty is readily legible in archetypal terms. Where he is a classic "sad sack" or permanent loser, she is a classic tomboy. But this archetypal aspect also makes Patty slightly more complex than Charlie Brown when it comes to a discussion of desire and its vicissitudes. As a number of critics have observed, the tomboy represents a paradigmatic instance of "female masculinity"—a historically marginalized category of identity that cannot be contained within the binary conception of gender difference dominant in so many of our institutions (including our institutions of aesthetic and cultural criticism).[3] Jack Halberstam, for example, elucidates the multiple forms of female masculinity, both as a critical tool and a way of being in the world, as follows:

> Sometimes female masculinity coincides with the excesses of male supremacy, and sometimes it codifies a unique form of social rebellion; often female masculinity is a sign of sexual alterity, but occasionally it marks heterosexual variation; sometimes female masculinity marks the place of pathology, and every now and then it represents the healthful alternative to what are considered the histrionics of conventional femininities.[4]

Halberstam's larger point is not merely that female masculinity has many modes and meanings but that the sheer irreducibility of the concept may help us "explore a queer subject position that can successfully challenge hegemonic models of gender conformity."

Academic criticism to date has not considered Peppermint Patty in these terms, but her queer potentiality has attracted plenty of attention in the culture at large. A cursory Google search, for example, turns up examples of femslash fanfic devoted to the exploration of Patty's relationship with Marcie in their adolescent years.[5] A similar search of the DeviantArt website yields a wealth of visual material: numerous depictions of Patty and Marcie as romantic partners ranging in content from the subtle to the explicit and employing a wide variety of artistic techniques, from pastiches of Schulz's style to manga-inspired renderings of the characters as teenagers to soft-edged color-pencil portraits of them as adults. Speculation about Patty's sexual orientation can also be traced in the more mainstream world of network television on such shows as *The Simpsons*, *Family Guy*, and *The Big Bang Theory*.[6] Still more recently and significantly, the July 10, 2015, issue of *Entertainment Weekly* used an image of Peppermint Patty and Marcie in reference to the landmark Supreme Court decision granting same-sex unions constitutional protection.[7] For the editors of this pop-culture news magazine, Patty and Marcie were (quite literally) the poster children for gay marriage.

Vikki Reich, a writer on issues of lesbian life at the blog Up Popped a Fox, also outed Patty and Marcie in a brief analysis of the TV special *A Charlie Brown Thanksgiving*.[8] Although Reich's reading could be regarded as somewhat belated, her blog and the comments that it inspired serve as a usefully extended example of an interpretive community engaging with the business of queering works of popular culture. Her essay concludes with a prophecy regarding the events proceeding from Patty's eventual discovery of her lesbian orientation:

> I predict Peppermint Patty and Marcie went to college, got drunk after a softball game and made out. They both immediately realized that they had been in love all along. After graduation, they moved to Portland, Oregon, rented a small house and got a black lab. Marcie is getting an advanced degree in library science and Peppermint Patty became a gym teacher.

The majority of Reich's respondents find her thesis persuasive, although some run the ball in different directions.[9] "I kind of hope Marcie ends up with a high femme who likes to take care of her," says one. "She's been kowtowing to P[eppermint] P[atty] for far too long now." Another initiates a short but thought-provoking discussion on whether Patty is actually "unknowingly transgender," concluding with the following observation:

> The thing I like most about PP is that ze DOES break the gender mold, even if ze's "cast" into another label to do so. Kids are only recently aware enough of QUILTBAGs to question whether ze's a lesbian, or a boy. I don't know when I caught on to the shared interpretation of hir as gay and I know my "waitaminute, trans?" realization was very recent, but as a kid I just thought it was COOL that SHE got called SIR.

Fig. 1.1: Charles Schulz, *Peanuts*, August 22, 1966. PEANUTS © 1966 Peanuts Worldwide LLC. Dist. by UNIVERSAL UCLICK. Reprinted with permission. All rights reserved.

If nothing else, Halberstam's general claim that popular representations of female masculinity can challenge the proscriptive gender norms of the dominant culture is confirmed by Reich and her respondents. Clearly, Peppermint Patty has been a locus of queer and transgender identification within an overtly straight popular media franchise for some years now. But what else can we learn from these acts of identification, once we have recognized them as such? If Schulz's *Peanuts* can be read as a queer or genderqueer text (and obviously it can), then where might a more sustained interpretation take us?

In my opinion, to think about *Peanuts* from the perspective of queer theory is to open the door upon a whole set of new readings of this ubiquitous, resonant, and beautiful work of American popular culture. I can only offer a preliminary sketch of such a project in this short chapter; but I will begin with a close reading of Patty's very first appearance, from August 22, 1966. First, let's be clear about the specifically *visual* challenge Schulz set himself when he decided to create a cartoon character who would at once refuse to adopt the normative behaviors and trappings of femininity while simultaneously remaining recognizably female to the casual reader. Schulz's technique tends toward minimalism and reduction: it was part of his genius that he could convey a wide variety of actions and moods with the simplest shapes and lines, and an astonishing range of emotional expressions with just a few dots and squiggles from his crow-quill pen. But this very talent for abstraction also led him to rely on emblematic details of clothing and haircut in his figure work in order to signify gender distinction and ethnic variance. This reliance is readily apparent if we pause to consider Schulz's cast members before Peppermint Patty's arrival: Shermy, with his severe crew cut; Schroeder and Linus, with their simple striped T-shirts and black short pants; Violet, with her long hair in either a ponytail or a bun; Lucy, with her dark locks, shoulder ruffs, and wide skirt (which has a wonderfully rigid, unbending quality, perhaps marking her out as the most aggressively "phallic" if not the most gender ambiguous of Schulz's girls); Sally, with her slightly impossible combination of waves and curls (a cartoon hyper-femme hairstyle if ever there was one); Frieda, with her "naturally curly" bouffant; and so on. With these accouterments, there was little chance of confusion with regard to the gender designations of these characters.

Looking again at Peppermint Patty's first appearance—and taking no cues from the dialogue for a moment, but focusing on the drawings alone—we can see Schulz pushing against the standard conventions of his idiom and resisting the emblematic tendencies of his own personal style to make sure that Patty's gender is ambiguous. Certainly, her clothes are not designed to provide any overt signals of gender; her short-sleeved and collared shirt is indistinguishable in cut from Roy's, and with her lower half obscured by a table we can't know if she is wearing a skirt or pants. (This matter would be resolved the following day, when Patty is shown wearing a pair of striped running pants and her soon-to-be-familiar default footwear, sandals.) Her hair adds to rather than resolves the potential for confusion: more unkempt than would be considered typical for a girl, it is nevertheless perhaps longer than would be typical for a boy.

A similar ambiguity around issues of identity, both in gendered and racial terms, also appears to have communicated itself to Patty's companion on the page, Roy. Roy was also a fairly new character at that time, introduced by Schulz the previous year. (Charlie Brown first meets Roy at summer camp; Roy expresses feelings of isolation that mark him out to Charlie Brown as a friend.) In most of his prior appearances, Roy wears a hat or cap, but for this scene with Patty, Schulz renders him with almost an Afro-style crop of dark, curly hair—a style unlike that of any other character in the series to this point. As is well known, Schulz did not officially write an African American character into the *Peanuts* cast until the summer of 1968, when he introduced Franklin (a politically self-conscious decision that has been extensively discussed elsewhere).[10] But Schulz was clearly pondering the representation of race before that date, having introduced José Peterson, a Latino-Swedish boy, in March 1967, more than a year prior to Franklin's arrival. Roy, introduced in June 1965, predates both José and Franklin, and while I am unaware of any statements by the artist regarding Roy's ethnicity, I think that Schulz may well have intended to render the character in a manner that would not immediately signify as phenotypically white, in a quiet step toward greater diversity. But whatever Schulz's intent with regard to Roy's ethnicity, the character's hair also renders him (in comparison with Schulz's other male characters) more difficult to read from the point of view of gender. In fact, if we try to look at these two characters as if for the first time, then neither really conforms to a restrictively normative cartoon standard of gender representation. Although some may insist that what we see here is a girl talking to a boy, that perception has more to do with the expectations we bring to the comic than it does with any obvious gender indicators in the drawings themselves.

My point is not that Schulz consciously intended to confuse his audience about the gender identity (or ethnicity) of either character, but simply that this first appearance of one of his most original and popular creations fairly abounds with intriguing ambiguities once we start to look for them. We might even say that, by self-consciously attempting to avoid crudely emblematic signifiers of gender while still pursuing his basic technique of representational abstraction, Schulz has here discovered—or rediscovered—the essential queerness of all children (to adopt an idea that is in some ways at least as old as Freud, and that has been most influentially articulated in recent years by Kathryn Bond Stockton).[11] Reduced to representational abstractions, Schulz's "Li'l Folks" are no longer clearly marked as male or female, and as such they stand as scandalous evidence that our ideas about gender do not "naturally" derive from the prior ground of the material body but are culturally imposed upon it.[12]

What's more, while some of these ambiguities might seem to be resolved by the strip's dialogue, on closer examination we discover multiple possibilities of signification in Schulz's writing of the scene, too. The basic situation, as we immediately glean from the first panel, is a conversation between Patty and Roy, who is writing a letter to Linus. In the second panel, Patty asks whether Roy's pen pal is "cute," a question we are presumably meant to understand as an amusingly direct expression of a young person's sexual curiosity—which, given the social and political mores of the era, would overtly signify as straight, and which would therefore seem in context to mark the speaker as necessarily female. But even if we assume this heteronormative interpretive context, the immediacy and bluntness of Patty's question could be said to cut against traditional gender expectations regarding female modesty. Patty's apparent assertion of a "normal" heterosexual identity is thus at once reaffirmed and undercut.

This double process repeats itself more emphatically in the following panel, when Patty asks Roy to tell Linus "what a real swinger I am." Nowadays, the noun "swinger" is almost always used in a sexual sense, if it is used at all, either to indicate an individual member of a couple who participates in partner swapping or, more generally, to designate a person who enjoys a number of different sexual relationships without requiring exclusivity. Historically, the term has also suggested a proclivity for bisexuality—"swinging both ways," as an older, slangy idiom once phrased it. In the mid-1960s, however, the word "swinger" could also function more innocently to designate a "person who actively seeks excitement and moves with the latest trends" (to cite the *American Heritage Dictionary* entry on the term), although the sexual associations were also fully available. In context, Patty probably intends to describe herself as a fashionable thrill seeker and trendsetter rather than boldly declare her sexual interests. What's more, she appears to do so in order to appear more interesting to a boy: specifically, Roy's friend Linus, who remains as yet unknown to her. This bit of dialogue would therefore again seem to establish Patty's heterosexual bona fides. But for all that, it's hard to entirely repress the other associations of the term "swinger"—even though many readers might be uncomfortable with the suggestion that those associations form part of Patty's conscious self-understanding at this moment. The innuendo is thus both there and not there, an absent presence that cannot be articulated without some acknowledgment of its likely-not-intended-ness but that nevertheless permits us to recognize Patty as a potential sexual dissident—and, indeed, that allows us to make this identification without needing to insist that Patty makes any such claim for herself.

At the same time, Schulz *does* portray Patty as performing an act of self-recognition here—or perhaps, more accurately, an act of self-*misrecognition*—in a manner that makes the moment even more intriguing, and slightly poignant. Notice that her sentence about being a "real swinger" trails off into a wistful ellipsis. Taken in conjunction with her emotionally expressive posture—her head propped in her hands as she stares dreamily into the middle distance—and however we understand her delightfully overdetermined self-designation, Patty is having a fantasy about herself more than revealing any objective truth about her personality. Schulz thus lets us know that whatever Patty means by the word "swinger," it is something she only *wishes* she could be, or something she would like to be thought of as being, or even something that she might become in the future, but that she isn't . . . yet. Indeed, I would suggest that Schulz here attains a level of psychological subtlety that critics are only just beginning to acknowledge in works of cartoon art. The structure of Patty's subjective experience of desire across these four panels is certainly quite complicated and could be explicated in a manner that will not sound unfamiliar to readers of Lacan: Patty's desire is to be desired by the Other, and as a result she misrecognizes herself.[13]

The dialogue of the final panel emphasizes this act of misrecognition, to comic effect. We know from the third panel that Patty wants to be thought of as a swinger, an attractively fashionable figure. The take-home message of her confident assertion about her ability to trounce Roy at wrestling in the fourth panel, however, is not that she is a swinger but rather that she is competitively sporty. If she *were* identified as a boy, such statements would probably lead some of us to label her a jock. But it has never been particularly fashionable to be a female jock—sports being another realm in normative culture where gendered double standards seem impervious to critique—and so the gulf between Patty's desired self and the diegetic "reality" of the strip is brought home with this last line.[14] It is this disjunction between aspiration and actuality that makes the moment work as a beat (to utilize the metrical vocabulary of dramatic timing) and gives her closing sentence the weight of a punch line.

This, then, is Peppermint Patty's introduction to the world: a deft four-panel sequence that establishes her rejection of the stereotypically feminine attributes of passivity, weakness, and deference with admirable economy of characterization—and that at the same time manages to explore the ambiguities inherent in identity, desire, self-knowledge, and the very act of cartooning itself, to gentle comedic effect and with an extraordinary lightness of touch. The elaborations of the interpretive process almost inevitably feel like an imposition in relation to work of such deceptive simplicity—and I would not even claim this to be one of Schulz's greatest comics. But Patty would inspire Schulz further in the coming years, eventually leading him to produce some of his most poignant comedy and some of his most insightful ruminations on the persistence of desire and the inevitability of failure. In the remainder of this chapter, I'll discuss several of those subsequent strips, and in the process I will address what many see as a clinching argument *against* the queer interpretation of the character: the notion that Patty has a "crush" on Charlie Brown.

As Patty and Marcie have become increasingly cited in the popular media and culture as figures of genderqueer identification, other commentators have responded (often in backlash mode) that such interpretations are based on an inadequate knowledge of the source texts. "Patty clearly has feelings for Charlie Brown!" they say, "and so she cannot possibly be queer!"[15] Of course, it would be simple enough to point out in response that this argument rests upon the presumption that expressions of heteroerotic desire nullify the possibility of homoeroticism—a position that is entirely invalidated by history and experience—and then let things go at that. But if we look again at the actual comics without imposing the ideology of heteronormativity upon them, we discover that Schulz is up to something much more emotionally delicate and interesting. For while it is certainly the case that Patty has intense feelings that emerge in relation to Charlie Brown, they don't ever coalesce into anything quite as simple as a crush.

Schulz intermittently explores this complicated emotional dynamic in his daily and Sunday strips from the early spring of 1971 through the late summer of 1972.[16] Strikingly, throughout this entire period, Patty never expresses direct romantic interest in Charlie Brown and generally insists that she only likes "Chuck" as a friend. Most of the time, in her own mind, she is the object of *his* crush and not the other way around. In numerous strips, Schulz represents Patty as absolutely sincere in the conviction that "poor Chuck" has fallen for her, and as insisting (sometimes with unintentionally cruel vehemence) that she will never return his feelings. (See, for example, the dailies for March 11, 13, 15, and 16; May 31; and October 8, 1971.) At the same time, these dailies run alongside others in which Patty appears to be awkwardly flirting with Charlie Brown. There's often a special tenderness to these strips, many of which end with the line: "You kind of like me, don't you, Chuck?" But even here, Patty is shown *telling* Charlie Brown what *he* feels (her "don't you, Chuck?" is a rhetorical speech tag, not a question), not directly revealing her own feelings. Taken in conjunction with the apparent lack of affect Charlie Brown displays, despite the intense feelings Patty attributes to him (as in the particularly hilarious daily of March 12, 1971), the combined results do suggest that Patty is caught up in what psychologists diagnose as the logic of disavowal and displacement: first repressing her own unacknowledged feelings for her friend and then projecting those emotions onto him. However, the upshot is that Patty never expresses an uncomplicated heterosexual *desire* for Charlie Brown, instead exhibiting a much more complicated and nuanced form of *anxiety*. Of course, numerous commentators have taught us to think of desire and anxiety as close cousins, and I'm not suggesting that the presence of the latter somehow cancels out the former. My point is simply that Schulz's representation of Patty's feelings is much more subtle, complex, and ambiguous than the simple notion of a normatively comforting "girlish" crush could ever hope to convey.

What's more, he offers a quite different explication of Patty's emotional investment in Charlie Brown in the course of an extended narrative arc of dailies published between June 5 and June 24, 1972. Patty learns from Marcie that "the little red-haired girl," the true object of Charlie Brown's obsessive passion, is also attending their summer camp. Patty is immediately and frantically desperate to meet this girl, and runs to find her; in fact, her need to meet this legendary figure is so urgent that when Marcie refuses to point out the little red-haired girl in a crowd, Patty even threatens to "slug" her (June 9–14). We never actually see the little red-haired girl ourselves, of course—Schulz understands as well as any Lacanian that access to the object-cause of desire must be continually deferred if the desirability of that object-cause is to be sustained—but after a tantalizing delay the details of Patty's encounter with this transcendent creature are reported retrospectively by Patty herself to Linus in a series of strips from June 20 to 23. No words were exchanged at their meeting, we learn. Instead, Patty tells us: "I finally saw the little red-haired girl that Chuck is always talking about. And you know what I did? I cried, Linus . . . I cried and cried and cried" (June 21). We are told the reason for her tears the following day: "I stood in front of that little red-haired girl and I saw how pretty she was . . . Suddenly I realized why Chuck has always loved her, and I realized that no one would ever love me that way . . . I started to cry and I couldn't stop" (June 22). It's a genuinely heart-rending episode, but if we simply interpret Patty's breakdown as a belated acknowledgment of the fact that she really does have a crush on Chuck, we fail to grasp the source of the pathos. Although her language is simple, the structure of Patty's feelings is, again, more complex than it first appears.

Schulz has already made apparent in the dozens of delightful cartoons that lead up to this moment that Patty's feelings about Charlie Brown are a confused mixture of contempt, affection, and frustration; and nothing in this scene suggests that has changed. What pains her is not that she can no longer disavow her "true" feelings for him, but a sudden awareness of the gulf between the little red-haired girl and herself in terms of their relative desirability, according to the normative standards of feminine beauty. It's not even that she wants to exchange her looks for those of the little red-haired girl, however. What she wants is for *someone* to love her in the same way that Charlie Brown apparently loves the little red-haired girl, and her tears are provoked by a devastating wave of self-conscious angst at the idea that this will never happen. Her dialogue is quite clear in this regard: "I realized then that no one would ever love me that way." Her grief thus turns on the issue of *how* she wants to be desired, not *who* desires her; indeed, from that point of view, the implication is that almost anyone would do. What Patty desires, in other words, is not any particular person but a particular experience of desire itself—a longing with which anyone can at least potentially identify because it is neither uniquely heterosexual nor confined to the logic of gender binarism. The queer identification with Patty is therefore not based on an inadequate reading of Schulz's text; on the contrary, it both responds to and helps us to identify a much more nuanced portrayal of the workings of desire within those texts.

Schulz clearly had a profound empathy for the particular fear that Patty here expresses—the fear that one might be deemed unworthy of love—and this empathy was the wellspring for some of his most exquisite Sundays from this same period of his career. Throughout the early 1970s, Schulz produced a series of strips in which Patty and Charlie Brown sit under a tree and discuss the nature of love, like the protagonists of a pastoral poem (as in the comics of May 16, June 13, and October 3, 1971, and March 5, April 16, May 21, August 6, and September 17, 1972). Patty is rarely satisfied with "Chuck's" responses, of course, and her dissatisfaction is generally the source of the humor in these highly emotionally nuanced pieces, which often manage to be funny and painfully moving at once. Consider, for example, this little masterpiece from August 8, 1975. The effect of the scene is underwritten by Schulz's employment of psychological irony; we feel that we know things about the characters that are perhaps less than fully apparent to the characters themselves. Patty asks her friend to explain love; after (sensibly) admitting that he can't, he makes the mistake of positing a hypothetical situation involving a "cute little girl." We never learn where Charlie Brown plans on going with this hypothesis, however, because Patty clearly senses that if his story is about a "cute" girl, then it's *not* a story that will include her. This

Fig. 1.2: Charles Schulz, *Peanuts*, August 8, 1975. PEANUTS © 1975 Peanuts Worldwide LLC. Dist. by UNIVERSAL UCLICK. Reprinted with permission. All rights reserved.

awareness gives her next questions their special force: "Why does she have to be cute, Chuck? Huh? Can't someone fall in love with a girl who isn't cute, and has freckles and a big nose?" What we hear, here, is Patty saying without saying: "What about me, Chuck? Can't someone fall in love with *me*?" But at the same time, neither Patty nor Charlie Brown seem fully aware that Patty is talking about herself (even though we as readers are so aware); if they were, perhaps the conversation would have gone differently. From the beginning, the attempt to articulate the nature of desire has run aground on misrecognition.

Still, never one to quit when he is behind, Charlie Brown tries to address Patty's questions by introducing a girl with "a great big nose" into his story. But this makes things worse, because while Patty may want to know that she can be desirable, she doesn't want to be identified as an unattractive caricature. Throughout the strip, in fact, Patty does not express the wish to be anything other than what she feels herself to be—this is *not* self-loathing that we are seeing—she just wants to know why there doesn't seem to be a place for someone like herself in the allegory of desire that Charlie Brown is attempting to spin. But this time, her anxiety at the possibility that she is excluded from a normative economy of desirability manifests not as grief, but rage—a rage that ends the conversation and leads her to abandon her hopeless friend under the tree, ruefully wondering what went wrong.

Some might be tempted to conclude from comics like this that Peppermint Patty has become an object of queer identification because she is positioned as excluded from the structures of desire within the world of Schulz's comics. Certainly, those who identify as queer or/and transgender have every reason to be sensitive to the exclusions of heteronormativity and might sometimes identify with Patty on that basis. But I think to rest the argument here risks an incomplete understanding of Schulz's achievement across the greater body of his work (which actually insists on Patty's lovability in countless ways, as no true *Peanuts* fan needs to be told). Schulz's cartoons suggest something more radical about the relationship between desire and failure, something like the lesson that Heather Love teaches in *Feeling Backward*. Love supplements the Lacanian insistence that desire is a paradoxical phenomenon sustained by frustration with the observation that in straight culture it is the queer who is made to bear the burden of this truth, which heterosexual ideology otherwise represses (proclaiming at every turn that actual "completion" in a monogamous romantic union is not only possible but the end result of healthy maturation).[17] Schulz is as Lacanian as they come in his insistence that failure is actually built into the experience of desire, but his comics refuse to foist this knowledge onto the queer "other." You can't get what you want in his universe, no matter who you are. As Charlie Brown observes in the final line of that exquisite Sunday, "you can't even talk about it." Indeed, after Schulz, we might see the inevitable failure of desire as a paradoxical form of validation, a testament to its intensity and verity, a confirmation of its power to simultaneously motivate us and arrest us, to break us open even as it makes us what we are.

What's more, and following Jack Halberstam's arguments in another book (from which I have borrowed my subtitle for this chapter), we might even begin to see Schulz's investment in failure as evidence not of his supposed depressive tendencies but rather as a sign of a fundamental (and exciting) rejection of the normative within his work.[18] Although closely identified with conventional American ritual celebrations and values (the baseball season, Valentine's Day, Christmas pageants, Halloween, the football season), and although often mistakenly identified as a "wholesome" form of children's entertainment (despite that fact that the artist addressed his work to adults), Schulz's cartoons subvert this superficial conservatism by refusing to participate in the fundamental American myth of success. Indeed, in his investment in failure, Schulz's work constitutes a fifty-year-long assault upon the core American belief that "success" is finally a matter of working hard and maintaining a positive attitude (as opposed to, say, a function of power structures that weigh race, class, and gender rather more heavily than one's capacity for irrepressible determination and good humor). Capitalist ideology offers up the bootstraps myth and encourages us, if at first we don't succeed, to try and try again (though always on the terms of the dominant culture, of course); but the continual defeats and frustrations experienced by Charlie Brown, Peppermint Patty, and the rest of the gang stand as a painfully funny refutation of such fatuous bromides. Similarly, when straight culture insists that a girl needs to put on a dress and be feminine to be worthy of love, Peppermint Patty's angry questions, her grief, and her frustrations stand in opposition to that cruel and unimaginative logic of identity. But so do her talents, her own capacity for love and friendship, her moments of joy—the many moments in the strip in which she gets what she needs, if not what she wants (for Schulz understood *that* difference, too). After all, from the very first, she imagines herself as a "swinger" even when no one else—including, perhaps, her creator—was capable of doing so; and who are any of us, at the end of the day, to insist that she is wrong?

In conclusion: Peppermint Patty's queerness is valuable not merely as a point of identification for the members of queer and genderqueer communities. It also provides a conceptual lens through which we can give Schulz his due as the author of some of our greatest queer comics of failure. Which is to say, it allows us to recognize the more fundamentally antinormative impulses of Schulz's work—including the politically subversive aspects of his investment in failure and his implicit recognition of the essential gender ambiguity of children. And finally, it helps us to recognize Patty as one of Schulz's most inspired inventions—"a rare gem," indeed—as well as a delightful figure of counterhegemonic desire. In a heterosexist culture, her tomboy status registers as a failure of "femininity." But in Schulz's queer comics, the failure is not Patty's; it belongs to the world.

NOTES

I am grateful to Lara Bovilsky, Charles Hatfield, Quinn Miller, and Howard Chaykin for their insightful and encouraging remarks on an earlier draft of this chapter.

1. With regard to sports, the key witness is Charlie Brown; with regard to academic failure, both Charlie Brown and Peppermint Patty; with regard to the failure of one's idols, the obvious (but not the only) example would be Linus's continually disappointed faith in the Great Pumpkin; and on the subject of romantic failure, one could cite almost every significant member of the cast.

2. This may be as good a place as any to say that my arguments are based solely on Schulz's newspaper comics and not on the animated television specials (which may be more familiar to a general reader). To my mind, these specials do not capture the comedy or the cruelty of Schulz's work, even when based on specific strips.

3. See, for example, Jack [Judith] Halberstam, *Female Masculinity* (Durham, NC: Duke University Press, 1998); the relevant essays collected in Matthew Rottnek, ed., *Sissies and Tomboys: Gender Nonconformity and Homosexual Childhood* (New York: New York University Press, 1999); and Michelle Ann Abate, *Tomboys: A Literary and Cultural History* (Philadelphia: Temple University Press, 2008).

4. Halberstam, *Female Masculinity*, 9.

5. See, for example, Senshi Sun, "Just One Kiss," FanFiction, June 10, 2013, at https://www.fanfiction.net/s/9374838/1/Just-One-Kiss.

6. Thus, in *The Simpsons* episode "No Loan Again, Naturally," Lisa says she suspects that Peppermint Patty is gay; in the *Family Guy* episode "Stuck Together, Torn Apart," Patty is depicted as living in a domestic partnership with Marcie; and in *The Big Bang Theory* episode "The Barbarian Sublimation," Raj and Leonard debate Patty's orientation. (Raj suspects that Patty is a lesbian; Leonard claims she is "just athletic.")

7. I thank my colleague Betsy Wheeler for drawing my attention to this reference.

8. Vikki Reich, "The Case of Peppermint Patty," Up Popped a Fox, November 21, 2012, at http://uppoppedafox.com/2012/11/the-case-of-peppermint-patty/.

9. Of at least twenty commentators, only two dispute Reich's reading.

10. See Tom Heintjes, "Crossing the Color Line (in Black and White): Franklin in *Peanuts*," *Hogan's Alley: The Magazine of the Cartoon Arts*, no. 18 (2012), at http://cartoonician.com/crossing-the-color-line-in-black-and-white-franklin-in-peanuts/, for the story of Franklin's creation; see also Clarence Page, "A *Peanuts* Kid Without Punch Lines," *Chicago Tribune*, February 16, 2000, at http://articles.chicagotribune.com/2000-02-16/news/0002160340_1_peanuts-charlie-brown-franklin, for a reflection on Franklin's personality, or lack of the same.

11. Kathryn Bond Stockton, *The Queer Child; or, Growing Sideways in the Twentieth Century* (Durham, NC: Duke University Press, 2009).

12. Although this phrasing will seem uncontroversial to some, others will no doubt find it problematic. While it is well beyond the scope of this essay to revisit the vexed question of the relationship between embodiment and identity, the pioneering texts in this regard are, of course, Judith Butler's *Gender Trouble* (New York: Routledge, 1990)

and *Bodies That Matter* (New York: Routledge, 1993), both of which have generated extensive bibliographies of commentary. For a more recent (and superbly cogent) summary of
the implications of the body/identity debate for transgender theory, I recommend Gayle
Salamon, *Assuming a Body: Transgender and Rhetorics of Materiality* (New York: Columbia
University Press, 2010).

13. See Jacques Lacan, *My Teaching*, trans. David Macey (London: Verso, 2009), 38:
"Desire full stop is always the desire of the Other. Which basically means that we are
always asking the Other what he desires."

14. This is not to say that "girl jocks" can never be objects of admiration and desire,
but simply that normative culture lavishes far more attention on male athletes than female ones. For a man of his generation, Schulz was unusually aware of gendered double
standards in the world of sports; he was a strong supporter of Title IX and made reference to that important piece of legislation in more than one strip.

15. See, for example, "Peppermint Patty Is Not Gay," Macaroni Waffles, July 6, 2015, at
http://macaroniwaffles.blogspot.com/2015/07/peppermint-patty-is-not-gay.html. The
author struggles to avoid the appearance of homophobia, claiming that he "can understand why gay viewers would relate to [Patty]," while insisting at some length that they
are wrong to do so. But he (perhaps unconsciously) reveals his prejudices when he asserts
that "Peppermint Patty and Marcie are just best friends and to insinuate anything beyond that is to suggest something strange about same-sex friendship," thereby insinuat-
ing in turn that same-sex relationships that go beyond being "just friends" are "strange."
This is not to say that the "Peppermint Patty Is Not Gay" argument could never be
thoughtfully made. After all, Patty is a comic strip character, not a real person. Comic
strip characters, like all fictional creations, do not have sexual desires and orientations
because they do not have subjective experiences of any kind, and so to that extent, at
least, Peppermint Patty cannot be gay. But neither can she be straight, bi, trans, asexual,
or anything else. Artists *produce* these and other subjectivity effects by manipulating
the tools of representation they have to hand, and it is part of the function of criticism
to analyze how those effects are generated and to consider the impact they have upon
readers and upon the culture at large.

16. Schulz would periodically revisit this dynamic over the next few decades, introducing new elements. For example, in the 1990s, Marcie also declares feelings for Charlie
Brown, although intriguingly this does not produce any concomitant rivalry with Patty;
in fact, the two of them work together to woo him. Schulz also depicted Patty as developing other attachments over the years (to Snoopy in the 1970s and to Pig-Pen in the
1980s). Alas, I do not have room to address all these strips here. I'm also aware that my
focus on Patty's failed relationship with Charlie Brown rather than on her (more successful or perhaps just differently failed) relationship with Marcie may be somewhat ironic
in context, but this really only means that that much queer critical inquiry is to still be done
with regard to Schulz's marvelous texts.

17. Heather Love, *Feeling Backward: Loss and the Politics of Queer History* (Cambridge,
MA: Harvard University Press, 2009).

18. Judith [Jack] Halberstam, *The Queer Art of Failure* (Durham, NC: Duke University Press, 2011). Halberstam's influence on my thinking is everywhere apparent throughout
this chapter.

-2-

"THERE HAS TO BE SOMETHING DEEPLY SYMBOLIC IN THAT"

Peanuts and the Sublime

ANNE C. McCARTHY

At the moment that the artistic or philosophical, that is, the language-determined,
man laughs at himself falling, he is laughing at a mistaken, mystified assumption
he was making about himself.

PAUL DE MAN, "THE RHETORIC OF TEMPORALITY"[1]

This chapter rests on two propositions: first, that there is a sublime aesthetic in *Peanuts*; and second, that this aesthetic arises most clearly in
the long-running "football gag" in which Lucy pulls the ball away from
Charlie Brown. The popular understanding of the sublime tends to look
a lot like the famous painting by German romantic artist Caspar David
Friedrich, *Wanderer above the Sea of Fog* (1818). The gentleman wanderer,
dressed in dark clothes with his back to the viewer, stands alone atop a
lofty summit, looking down at a rugged, foggy landscape while mountain
peaks rise in the distance, stretching as far as the eye can see. On the
one hand, the vastness and obscurity of the view that unfolds before
this solitary walker suggest human insignificance in the face of nature's
power and the forces of geologic time. On the other hand, the visual
prominence of the downward-gazing human figure leaves an undeniable
impression of mastery and dominance—is it not, after all, the human
imagination that renders such vistas meaningful? As is typical in the
romantic tradition, the wanderer becomes significant by recognizing and
thus transcending his insignificance.

Friedrich's painting represents one version of what the philosopher
Immanuel Kant in the *Critique of Judgment* (1790) calls the "negative

29

pleasure" of the sublime.[2] While beautiful objects attract us straightforwardly, the sublime is more likely to begin as an experience of repulsion
and fear or as the kind of cognitive breakdown that occurs when we try
to perceive more than our physical senses or thinking mind can handle.
Yet in the awareness of this cognitive breakdown, it becomes possible
to transcend this initial moment of frustration. We may not be able
to use our senses to grasp the infinite, Kant's argument goes, but our
reason—not subject to the limits of our bodies or feelings—can con-
ceptualize infinity and therefore can summon a certain kind of power
in the situation.[3] Reason elevates the subject, offering a momentary
glimpse of a more-than-sensory reality. One of the best contemporary
definitions of the sublime has been offered by the literary scholar Christopher Hitt, who emphasizes how the sublime "jolt[s] us momentarily
out of a perspective constructed by reason and language," resulting in
"heightened understanding."[4] Kant talks about the sublime in terms like
"superiority," "elevation," and "freedom"—the idea being that people can
both recognize that they cannot resist nature's power and nonetheless
face that power without fear. However, we might, following Hitt, allow
the possibility that this experience of elevation has less to do with the
consolidation of power than it does with realigning our relationship to
reality—a reality that post-Kantian philosophy has increasingly come
to see as structured not by some inaccessible order of reason, but by
contingency.[5]

Traditionally, the natural world has been the privileged place for experiencing this feeling, but Kant cautions his readers against clinging
too tightly to certain "sublime" images or places:

> [T]rue sublimity must be sought only in the mind of the judging
> person, not in the natural object the judging of which prompts this
> mental attunement. Indeed, who would want to call sublime such
> things as shapeless mountain masses piled on one another in wild
> disarray, with their pyramids of ice, or the gloomy raging sea?[6]

This is a somewhat weird contention, and the short answer to Kant's
obviously rhetorical question is, of course, just about everyone. There's
a reason why Friedrich's wanderer is so iconic (and, perhaps, why the
walls of Schulz's Redwood Empire Ice Arena in Santa Rosa, California,
display 1960s-era photographs of the Swiss Alps). But by decoupling the
idea or the form of sublime experience from the images that are generally

associated with it, Kant leaves room in his theory for more unconventional and even more subtle sublimes. While it might be somewhat easier to encounter the otherness of the world and a sense of our own place in it by struggling to the top of a mountain, such insight doesn't depend on being in a certain place or looking at a certain thing. The experience of the sublime is inherently spontaneous, happening each time as if for the first time. The moment it starts to conform to a rule or become the object of expectation, it begins to slip away, like a football perpetually proffered and perpetually withdrawn.

Simply put, the sublime reveals that the world may be a whole lot stranger than we think it is. When we encounter things that are inassimilable, what we are encountering is the discontinuity between the world as we think it should be and the world as it is. Samuel Taylor Coleridge, an early adopter of Kantian aesthetics, describes the sublime as the "suspension of the Comparing powers"[7]—the suspension, that is, of the very structures of expectation that make the world appear to be other than what it is. So, while it is easy to assume that considering nature as "a might that has no dominance over us"[8] is the ultimate in anthropocentric hubris, it may be more productive to think of it less as a denial of reality than as a way of coping with it, and perhaps even enjoying ourselves along the way.

Granted, it still may not be immediately clear what this has to do with *Peanuts*. All Charlie Brown wants to do, after all, is kick that football. Charles Schulz always avowed the necessity of Charlie Brown's failure in this endeavor: losing is funnier than winning, but, more to the point, perpetual losing is funnier than winning once and then going back to losing. But if there's nothing funny about kicking the football, it doesn't necessarily follow that not kicking it *is* funny. We could see Charlie Brown falling for the trick once, twice, even six or seven times. There are forty-one football strips.[9] To imagine him falling for this trick forty-one times necessitates a strenuous suspension of disbelief. More than that, it requires letting go of the assumption that we know what these strips are about. Forty-one is not a number that invites theorization or interpretation: what does it mean to do something forty-one times? If it is dwarfed by the more than seventeen thousand total strips Schulz produced, it is nonetheless a large enough number to invite imprecision or a kind of mental fuzziness. In my own experience, at least, the material unwieldiness of this set of strips is accompanied by a sense of cognitive overload. I have a strong sense of what this series is about in general,

and certain individual strips (and their dates) stick in my mind, but I'm
constantly realizing that there's something I've missed along the way. In
practice, I can only hold a certain number of strips in my head. As soon
as that number is exceeded, something else has to go.[10]

All of that notwithstanding, there's much to be gained from a more or
less systematic reading of the football strips.[11] Lucy pulls the football away
from Charlie Brown for the first time in 1952, but it takes a couple of years
after that for the gag to get off the ground. There are no football episodes
in 1953, 1954, or 1955. By the gag's third iteration in 1957, however, the
pattern of holding and pulling away is well established. The repetitive
nature of the event is explicitly acknowledged by Charlie Brown. "She
did it again!" he exclaims, as Lucy's action sends him flying into the air.
Another defining visual element of the gag emerges in 1958, when Charlie
Brown first approaches the football by running right to left—running,
that is *against* the direction of reading. The directional change forces the
reader to make a barely perceptible U-turn in the viewing of the strip,
creating a minor rupture in the gag's unfolding. It draws attention to the
impossible moment of decision, suggesting that Charlie Brown is never
entirely carried along by compulsion. This remains one of the most consistent visual elements of the football gag, to the point that it can seem
almost "natural," at least until it's compared to the very early versions of
the strip. This reversal—of direction, but also of expectation—encodes
the possibility of sublime experience, the inhibition or suspension that
momentarily realigns the subject's relationship to the world.

The strips of the 1950s and 1960s play out in ways that Robert Short
codifies in *The Gospel According to Peanuts*: "The classic *Peanuts* commentary on this rather pessimistic view of human nature is the running gag
every year when Charlie Brown's courageous views on man's freedom and
goodness are invariably brought back to earth by Lucy."[12] Short invokes
the football gags—already deemed "classic" in the mid-1960s—to illustrate the fallenness and the impotence of human nature. This is certainly
a plausible reading of the early strips, with their inconclusive banter
about trust and truthfulness. However, despite the timelessness that
Short attributes to these themes, the strips themselves have not aged
particularly well, given, among other things, their frequent recourse to
gender-based punch lines ("A woman's handshake is not legally binding"
[1963]; "Never listen to a woman's tears, Charlie Brown" [1969]; "This
year's football was pulled away from you through the courtesy of women's
lib" [1971]). But even these gags are as much about discontinuity and

Fig. 2.1: Charles Schulz, *Peanuts*, October 11, 1970. PEANUTS © 1970 Peanuts Worldwide LLC. Dist. by UNIVERSAL UCLICK. Reprinted with permission. All rights reserved.

contingency as they are about inevitability and stasis. Charlie Brown's right-to-left dash is an early indication of the gag's resistance to a binary, programmatic reading that identifies one unified meaning in the sequence.

The first explicit shift from the poetics of repetition to the aesthetics of contingency occurs in 1970. This is the first of the football strips to open an explicit gap between text and image. Charlie Brown's reaction to Lucy's suggestion takes on comically biblical proportions: "How long, O Lord?" he cries, shaking his fists at the heavens that lie beyond the upper boundary of the panel. But after this, neither Lucy nor Charlie Brown mentions the football again. Lucy offers no elaborately absurd justification to "trick" Charlie Brown. Charlie Brown offers no rationalization for the act in which he is about to engage; he does not promise to kick the ball to the moon, Omaha, Bullhead City, or the edge of the universe. This scrambles many of the binaries that are perceived to drive the joke from earlier instances. It is no longer simply about the perception of stupidity, the solicitation of trust, or even the possibility that someday Charlie Brown himself might take control of the situation. Lucy quotes part of the divine intention as communicated to Isaiah—the verse is Isaiah 6:11—as Charlie Brown walks away from her to position himself for the run toward the football.

Schulz, of course, had been placing scripture in the mouths of his characters for some time already. But this is the first time he does so in the context of the football gag, and it is different in kind from, say, Linus's recitation of the gospel in *A Charlie Brown Christmas* or even the theological debates that arise on the baseball field.[13] In both of these instances, there is a more or less directly referential relationship to what the scene or strip is "about." In the case of the baseball strips, in fact, the joke is directly related to the invocation of scripture—"I don't have a ball team, I have a theological seminary!" The relationship is more complex in the 1970 football strip. The context of Isaiah's question, as cited by Charlie Brown, is that of the Lord's vengeance against Israel. At the beginning of Isaiah 6, the prophet himself receives absolution from the Lord, but as the price of that forgiveness, he must obey these instructions:

> Go, and say this to the people:
> "Hear and hear, but do not understand;
> see and see, but do not perceive."
> Make the heart of this people fat,
> and their ears heavy, and shut their eyes.
> lest they see with their eyes, and hear with their ears,
> and understand with their hearts,
> and turn and be healed. (Isaiah 6:9–10)

This injunction to deliver a message of misunderstanding provokes Isaiah's cry. How long must he, the divinely pardoned prophet, declaim God's refusal to extend that mercy to others? Or, rather, how long will God prevent the people from reaching the understanding that would give them access to his mercy? We already know from Lucy how he responds to Isaiah's question: until the judgment is final and complete, or until the time at which his people finally realize that their own efforts to save themselves cannot possibly succeed.[14]

Yet Isaiah, at least in Lucy's gloss, resists the apocalyptic "finality" of this judgment. This comment appears in a speech balloon over the iconic image of Charlie Brown's right-to-left rush toward the ball. Both Charlie Brown and Isaiah seek the deferral of endings, the suspension of mastery and calculation against seemingly intractable odds. As Charles

Hatfield rightly observes: "[T]he irony in *Peanuts* simply spikes an irony always already implicit in comics: the incommensurability of, or tension between, image and word. Schulz's combination of child personas and adult chatter underscores comics' lack of a perfect fit between the visual and the verbal, a lack or gap that, we might say, compels us readers to reconcile these disparate elements."[15] The gap that begins to open up in the football episodes, however, reveals an even deeper incommensurability: a constitutive discontinuity between form and content. The punch line—"All your life, Charlie Brown, all your life"—does not reconcile the two levels of discourse but rather marks the site of the discontinuity between them. The rupture here does not relate to the presence of adult observations coming from children but instead suggests a potentially endless recursion of pulled-away footballs, always just out of reach, gesturing toward the sublime abyss that exists beyond the borders of the strip and in the gutters between panels. This is one of the moments when *Peanuts* evades calculation and exceeds representation, language, and even meaning.

The sublimity of the football gag arises somewhere between the words and the images. There are episodes that include hardly any dialogue (as in 1986) and one where the entire holding and pulling away sequence takes place offstage and is narrated by Sally (1994). But arguably the most perfect realization of this relationship appears in 1973. The joke depends on the viewer's ability to hold word and image in suspension. Charlie Brown does gain a certain kind of insight here, but it comes only when it can be of no use to him—he can see clearly only from this impossible position in midair, which itself is a visual echo of some of those earlier strips. This is a particularly apt representation of sublime "elevation," because it is possible for Charlie Brown to achieve this height only by trying to do something else—that is, by trying and failing to kick the football. It wouldn't work if he planned it. The experience of the sublime frequently unfolds as an unexpected flash of insight at the moment of failure or of the most extreme ungroundedness, a moment of suspension taken out of time and made the subject of an endlessly reproduced panel in a comic strip.[16]

The third certainty—the answer to the riddle and the subject of the strip's visual narrative—is never directly named, despite Lucy's insistence that it was "so obvious."[17] It *is* obvious (as the first panel's representation of Charlie Brown's head being crushed by a giant football implies), but only until you try to articulate it. For instance, is the third certainty that

Fig. 2.2: Charles Schulz, *Peanuts*, November 11, 1973. PEANUTS © 1973 Peanuts Worldwide LLC. Dist. by UNIVERSAL UCLICK. Reprinted with permission. All rights reserved.

Lucy will always pull the football away, or that Charlie Brown will never kick it? Charles Schulz floated both possibilities, but they aren't mutually interchangeable, even within the horizon of the forty-one football episodes. The problem is with the notion of transcendence itself, with the appeal to an overarching rule or order. But what Charlie Brown might be realizing, however obliquely, is the "certainty" of contingency itself, a fundamental discontinuity in the world that is accurately replicated in the separation of word and image that structures so much of *Peanuts'* humor. The 1982 and 1996 episodes offer variations on this theme. In the October 10, 1982, strip (one of Schulz's best), Charlie Brown approaches the football while musing on his failure to discover whatever is "deeply symbolic" in this ritual. He admits that he has missed the symbolism; in the final panel, Lucy observes that he has also missed the ball. Charlie Brown again misses the symbolism in 1996 and wonders if he has fared any better when it comes to reality.

But perhaps Charlie Brown's "problem" lies not in his inability to grasp the symbolism, certainty, or deeper meaning of the situation, but rather in his investment in a world that has to make sense.[18] Ultimately, there isn't really a good reason why Lucy acts the way she does. Nor is there a reason why Charlie Brown plays his part. Any explanations that we come up with can only be partial and provisional, denying the force of these forty-one instantiations.[19] This may sound nihilistic, but it doesn't need to be. There's a remarkable amount of possibility, of flexibility, that arises when what was previously thought to be essential is redefined as contingent—ungroundedness is scary, but it's also generative. In the paradoxical logic of the sublime, Charlie Brown finds out that he is not a match for Lucy in terms of wit or swiftness of kick, yet he also finds himself to be more than adequate to the larger task of seeing both the kicking and not kicking of the football outside of an economy of meaning. Regardless of the specific circumstances visited upon him each year, there is always implicitly a point at which we must imagine Charlie Brown running so fast that he could no longer stop himself even if he tried—a point, that is, at which he gives himself over fully to the suspension of comparison and calculation and renders himself vulnerable to the "jolt" of an encounter with inexorable reality.

This point becomes clearer when we consider a small subset of football gags that don't follow the usual pattern. These involve the presence of other characters in addition to Charlie Brown and Lucy, and the most interesting aberrations are connected to stronger-than-usual impositions of narrative form. But these attempts to contain or otherwise dilute the sublime energy of the football gag have an interesting result: in none of these cases does the reader witness Charlie Brown's attempt to kick the ball. If the failure is still implied in some of these (particularly in the 1994 episode), others remain more ambiguous. For instance, when Charlie Brown decides in 1983 that he has finally had enough, he walks away from Lucy, telling her, "I'm glad you're the only person who thinks I'm that stupid." He turns around to find, in the last panel, a group of other characters—Snoopy, Woodstock, Sally, Peppermint Patty, and Marcie—each holding a football. Charlie Brown's next move remains undetermined, but we assume that he does not run at all these temptations (a circumstance that undercuts any ostensible "compulsion" to participate in these scenes). Confirming the widely held opinion of Charlie Brown's stupidity more emphatically than the other football strips do, this punch line closes off possibility. Here, the joke can only be "about" Charlie Brown's foolishness. This approach, however, could very much have been a dead end for Schulz; there was not another football strip until 1986.

The 1995 football episode is perhaps the most direct example of the way that the joke misfires in the presence of narrative demands. This year, Lucy suggests to Charlie Brown that he could sue her if she pulls the ball away. In the final panel, Charlie Brown runs toward the ball, followed by Snoopy in his "Joe Lawyer" guise.[20] The ending of this strip remains necessarily undetermined. We know that Charlie Brown cannot actually kick the ball without destroying the integrity of any future football strips. But under the conditions of this particular joke—which evokes the rule of law and of cause and effect—Lucy's pulling the ball away would trigger a specific set of narrative consequences. A lawsuit, even one handled by Snoopy, would again threaten to end the gag. What this suggests is that the football gags need to remain outside of narrative structures in order to make sense. What's more, to the extent that they possess a structural significance for *Peanuts* as a whole, they help to ensure that whatever happens, *Peanuts* remains something other than a narrative with a beginning, middle, and end. It becomes difficult, if not impossible, to tell an ongoing "story" about Charlie Brown's attempts to kick the football, and this may be one reason why the paradigmatic football gag is always a self-contained Sunday strip.

The football gag reaches its limit—I hesitate to say its ending—in 1999. The last football episode ever published belongs to the category of "misfires" in that it includes a third character (Rerun, the much-maligned youngest Van Pelt) and does not depict what happens when Charlie Brown reaches the football. At the beginning of the episode, Rerun arrives, as if from another world, to call Lucy to lunch. He represents an order of authority and temporality that has long been absent from the strip: the message comes from their mother. Why, after so long, is Lucy willing to acquiesce to parental demands—demands that suddenly assume an unprecedented priority over her own wishes? For a moment, these characters are almost real children. Yet the football gag operates according to its own insistent temporality. The time is now, and Lucy thus hands the ball over to her brother: "Rerun can take my place." Charlie Brown sees this substitution as an opportunity: "Rerun will never pull it away. He just wouldn't," he muses as he walks toward his starting position. We never find out whether or not this is true, for Rerun's presence disrupts the repetitive force of the gag. The concluding panel, usually the space where Lucy gets the final word as she stands over a prone Charlie Brown, is in this episode a site for her frustration. To her anxious inquiries—"Did you pull the ball away? Did he kick it? What happened?"—Rerun replies, "You'll never know." Lucy's last word is an anguished scream. Uncharacteristically, Charlie Brown is nowhere to be found in the final panel. The last view we have of him is in the third-to-last panel, running toward the ball, right to left, declaring, "So here we go!" Despite all the evidence, it can never be said with any certainty that Charlie Brown *never* kicks the ball, only that we do not see him do so. What remains is contingency and the inexhaustible possibility: "So here we go!"

Here we go, indeed—not toward the ball, precisely, but toward the gutter between panels, a structural discontinuity that is one of the defining features of the modern comic strip. There is grace in this open-ended finale. It manages to offer possibility without nurturing false hope, and it reminds us that we have not yet finished reading *Peanuts*.[21] "You'll never know" turns out to be an answer after all. When we suspend the binary constructions usually placed on this event (Charlie Brown versus Lucy, failure versus success, credulity versus cynicism) in favor of a sublime aesthetic that attends to the stranger dimensions of the football strips, it becomes clear that *Peanuts* is fundamentally about the experience of coming face-to-face with the illegibility of the world. Transcendence, such as it is, occurs in the aggregate of the football episodes, in the force of more than forty years of falling on one's back, having the ball pulled away, and glimpsing a world that, paradoxically, attains the appearance of stability by repeating scenes of contingency. Charlie Brown's error lies not in his trust of Lucy but in his attempts to analyze his situation for a deeper or hidden meaning and thus to master the play of running and pulling away. His crash landing is also the crash landing of a desire to uncover hidden continuities in a constitutively discontinuous world.

Which is all to say that *Peanuts* is an intensely strange textual and material object. Reading it demands something like the Coleridgean "suspension of the Comparing powers"—not to mention our conventional notions of time, causality, even ethics—to experience it. The meaning of the name "Peanuts" exists somewhere between the levels of the individual strip and the entire oeuvre, somewhere in the play of repetition and discontinuity. What the sublime of *Peanuts* lacks in visual impressiveness and overwhelming natural force, it makes up in the ability to reveal another set of essential truths about this concept: that contingency is everywhere, that mastery remains elusive, and that the experience of sublime expansion is an uncertain, ongoing, and open-ended process. Beyond questions of failure and success, beyond even the football itself, the sublime of *Peanuts* asks what it might mean to give up (however temporarily) that search for underlying meaning.

NOTES

1. Paul de Man, "The Rhetoric of Temporality," in *Blindness and Insight: Essays in the Rhetoric of Contemporary Criticism*, 2nd ed. (Minneapolis: University of Minnesota Press, 1983), 214.

2. Immanuel Kant, *Critique of Judgment*, trans. Werner S. Pluhar (Indianapolis: Hackett, 1987), 98.

3. The things that we call sublime, Kant says, "raise the soul's fortitude above its usual middle range and allow us to discover in ourselves an ability to resist which is of quite a different kind, and which gives us the courage [to believe] that we could be a match for nature's seeming omnipotence" (*Critique of Judgment*, 120).

4. Christopher Hitt, "Toward an Ecological Sublime," *New Literary History* 30, no. 3 (Summer 1999): 617, 611.

5. This argument has been made most forcefully by the French philosopher Quentin Meillassoux, who proposes that "everything and every world *is* without reason, and is thereby *capable of actually becoming otherwise without reason*" (*After Finitude: An Essay on the Necessity of Contingency*, trans. Ray Brassier [London: Continuum, 2008], 53, emphasis in original). Meillassoux is part of a broader group of post-Kantian philosophers working in the area known as speculative realism (or speculative materialism). For an accessible overview of this field, see Steven Shaviro, *The Universe of Things: On Speculative Realism* (Minneapolis: University of Minnesota Press, 2014).

6. Kant, *Critique of Judgment*, 113.

7. "I meet, I *find* the Beautiful; but I give, contribute, or rather attribute the Sublime. No object of Sense is sublime in itself; but only as far as I make it a symbol of some Idea. The Circle is a beautiful figure in itself; it becomes sublime, when I contemplate eternity under that figure.—The Beautiful is the perfection, the Sublime the suspension, of the Comparing Power" (Samuel Taylor Coleridge, *Shorter Works and Fragments*, 2 vols., ed. H. J. Jackson and J. R. de J. Jackson [Princeton, NJ: Princeton University Press, 1995] 1:596–97).

8. Kant, *Critique of Judgment*, 119.

9. In the interest of clarity, I'm counting only the gags that appear in Sunday strips, excluding the first time Charlie Brown missed the ball when Violet refused to hold it in place (November 14, 1951); the series of 1979 daily strips in which Lucy promises never to pull the football away again if Charlie Brown is released from the hospital; and, finally, a 1990 story line between Charlie Brown and Peggy Jean. The football gag takes on a fundamentally different status when deployed as part of a longer narrative, and to do justice to this would require a separate essay.

10. To put this in Kantian terms, "when apprehension has reached the point where the partial presentations of sensible intuition that were first apprehended are already beginning to be extinguished in the imagination, as it proceeds to apprehend further

ones, the imagination then loses as much on the one side as it gains on the other; and so there is a maximum in comprehension that it cannot exceed" (*Critique of Judgment*, 108).

11. I used Derrick Bang's list of football strips to locate them on GoComics.com, which hosts a digital archive of the full run of *Peanuts*. See Derrick Bang with Victor Lee, *50 Years of Happiness: A Tribute to Charles M. Schulz* (N.p.: Peanuts Collector Club, 1999), 128–34.

12. Robert Short, *The Gospel According to Peanuts* (Richmond, VA: John Knox Press, 1965), 42.

13. Only one other football strip contains a direct quotation of scripture. In 1980, Lucy recites the famous "to everything there is a season" passage from the book of Ecclesiastes, adding her own item at the end: "And a time to pull away the football."

14. Coincidentally, years before this strip appeared, Short cited the same passage from Isaiah to describe the human condition. In his gloss on these verses: "Man is trapped in his own blindness, in the circle of his own humanity. Apart from God's mercy, men cannot even 'turn for [God] to heal them.' This is why when a man *does* turn to God, this revolution, or reversal, always has the aspect of a *miracle*, it is a revolution which occurs in *spite* of man's own best efforts rather than *because* of them" (*The Gospel According to Peanuts*, 12).

15. Charles Hatfield, "Redrawing the Comic-Strip Child: Charles M. Schulz's *Peanuts* as Cross-Writing," in *The Oxford Handbook of Children's Literature*, ed. Julia L. Mickenberg and Lynne Vallone (Oxford: Oxford University Press, 2011), 176.

16. Something like this is suggested by the final two-page spread in Charles M. Schulz, *You Don't Look 35, Charlie Brown* (New York: Holt, Rinehart and Winston, 1985), a collage of panels showing just the pulling-away moment of many different strips.

17. "Obvious?! It may be obvious to you, but it's sure disobvious to me!"—Lucy, July 6, 1974.

18. This is different, of course, from saying that there are no deeper meanings in the strip, which was a refrain often repeated by Schulz.

19. Meillassoux writes: "Instead of laughing or smiling at questions like 'Where do we come from?,' 'Why do we exist?,' we should ponder instead the remarkable fact that the replies, 'From nothing. For nothing' really *are* answers, thereby realizing that these really were questions—and excellent ones at that" (*After Finitude*, 110).

20. Peter Sanderson suggests that Snoopy's lawyer persona "surely represents the side of any professional that somehow sees himself inadequate to his responsibilities and as misplaced in his role as a dog might be" ("*Peanuts* Unshelled," *Comics Journal* 75 [September 1982]: 29). More than that, the law itself is out of place, as it must always be in matters of aesthetics and ethics.

21. This is an important point to stress when, thanks to *The Complete Peanuts*, it is now possible to read the entire run of the strip in order from beginning to end. We would be wrong, I think, to privilege this sequential, linear reading *too* much. Part of reading *Peanuts* is appreciating the also strange flexibility of time that made the strip's longevity possible, the sometimes odd juxtapositions of strips from different years in the reprint books and anniversary tomes, and the overall vastness of the endeavor. Even though we have all of the *Complete Peanuts*, *Peanuts* still remains, in some fundamental way, ungraspable and incomplete.

SAYING, SHOWING, AND SCHULZ

The Typography and Notation of *Peanuts*

ROY T. COOK

In 1985, Will Eisner wrote that in comics "[t]ext reads as image," emphasizing that text in comics typically functions both as the bearer of linguistic content and as an integral part of the image on the page.[1]

This insight—roughly put, that a change in the nature of the text of a comic (e.g., changing the font) constitutes a change in the aesthetic nature, if not the identity, of the comic—is an important one. But it only scratches the surface with respect to the complicated functions that text plays in comics, and with respect to the interrelations between text and pictures, and between textual content and pictorial content, in comics.[2] In addition, musical notation in comics plays a similar and similarly complicated role to that played by text (hence, Eisner could have added: "Musical notes read as image!" to his pronouncements). The purpose of this chapter is to begin to flesh out some of the functions of and interrelations between text and other forms of notation (especially musical notation) in comics.

I will carry out this investigation by closely examining a particularly interesting case study: the use of text and musical notation in Charles Schulz's *Peanuts*. As we shall see, Schulz was well aware of the pictorial role that various textual or text-like notations can and do play in comics, and how that role can be manipulated in order to draw attention to the nature of comics, the nature of text and other notations in comics, and aspects of the nature of art itself. Schulz's *Peanuts* strips often play with the conventions governing how we are meant to interpret both the notational and visual elements within comics panels, subverting these conventions in two ways: first, by constructing comics in which two or more standard conventions regarding how we are meant to interpret panels conflict with each other, pushing the reader's attention "outside" the strip in order to reflect on the narrative incoherence that results, and second, by adopting novel (nonstandard and hence strip-specific) conventions regarding how we are meant to understand musical notation, providing his comics with an additional level of narrative depth—one unrecognized by readers not in on the convention in question.

Before examining the ways that Schulz manipulated and subverted the conventions governing the interpretation and understanding of various kinds of notation, however, a basic account is needed of what, exactly, the standard conventions governing such content are. In the next section I will develop a rough and necessarily incomplete account of these conventions. The following two sections then use this theoretical framework to construct a detailed analysis of the ways that Schulz routinely combined, contradicted, and added to these conventions in *Peanuts*. The chapter concludes with some brief observations regarding what all of this might imply about Schulz's own attitude toward the nature of, and art status of, the comics medium.

COMICS AND CONVENTION[3]

All art forms, including comics, are governed by a wealth of conventions regarding how we are meant to understand them. Some of these conventions are general and apply to many or all fictions or to many or all artworks—for example, the conventions governing the meaning of English vocabulary. Others are specific to particular forms, formats, or genres—for example, the conventions governing our interpretation of Hollywood musicals, which do not involve concluding that characters are insane based on their habitually breaking into song and dance, an assumption we likely would, and in many cases should, make if confronted with the same behavior in other genres.

Thus, we should not immediately assume that the conventions governing the interpretation of textual fictions are the same, or even relevantly similar to, the conventions governing the interpretation and evaluation of pictorial fictions (or that the conventions governing portions of a fiction that are textual or notational are the same as the conventions that govern those parts that are pictorial). As a result, we should expect the norms and conventions governing comics—an art form notable for its *mixing* of text and image—to involve not only different conventions governing the interpretation of images and of text (or, more generally, notation) but also complicated interactions between these conventions.[4]

We can further develop this point by noting that comics is a multimodal medium: content in comics is conveyed to the reader in more than one communicative mode (e.g., the visual and the textual), and these distinct modes function in very different ways (and should thus be expected to be governed by distinct conventions). Randy Bomer describes multimodal media as those productions

> where print and image do the work of meaning together, where sound and music contribute to the perspective readers are asked to take, where bodily performance works in tandem with the written word, where print itself is animated and choreographed.[5]

Importantly, comics are not multimodal *merely* in virtue of the presence of both text, and the textual communicative mode, and image, and the pictorial communicative mode. In addition, text can appear within a comics panel in (at least) four different, completely standard and familiar (to comics readers, at least), submodes. Thus, comics are multiply multimodal, communicatively articulated at both the coarse-grained level of text versus image and at the more fine-grained level involving distinct textual communicative modes.

Before I formulate and examine the relevant conventions governing the interpretation of text (and other notations) and images in comics, a disclaimer is in order: in what follows, I am implicitly assuming an account of the nature of fiction based on the theories of Kendall Walton, in which fictions are understood to be (or to encode) implicit instructions for a game of make-believe, and claims are true-in-the-fiction if and only if we are required to imagine them to be true when competently playing the relevant game of make-believe.[6] Thus, the conventions regarding how we are meant to interpret text and images in comics are conventions regarding what we are meant to imagine when confronted with certain kinds of text or images. Most of the arguments given below, however, can be easily reformulated within other accounts of the nature of fiction—a task I leave for the interested non-Waltonian reader.

We begin our examination of the conventions governing comics with the simplest case, simple in virtue of the fact that it involves only a single communicative mode: images. Images in comics usually (although not always) function in a single, uniform manner—they represent how things appear.[7] We can sum up with the following *pictorial content convention*:

> *Pictorial Content Convention*: When confronted with pictorial content, we are to imagine seeing the people, objects, environments, actions, and events in question, and to imagine that those people, objects, environments, actions, and events appear to us as they appear in the image.[8]

Note that we are not meant to imagine that things in the fiction look just like they look in the image—that is, we *do not* assume that the images in comics panels accurately represent how things standardly (albeit fictionally) appear to characters in the fiction. Rather, we are to imagine that things in the fiction appear to us, when we imagine seeing them, just as they look in the image. In other words, pictorial content in comics cues an inferential process: we imagine that we see the people, objects, environments, action, and events depicted in the panel, and we imagine that those people, objects, environments, actions, and events appear to us as they appear in the panel, and we then infer, based on these imaginative acts and other information, various claims regarding what these people, objects, environments, actions, and events actually look like within the fiction.[9]

With images out of the way, we can move on to the case of primary interest here: text. The first way that text standardly appears within a comic is as a part of an image. Examples of this textual communicative mode include images of street signs, graffiti, books, newspapers, and other elements of the fictional world that display text. Text that appears in this mode is nothing more than a special case of the pictorial content convention, since in such instances the text in question is nothing more than a part of the image. Thus, we obtain the *pictorial text convention*:

> *Pictorial Text Convention*: When confronted with pictorial text, we are to imagine *seeing* the text in question, and to imagine that it appears to us as it appears in the image.

Put bluntly, pictorial text is a picture of text, and our imaginings should treat it as such.[10]

Next up is the textual communicative mode that has received perhaps the most attention in comics studies—text that appears within smooth or scalloped speech or thought balloons (or bubbles). Balloons prescribe that we imagine that the characters speak or think the text contained in the bubble, hence the *balloon text convention*:

> *Balloon Text Convention*: When confronted with balloon text, we are to imagine *hearing* (or telepathically *sensing*?) the relevant characters speaking the dialogue (or thinking the thoughts) textually represented.

Note that, although the balloons containing the speech or thoughts of characters in a comic might obstruct portions of our view of the pictorial content contained in the comic panel, we are not meant to imagine either that we see the balloons themselves or, when interpreting the pictorial content of the panel, that portions of the scene are mysteriously obstructed from view.[11]

Along lines similar to the pictorial conventions above, we are clearly meant, when confronted with speech balloons, to imagine not only that the characters speak (or shout, etc.) the text contained in the balloon but also that we hear the text being spoken (or shouted, etc.).[12] As indicated by the questioning parenthetical remark, it is not exactly clear what thought balloons ask us to imagine, however: if we apply the same template to thought balloons, we would be required to imagine not only that characters think the text contained within the balloon but also that we somehow experience those thoughts ourselves. But it is not clear exactly what it would be like to imagine such a thing. This issue deserves further theoretical scrutiny but is orthogonal to our present concerns, so having noted it we can move on.

Narrative text—the descriptive text that appears in small rectangular boxes, often attached to panel borders—activates the following *narrative text convention*, at least when the narration is in the form of seemingly omniscient third-person description:

> *Narration Text Convention*: When confronted with narration text, we are to imagine people, objects, environments, actions, and events as they are described in the narrative text. Hence, narration text functions (roughly) the same way that descriptive text does in literature.

In short, this style of third-person narration functions in much the same manner as text functions in primarily textual narrative forms such as novels.

Other forms of narration text within comics activate somewhat different conventions regarding what we are meant to imagine. For example,
first-person film noir–style narration does not necessarily describe how
things are in the fiction but is instead better understood as a prescription
to imagine that the narrator (usually the protagonist or other prominent
character) believes that things are the way she describes them or, perhaps,
that she wants us to believe things to be as she describes them.[13] Thus, a
completely adequate account of narration text in comics would require
a rather more subtle, more nuanced account than the single convention
just formulated. Since none of the examples we are concerned with below
concern narration text, however, we can set aside more ambitious treat-
ments of this particular communicative mode for another time and focus
instead on those modes that are present in the cases of interest here.

The final mode in which text standardly appears within comics is
sound effects (or SFX) text: the "BAMF"s, "THWIP"s, and "SNIKT"s that
appear within the panel, often in bold, brightly colored block letters,
indicating loud or important sounds occurring within the fiction. The
following *SFX text convention* captures at least part of the convention
regarding what we are to imagine when confronted with such text:

SFX Text Convention: When confronted with SFX text, we are to
imagine *hearing* a sound appropriately related to the events depicted and onomatopoetically suggested by the SFX.

Like balloon text and narration text (but unlike pictorial text), SFX text
does not require imagining that we see the text in question, despite the
fact that the text is incorporated directly into the panel rather than being
relegated to narration boxes separated from the panel by borders, or to
balloons (which are perhaps better read as sitting "outside" or "atop" the
panel rather than being contained in, or being a part of, the content of
the panel itself). A few complications are worth noting, however.

First, the fact that the presence of SFX text does not trigger a convention requiring us to imagine that we (or the characters in the fiction)
see the text does not mean that such text never triggers conventions
requiring us to imagine seeing *something*. In fact, it seems likely that
SFX text indicating the sound of, say, an explosion is also meant to visually represent the explosion itself—in other words, some SFX text can
do double duty, representing the sound of an explosion as well as the
appearance of the explosion. Thus, a "BOOM" depicted in shades of red
and orange, and drawn using sharp-edged, burst-like characters, almost

certainly is meant to (and indeed does) play this double duty. Of course, even in such cases, neither the reader nor the characters are to be imagined to see the letters in question—that is, the "BOOM"—even if they are meant to imagine an explosion or collision whose visual characteristics are suggested by (and are perhaps even similar to) the shape, color, and other visual characteristics of the letters themselves.

Second, and more importantly for present purposes, musical notes occurring within a comics panel function very similarly to SFX text.[14] Since musical notion is not, strictly speaking, text, and hence not a literal instance of SFX text, but is instead a different (and, in various ways, different type of) notational communication, we need to provide a separate convention—the *musical notation convention*—for the sorts of imaginings that are usually prescribed by the presence of musical notes within a comics panel:

> *Musical Notation Convention*: When confronted with musical notes within a comics panel, we are to imagine that an appropriate piece of music is being played (or sung, or that a recording of such is being played, etc.), and we are meant to imagine *hearing* that music.

Importantly, musical notes floating free (or even embedded within a staff) within comics panels do not, typically, represent any *particular* piece of music—thus, we are not usually required to imagine a particular piece of music when interpreting musical notation appearing within a comics panel (although context will often determine the broad type of music to be imagined, for example jazz versus rock). On the contrary, when a particular piece of music is intended, this is usually indicated by appropriate narration text, dialogue, or singing on the part of one or more characters.

Of course, this is only a brief, and imperfect, account of the conventions that govern the pictorial and textual components found within typical comics panels. Additional conventions would also be needed, for example, to handle emanata—conventional pictorial elements such as motions lines, scent lines, dust clouds, and little birds circling the heads of stunned characters—since these symbolic elements are not meant to be imagined to be seen but instead involve further, medium-specific conventions regarding the information they provide (roughly speaking: emanata are metaphorical, and particular conventions govern each such metaphor).[15] There are no doubt other standard uses to which both images and text are often put within comics that do not fit any of the conventions listed above. But the six norms outlined above are enough to carry out the task at hand—to examine some underappreciated formal experimentation with text and musical notation in Schulz's *Peanuts*.

CONVENTION AND TEXT IN *PEANUTS*

The first example we shall look at is the October 1, 1954, *Peanuts* strip (fig. 3.1), in which Violet and Patty are watching Charlie Brown play football. Charlie Brown shouts out a series of signals before hiking the ball, and in the final panel Patty remarks: "Have you ever seen such fancy signals?" The balloon in the third panel containing the fancy signals in question is, at first glance, merely a standard speech balloon reporting Charlie Brown's football signals (albeit one rendered in a highly stylized and ornate manner). Thus, according to the conventions sketched above, we are meant to imagine that Charlie Brown speaks these signals and that we hear him do so (as do Violet and Patty). Further, we are not meant (again, at first glance) to imagine that we can see the balloon itself or text contained in the balloon—hence, the style of the typography (other than emphasis, which affects what we are imagined to hear) ought to be irrelevant to the narrative content of the strip (although, as Will Eisner reminded us at the beginning of this chapter, typographic style can have other, less direct effects on our interpretation of this, or any other, strip).

But merely applying the balloon text convention to signals enunciated by Charlie Brown in the panel in question provides a wholly inadequate understanding of the strip, missing its very point. There are two pieces of evidence that point toward a more complicated interpretation. First, the text in the balloon is rendered in extremely ornate, hand-drawn fonts, with a different "look" for each number in the series, suggesting that their appearance *is* relevant to interpretation, despite the dictates of convention. Second, and even more telling, Patty does not say "Have you ever *heard* such fancy signals?," which is what we would expect if this text were functioning along standard, convention-bound lines. Instead, she says "Have you ever *seen* such fancy signals?," indicating that she can see the signals, and hence that we should imagine that we can see them too.

In short, the fancy typography used in the balloon in the third panel, combined with the otherwise puzzling comment by Patty in the fourth panel, indicate that we should break with convention and apply the

Fig. 3.1: Charles Schulz, *Peanuts*, October 1, 1954. PEANUTS © 1954 Peanuts Worldwide LLC. Dist. by UNIVERSAL UCLICK. Reprinted with permission. All rights reserved.

pictorial text convention (or something much like it) to the contents of Charlie Brown's speech balloon. In short, we should not only imagine that Charlie Brown speaks the signals in question, and imagine hearing him do so, but we should also imagine that we (and Patty and Violet) *see* the spoken symbols, and imagine that when we see them they appear to us as they appear in the panel (i.e., we imagine that we *see the sounds*, and they look to us much like the symbols within this speech balloon).[16]

Note that properly appreciating the strip requires more than that we switch from one reading (signals as textual) to the other (signals as pictorial). The strip is not ambiguous between the two relevant imaginative acts but instead requires that we somehow sustain both readings—that is, perform both imaginative acts—at the same time. The problem, however, is this: while there is no doubt that we can imagine that we hear the signals spoken by Charlie Brown, and there is no doubt that we can imagine seeing those very same signals (nonstandard though the latter imagining might be), there is some very real doubt regarding whether we can coherently imagine that we hear the signals and see them (i.e., those very same signals) *at the same time*. In short, the content of this strip, taken as a whole, is asking us to perform an imaginative act that might well be impossible to carry out, and even if it were possible (i.e., even if we could imagine, of some entity, that it is both a sound that we hear and an object that we see, at the same time), such bizarre and nonconventional (in a very literal sense) imaginative acts are liable to produce some rather substantial cognitive dissonance.

In short, this strip is paradigmatically metafictional: it is impossible to contemplate this strip without being forced "outside" the world of the strip in order to contemplate the various mechanisms by which meaning is made within the strip.[17] The particular metafictional strategy adopted by Schulz in this strip is a phenomenon that I have elsewhere called *multimodal metafiction*:

Multimodal Metafiction: Metafictional effects generated by the presence of a single narrative element that instantiates two or more
communicative modes at work within the fiction, thereby activating two or more conflicting conventions regarding proper interpretation of the fiction (i.e., regarding what we are meant to imagine
when experiencing the fiction).

Importantly, multimodal metafiction of the sort we have located in the
October 1, 1954, strip requires, by definition, that the medium in which
the metafiction is produced is multimodal. While this does not require
that the work in question be a comic, it does imply that comics, with
its characteristic mix of textual and pictorial elements, and the various
distinct communicative modes in which text can occur, will be a fertile
ground for locating and studying examples of this phenomenon.

Before moving on to examine the role of musical notation in *Peanuts*,
it is worth noting that the October 1, 1954, strip is not an isolated instance of this phenomenon. Other examples abound, including the June
2, 1977, strip, in which Peppermint Patty's *Z* emanata, indicating that she
is sleeping, transform from block to cursive when she is awakened by a
teacher asking her if she has been working on her handwriting; the April
9, 1979, strip, in which Woodstock convinces Snoopy that he would be a
good grocery clerk by producing a speech balloon containing a bar code;
and the February 16, 1980, strip, in which Peppermint Patty tells Marcie
that she is in love, her dialogue rendered in a schoolgirl script complete
with hearts for punctuation and Marcie's drowsy reply replacing the
hearts with *Z*s.

CONVENTION AND MUSICAL NOTATION IN *PEANUTS*

Schulz also uses musical notation to generate multimodal metafiction
throughout *Peanuts*—in fact, if one were to catalog all instances of overtly formally experimental, nonconventional metafiction in *Peanuts*, it is
likely that multimodal metafiction achieved via the nonstandard use of
musical notation would be the largest category. The August 20, 1980,
strip is typical: in this strip we see Snoopy roller-skating down the sidewalk, wearing headphones. Musical notes drift behind him, activating
the musical notation convention, instructing us to imagine that Snoopy
is listening to music on his headphones (and that, further, we are to

imagine hearing that music—disco, perhaps?). In the third panel, we see Woodstock coming up from behind Snoopy on his own pair of little roller skates, with the music from Snoopy's headphones drifting overhead, presumably indicating that we are meant to imagine that Woodstock can hear the same music. Things change dramatically, however, in the fourth panel, where we find Woodstock halted, looking bewildered, with the (now somehow physical) musical notes draped over his head.

Peanuts is chock-full of strips like these, in which musical notation is transformed from a nonpictorial indication of the presence of music (and hence an encoding of the prescription to imagine that we, and the characters, are hearing music) to a pictorial representation of the presence of musical-notation-shaped physical objects that are: used as a cage to entrap Woodstock (April 17, 1978), pushed aside to make room for a nap by Snoopy (May 10, 1980), used as a helicopter-like flying machine by Woodstock (July 20, 1980), wrestled with by Snoopy (May 2, 1981), used as a trampoline by Woodstock (December 21, 1981), scattered by a tumbling Woodstock (December 27, 1981), and used as a bed by Snoopy (July 2, 1982).[18]

These examples involve a conflict between a different set of conventions than the text-involving instances of multimodal metafiction discussed in the previous section. In the former cases, we had what appeared at first glance to be text of one sort or another turn out to also require activation of the pictorial content convention, forcing us to simultaneously interpret the text as both something that is heard and something that is seen. Although the conventions are different in the August 20, 1980, strip and the other music-oriented strips cataloged in the previous paragraph, the upshot is the same: in each of the strips involving apparently physically, causally efficacious musical notes (or staffs), a full interpretation of the strip requires activation of both the musical notation convention, by which we understand the musical notes to indicate the presence of music, and the pictorial content convention, by which we understand the notes to be physically present in the scenario depicted in the panels. Thus, although there are no doubt subtle differences between the text-involving instances of this phenomenon and the musical notation–involving instances, there is much apparent similarity, and, at this point, the reader might be forgiven for wondering why we need an entire section of this chapter to cover music.

Transforming notes so that they become physical inhabitants of the fictional world within which *Peanuts* takes place is not the only way in

Fig. 3.2: Charles Schulz, *Peanuts*, August 20, 1980. PEANUTS © 1980 Peanuts Worldwide LLC. Dist. by UNIVERSAL UCLICK.
Reprinted with permission. All rights reserved.

which Schulz manipulates musical notation to achieve unconventional (or, perhaps better, given what is coming: extraconventional) effects in his work, however. Another important aspect of Schulz's use of musical notation in *Peanuts* has been extensively studied by musicologist William Meredith, who curated a museum exhibit on the role of music in *Peanuts* titled *Schulz's Beethoven: Schroeder's Muse*.[19] Although Meredith uncovered many important and previously unnoticed facts regarding the role of classical music in *Peanuts* and the role this same music played in Schulz's life outside the cartoon, the most important observation for our purposes is this: the drawn musical notes of many of the pieces played by Schroeder in the strips are actual transcriptions of Beethoven's work, and Schulz was often very careful to include works that fit the content or theme of the strip.

The January 25, 1953, strip is a typical example of this phenomenon: in this strip, we are given nine panels depicting Schroeder engaging in various kinds of athletic training, followed by a panel depicting a healthy breakfast, and then the penultimate panel showing Schroeder walking determinedly, with fists clenched, toward some task or goal. In the final panel, we finally discover what all this training and game-facing is for, as Schroeder begins playing an extremely complicated piece of music, as indicated by the very complicated musical notation used to represent (via activation of the musical notation convention) the presence of such music.[20]

It will be unsurprising to many readers that the musical notation in this panel looks authentic, and it would indeed be a difficult piece to actually play (especially, one presumes, on a child's toy piano). The fact that Schulz was both a fan of, and extremely knowledgeable about, classical music is well documented.[21] What is more surprising, however, is this: the musical notation in the final panel is a transcription of the beginning of Beethoven's *Hammerklavier* Sonata in B-flat Major (op. 106), widely considered to be Beethoven's most difficult work for piano.[22]

The use of an actual, nearly impossible to play musical work in the January 25, 1954, strip enriches an already subtle and amusing strip. For readers not intimately familiar with the *Hammerklavier*, the strip amusingly shows Schroeder training like an olympic athlete before attempting to perform a particularly difficult piece of music. For those who do recognize those first few bars of music, however, the strip exhibits additional layers of intertextual depth, since such readers will recognize the difficulty of the piece (and might very well recall having attempted to play the work in question themselves, and the extensive preparation that such an attempt would have required). The explicit (even if somewhat difficult for nonexperts to detect) reference to a particular work by Beethoven also enriches Schroeder's backstory as an acolyte of the famous composer, adding extra layers of complexity to other strips in which he celebrates Beethoven's birthday or berates Lucy for her insufficient veneration of the German composer.

This strip would, like the textual instance of multimodal metafiction we examined in the previous section, be of limited interest if it were an isolated instance. But Schulz peppered his Schroeder strips with a wide variety of excerpts from Beethoven's oeuvre. Some examples:

- The Pathétique Piano Sonata in C Minor (op. 13) in the June 9, 1968, March 20, 1969, and April 15, 1985, strips.
- The Little Pathétique Piano Sonata in C Minor (op. 10, no. 1) in the September 12, 1968, strip.
- The Moonlight Piano Sonata Quasi Una Fantasia in C-sharp Minor (op. 27, no. 2) in the August 7, 1952, April 23, 1953, and April 29, 1957, strips.
- The Bagatelle in G Minor (op. 119, no. 1) in the December 15, 1974, strip.
- The Piano Sonata in A Major (op. 2, no. 2) in the April 17, 1960, strip.
- The Piano Sonata in A-flat Major (op. 110) in the December 15, 1968, strip.
- The Piano Sonata in B-flat Major (op. 22) in the September 27, 1960, strip.
- The Piano Sonata in D Major (op. 28) in the October 10, 1963, strip.
- The Piano Sonata in F-minor (op. 2, no. 1) in the February 4, 1963, strip.

Fig. 3.3: Charles Schulz, *Peanuts*, January 25, 1953. PEANUTS © 1953 Peanuts Worldwide LLC. Dist. by UNIVERSAL UCLICK. Reprinted with permission. All rights reserved.

In addition, the *Hammerklavier* was also referenced in the March 25 and April 14, 1952, strips.[23]

As a result, it is clear that Schulz hoped (and intended) that at least some of his audience would decode these musical allusions, identifying the music included in the strip and enriching their understanding of the gag, and of the larger fictional universe within which *Peanuts* takes place, in the process. In short, it seems reasonable to conclude that Schulz's inclusion of these bits of music amounts to his adopting an additional, strip-specific convention regarding the proper way in which to understand and interpret the presence of musical notation in *Peanuts* strips. In addition to prescribing that we imagine the presence of appropriate music, and that we imagine that we hear the music in question (and, when appropriate, that the characters do as well), a full and complete interpretation of a *Peanuts* strip that includes musical notation involves acting in accordance with something like the following *Peanuts*-specific *musical notation convention*:

Musical Notation Convention 2: When confronted with musical notes within a *Peanuts* panel (especially when those notes are embedded in a staff), we are often meant to identify the particular piece by Beethoven being referenced, and we are further meant to imagine that the work in question is being played, and we are meant to imagine hearing *that particular work*.[24]

In short, a full understanding of many *Peanuts* strips involves recognition of particular pieces of Beethoven's music (and an ability to imagine hearing those works). This, in turn, requires rather specialized knowledge—which, presumably, most intended readers of the strip don't have.

Of course, we shouldn't fall into the trap of thinking that, as a result, the typical (non–classically trained) reader of a *Peanuts* strip featuring Beethoven's work in this manner misunderstands, or fails to understand entirely, the strip in question. Comics (and other works of art) are not like items on a high-school vocabulary test, which you either understand or you don't. Rather, comics in general, and *Peanuts* strips in particular (like any narrative work of art) involve complex networks of meaning(s), and different consumers of such works are likely to recognize, emphasize, reflect on, and report different aspects of this complex manifold of content. Failing to recognize a somewhat obscure intertextual reference in a work of art does not imply that one has failed to understand the work generally, although it does imply that there is a part of the work that one hasn't understood. And the role that music plays in *Peanuts*—and the notational quotation of Beethoven's music in particular—is just such a part, one that we all are only just beginning to understand. I make no pretense to have fleshed out a full account of all of the interpretative consequences that these explicit references to Beethoven's music entail; rather, the task undertaken here is the more modest one of highlighting the issue and providing one possible framework within which more progress might be made.

Before moving on, it is worth mentioned the amazing November 20, 1997, strip, since the jack-of-all-trades musical notation in this strip plays all of the roles described above. At the far left of the strip, which consists of a single elongated panel, we see Schroeder playing the piano, and the first few bars of the *Pathétique* Sonata indicate the particular work we are meant to imagine. But at the middle of the panel the notes begin to "fall" out of the staff to the ground, and then they line up, marching across the panel toward the far right edge. Snoopy is attempting to walk on top of the row of musical notes, with "Ouch! Oo! Ow! Ouch!" in his thought balloon. Thus, in this panel we have musical notation

Fig. 3.4: Charles Schulz, *Peanuts*, November 20, 1997. PEANUTS © 1997 Peanuts Worldwide LLC. Dist. by UNIVERSAL UCLICK. Reprinted with permission. All rights reserved.

that activates both the pictorial text convention (like the musical notes draped across Woodstock's nose in the August 20, 1980, strip) and our new, *Peanuts*-specific version of the musical notation convention indicating that these same notes represent a particular piece of music—the *Pathétique*. One wonders what Beethoven would have thought if he had seen the notes of his sonata leaping from the staff and marching off in single file toward the panel border!

Two final, interconnected comments about the inclusion of these Beethoven passages in *Peanuts* are worth making. First, the intertextual nature of these strips, referencing and incorporating supposedly "high-art" works by Beethoven within the lowbrow medium of the newspaper comic strip, engenders a sort of metafictional (but not multimodal

metafictional!) effect that is, in virtue of its engagement with and interrogation of the traditional high/low or fine/popular art distinctions,
worthy of more attention than we can give here. Closely connected to this
is the second point: Schulz's own assessment of comic strips in general
(and *Peanuts* in particular) as inferior to "real/high/fine" art and as of
primarily commercial, rather than artistic, value is well known. The following comment by Schulz is typical:

> I seriously doubt that cartooning is a pure form of art for many rea-
> sons. For one reason, you have to please an editor, and no art form
> can exist when it has to please an immediate audience. Also the
> true test of art—my own definition, right or wrong—is how well
> it speaks to other, future generations. If a cartoon lasts generation
> after generation, is reprinted over and over, and speaks just as well
> to the fifth generation as to the generation in which it was drawn, I
> suppose it could be labeled as art just as much as a painting could.
> If it gives joy 100 years from now, then it's just as much a work of
> art as a painting.[25]

One irony of this passage, of course, is the fact that *Peanuts* is, among ex-
tant comic strips, one of a handful that seem likely to meet Schulz's read-
one-hundred-years-from-now criteria. Independently of Schulz's specific
beliefs regarding what makes something art (and independently of the
obvious inadequacy of that criterion), what is clear from this passage is
that Schulz characterizes comics as aesthetically inferior to the art forms
with which he entertained himself when not cartooning—notably literature and music. But the explicit inclusion of the excerpts from Beethoven
would seem to be in tension with (or, at the very least, worthy of being
interpretationally juxtaposed with) Schulz's well-publicized assessment
of cartoonists as craftsmen, not artists. If comics aren't art (or aren't
likely to be art), then why go to such lengths to imbue them with the
very sort of multiple layers of referential and narrative complexity often
indicative of (good or great) art—referential and narrative complexity
that, in this case at least, is likely to go unrecognized and unremarked
by the majority of the audience for the work?

CONCLUSION

Peanuts is often thought of as little more than a cute comic strip chronicling the cute (and often poignant) escapades of a group of kids—in other words, as nothing more than a run-of-the-mill family-oriented humor strip, albeit a brilliantly crafted, often nearly perfect run-of-the-mill family-oriented humor strip. Schulz's simple, minimalist drawing style and his tendency to focus on the funny, touching, or sad aspects of small, everyday events has encouraged interpretations of the comic (by fans and scholars alike) that fail to recognize its structural complexities. One such locus of complexity is the continued formal experimentation with the comic strip form that was an occasional, but nevertheless continuous and unrelenting, part of Schulz's legacy to comics. Here we have focused on just one aspect of this formal interrogation of the comics form—Schulz's masterful manipulations of text and musical notation—but hopefully this is enough to demonstrate that *Peanuts* is a technically complex, often experimental, and always masterful comic, and a genuine masterpiece of American art, one that deserves much more theoretical scrutiny that it has received up to now.

NOTES

1. Will Eisner, *Comics and Sequential Art* (Tamarac, FL: Poorhouse Press, 1985), 10.

2. Note that, given Eisner's insight, this sentence is not redundant, since nonpictures (e.g., text or musical notation) can nevertheless contribute to the content of a page in roughly the same manner as pictures do—that is, they can have pictorial content.

3. This section incorporates, and further develops, ideas I first explored in "Morrison, Magic, and Visualizing the Word: Text as Image in *Vimanarama*," *Imagetext* 8, no. 2 (2015), at http://www.english.ufl.edu/imagetext/archives/v8_2/cook/, which examines multimodal metafiction in Grant Morrison's *Vimanarama*.

4. Of course, a work is not required to involve this sort of interaction in order to be a comic: "silent" or "mute" comics (e.g., the comics collected in Marvel Comics' *Nuff Said* [2002] trade paperback anthology), which tell a story solely through the use of pictures, are uncontroversial cases of comics lacking this sort of interaction, while my essay "Comics without Pictures; or, Why *Batman* #663 Is a Comic" (*Journal of Aesthetics and Art Criticism* 69 [2011]: 285–96) explores the more controversial possibility of comics containing text but no pictures.

5. Randy Bomer, "Literacy Classrooms: Making Minds out of Multimodal Material," in *Handbook on Teaching Literacy through the Communicative and Visual Arts*, ed. James Flood, Shirley Brice Heath, and Diane Lapp (New York: Lawrence Erlbaum, 2008), 354.

6. See Kendall L. Walton, *Mimesis as Make-Believe: On the Foundations of the Representational Arts* (Cambridge, MA: Harvard University Press, 1993) for the canonical formulation of this account, and Patrick Maynard, *Drawing Distinctions: The Varieties of Graphic Expression* (Ithaca, NY: Cornell University Press, 2005) for an insightful application of Walton's ideas to pictures.

7. Of course, images can appear in comics and play roles other than that specified by the pictorial content convention, and no claim is made that understanding the pictorial content convention is sufficient for understanding all of the different ways that pictures might function within comics. The point is that when images (other than emanata—see below) *do* play roles other than that specified by the pictorial content convention—for example, the use of images in speech or thought balloons to indicate ideas—they are typically functioning in a nonstandard, nonconventional role, one that usually forces the reader to actively consider the manner in which the image is representing (i.e., to treat the image as metafictional in some sense), rather than simply interpreting it in accordance with standard and established comics storytelling conventions.

8. It is worth emphasizing that the pictorial content convention really is a convention—that is, it is a tacit agreement regarding how agents are meant to act. There is nothing in human nature or the natural world that requires that we interpret the pictorial content of comics in the manner in which we do. Rather, this rule, and each of the various other rules for interpretation discussed below, is the result of regularities in interpretational behavior that determine how interpretation *should* be carried out. The normative nature of these conventions is not incompatible with their open-endedness, however: these conventions govern how we ought to interpret comics without necessarily implying that there is a single correct way to apply them. For an in-depth discussion of both the contingency and normativity of conventions, see David Lewis, *Convention: A Philosophical Study* (Oxford: Blackwell, 1969).

9. Reflecting on *Peanuts* is enough to see that something like this account of the imaginative acts associated with images must be right: anyone who concludes that he is reading science fiction when reading *Peanuts*, based on the giant heads possessed by all of the characters, is misunderstanding the fiction (and, in fact, misunderstanding how comic art works). We are not meant to imagine that Charlie Brown actually has a head too big to be supported by his body, but we are meant to imagine that he looks that way when we imagine seeing the events depicted in the strip. For further detailed discussion of the gap between how things appear in panels and how we are meant to understand them to look in the fiction, and a detailed defense of understanding this gap along the lines sketched above, see Roy T. Cook, "Drawings of Photographs in Comics," *Journal of Aesthetics and Art Criticism* 70 (2012): 129–38; "Does the Joker Have Six-Inch Teeth?," in *The Joker: A Serious Study of the Clown Prince of Crime*, ed. Robert Moses Peaslee and Robert G. Weiner (Jackson: University Press of Mississippi, 2015), 19–32; and "Judging a Comic by Its Cover: Marvel Comics, Photo-Covers, and the Objectivity of Photography," *Image and Narrative* 16, no. 2 (2015): 14–27. All three of these essays are deeply indebted to Maynard.

10. The reader should take care not to confuse the common and unremarkable presence of pictorial text in comics with Scott McCloud's more esoteric notion of *montage*

text. Montage text—one of McCloud's seven ways that words and pictures can interact within a comics panel—is (inadequately) defined by McCloud as those combinations "where words are treated as integral parts of the picture" (*Understanding Comics: The Invisible Art* [New York: William Morrow, 1993], 154). Although he does not say as much, it is clear from McCloud's examples (words such as "cash flow" floating around a sweat-beaded head, happiness expressed by large letters filling the panel, and a human figure made up of rows of type) that montage text is meant to be restricted to those cases in which pictorial elements are *composed* of text, which must be both read and seen. Thus, montage text is an instance of multimodal metafiction (a notion introduced below), but, as we shall see, not all multimodal metafiction involves montage text.

11. Thus, balloons cue another inferential process, since we must infer what to imagine lies "behind" the balloons based on the portions of the scene not obstructed by balloons, contextual clues, and other relevant information.

12. Of course, things are more complicated here, as well. For example, sometimes we are given text embedded in angle brackets "< . . . >" indicating that (in Anglo-American comics) the English text within the brackets is a translation of the non-English expressions that we are meant to imagine spoken, where the particular language in question is usually clear from context. In such cases, we are not meant to imagine that the English text within the brackets is spoken, nor are we meant to imagine that we hear it spoken. Instead, we are meant to imagine that some non-English "equivalent" of the text in brackets is spoken, and we are meant to imagine that we hear this "equivalent" being spoken. Problematically, this scenario seems to require that we do things that we are incapable of doing, in cases where we do not know what the relevant translations are.

13. As this observation makes clear, the usual concerns regarding the reliability of various sorts of narrators apply to all types of narration text.

14. Of course, musical notation might also (and often does) play a role analogous to pictorial text, in which the musical notation is a part of the picture, and hence prescribes that we imagine *seeing* the notation but does not prescribe that we imagine *hearing* anything.

15. For an amusing catalog of common emanata used in comics, see Mort Walker's *Lexicon of Comicana* (Lincoln NE: iUniverse Press, 1980).

16. Note that the gap between imagining that things *appear* to us in a certain way, and imagining that they *are* that way, prevents the prescription to imagine that we see the signals from collapsing into outright coherence. While it is not clear that we can imagine that sounds genuinely look a particular way (e.g., that they would look a certain way to normal, nonsynesthesic perceivers), we can imagine that sounds appear to us as looking a certain way (i.e., we can imagine ourselves to be having synesthesic experiences).

17. For an early examination of metafiction in comics (including a brief discussion of metafiction in *Peanuts*), see M. Thomas Inge, *Anything Can Happen in a Comic Book: Centennial Reflections on an American Art Form* (Jackson: University Press of Mississippi, 1995); and for an extended survey of various sorts of metafiction occurring in *Peanuts* strips, see my "Schulz, *Peanuts*, and Metafiction," *International Journal of Comic Art* 14, no. 1 (2012): 66–92.

18. For the reader who does not have the entire run of *Peanuts* handy, it is worth noting that in some of these cases—notably the cage and the trampoline—it is a musical staff full of notes with which the relevant character interacts, not merely individual musical notes.

19. The exhibit was housed at the Charles M. Schulz Museum and Research Center in Santa Rosa, California, from August 2008 to January 2009, and at the Ira F. Brilliant Center for Beethoven Studies at San Jose State University from May 2009 to July 2009. An excellent online version of the exhibit is now housed at the website of the American Beethoven Society, at http://absadmin.users.sonic.net/schulz/pages/page1.html.

20. As already noted, the kind and complexity of the musical notation used to represent the presence of music can also suggest the kind and complexity of the sort of music that we are meant to imagine. Nevertheless, in standard cases, this still falls far short of determining a particular piece of music that we are meant to imagine hearing.

21. Ironically, given the centrality of Beethoven to *Peanuts*, Schulz actually preferred Brahms to Beethoven (a fact humorously referenced in the September 4, 1953, strip, in which Schroeder suffers a moment of existential dread after carelessly admitting that he sometimes prefers Brahms to Beethoven). Schulz thought that the name "Beethoven" looked funnier on the page, however, and thus Schroeder's obsession was born.

22. For further discussion of the *Hammerklavier* and its role in this strip, see Cook, "Schulz, *Peanuts*, and Metafiction."

23. The online *Schulz's Beethoven, Schroeder's Muse* exhibit hosted by the American Beethoven Society features each of these strips paired with digital files of performances of the referenced music along with detailed commentary.

24. This convention, like any convention, must be defeasible: Schroeder occasionally plays other particular works of music that are indicated by accurate musical notation, such as his performance of the "Spinning Song" (op. 67, no. 4) by Felix Mendelssohn for an appreciative Snoopy in the January 30, 1957, strip.

25. Charles Schulz, "*Atlanta Weekly* Interview," interview by Eugene Griessman, *Atlanta Weekly*, November 15, 1981, 177; reprinted in M. Thomas Inge, *Charles M. Schulz: Conversations* (Jackson: University Press of Mississippi, 2000), 111–20.

IDENTITY AND PERFORMANCE

-4-

CONSUMING CHILDHOOD

Peanuts and Children's Consumer Culture in the Postwar Era

LARA SAGUISAG

The debut of Charles Schulz's *Peanuts* on October 2, 1950, seems expressive of the postwar period's preoccupation with the subject of childhood. Americans who grew up during the Great Depression, lived through wartime, and were witnessing the onset of the Cold War were keen to ensure that their children were sheltered from the perceived complexities and dangers of the adult world.[1] Of course, adult efforts to protect children and to draw boundaries between childhood and adulthood were not without precedent. In the late eighteenth century, the notion that innocence was an inherent quality of childhood—and that adults were tasked to safeguard this innocence—began circulating among white, urban, middle-class families. Consequently, the material culture associated with childhood, such as toys, books, furniture, and clothing, reflected and conveyed adults' desires to maintain childhood as a pure, carefree stage of life.[2] In the nineteenth century, the image of childhood innocence became more widely accepted, and by the Progressive Era, this ideal spurred many reformers to campaign for initiatives that they viewed as necessary to prolong childhood, such as the abolishment of child labor, the mandating of school attendance, and the establishment of playgrounds and kindergartens in urban spaces.

Many efforts that sought to "save the child" were attempts to monitor and censor mass entertainments. Anthony Comstock, writing in 1883, denounced dime novels as "traps for the young." In the early twentieth century, the educator and reformer Percival Chubb waged a campaign that sought to "improve" comic strip supplements, and some of his contemporaries called for the regulation of nickelodeons. In the post–World War II era, similar crusades were waged against television and comic books. Parents, educators, civic leaders, and psychologists claimed that these forms of entertainment were prematurely exposing the young to the world of adults, and that the popularity of these media was directly correlated to the purported rise of juvenile delinquency. Moreover, many adults believed that children were too passive and naïve to resist commercialization and were thus easily swept up in a culture that was increasingly defined by consumption.

This chapter places *Peanuts* in the context of the radical expansion of children's consumer culture in the postwar period. It examines the ways the strip depicts, interrogates, and celebrates young people's relationships with goods and entertainment. Focusing on episodes published in the 1950s, I argue that *Peanuts* expresses ambivalence over children's practices of consumption. Some of the strip's episodes suggest that children are victimized by a distracting, excessive consumer culture. In a sense, Schulz positions the strip as an alternative to "harmful" popular media such as television and comic books. He presents *Peanuts* as wholesome fare, a gag strip that uses light humor and that insists that certain spaces—the comic strip, the suburb—could serve as safe havens for children.

However, the strip also proposes that commercialization and child-centered entertainments are not necessarily corrupting forces and that children are not necessarily corruptible. The young characters display savvy and enterprise as they use and share commercial products. *Peanuts* illustrates the ways children are able to play and exercise creativity not in the absence, but through the use, of consumer goods. In other words, Charlie Brown and his friends are able to perform childhood innocence not by avoiding but by participating in the adult market. Furthermore, even as the strip appears to be more "innocent" than contemporary television shows and comic books, it remains a commercial form that trades on images of childhood. Ultimately, *Peanuts* implies that children's engagement with consumer culture is inevitable.

BABY BOOM: THE EXPANSION OF CHILDREN'S CONSUMER CULTURE IN THE POSTWAR PERIOD

In the late 1940s and early 1950s, many adults were concerned, even agitated, by the effects of commercialization and expanding consumer culture on childhood. During this period, however, advice literature touted consumer goods as necessary elements in establishing a blissful, stable nuclear family. Members of the middle class were encouraged to practice robust consumption as a means of responding to the trauma and tumult of the Great Depression and World War II. Lynn Spigel describes how advertisements for household appliances such as washing machines and blenders worked to secure working women in the home, as they promised that such technological innovations would help facilitate intimacy with husbands and children.[3] Much marketing and advice literature of the period was also keenly focused on the perceived needs and wants of the child, encouraging parents to purchase goods and design "child-friendly" spaces in the home in order to cultivate their children's physical, mental, and emotional health. The migration of American middle-class families from cities to suburbs was linked to the belief that yards and sizable homes that could accommodate playrooms and children's bedrooms were necessary to the development of the child.[4] The expansion of the educational toy industry expressed how children's playthings were increasingly seen as indispensable to stimulating creativity, a quality that, in the postwar period, was understood as essential to social progress.[5] As Amy F. Ogata puts it, "the making of the 'child-sized world' in the home was an ongoing project for postwar middle-class families who labored to meet the social expectations of a popular culture that was increasingly obsessed with family life."[6]

Parental efforts to shape a "child-sized world" in the home was supported by a market flooded with products specifically designed for and directed at child consumers. Gary Cross reminds us that producers have recognized children as a viable market in decades prior: in the 1900s, advertisements for children's toys were prominent in catalogs and children's magazines; in the 1930s, radio programs and film matinees aimed at young audiences were accompanied by commercials for children's products; the comic book also emerged in the 1930s, a publication that was at once a commercial product and a venue for marketing other merchandise.[7]

In the postwar era, with the entry of television into American homes, producers became more vigorous in creating and marketing goods and entertainment for consumption by children and adolescents. Thus, the 1950s was marked by the arrival of what Steven Mintz calls "postmodern children," as young people increasingly became "independent consumers and participants in a separate, semiautonomous youth culture."[8]

The February 1, 1953, episode of *Peanuts* illustrates how children in the postwar period were being ushered into the role of consumer. Patty and Lucy walk into a dime store to examine and appreciate the variety

Fig. 4.1: Charles Schulz, *Peanuts,* February 1, 1953. PEANUTS © 1953 Peanuts Worldwide LLC. Dist. by UNIVERSAL UCLICK.
Reprinted with permission. All rights reserved.

of objects that were especially made for children. Certainly, the episode
makes clear that both Patty and Lucy are still too young to be fully integrated into the culture of consumption. Neither child has the money to
purchase any of the toys; the episode revolves around the gag that Lucy is
too short to see over the counter. But as even as the girls lack purchasing
power, Patty insists that they could derive pleasure from simply *looking*
at the toys. For her, visiting the dime store is "a lot of fun even if you
can't buy anything." She takes delight in seeing the toys laid out on the
counter, perhaps exuberant over the promise that, in a few years, she
will be able to purchase these toys on her own.

As Patty visually consumes the toys, she appears to delight most in
the diminutive size of the objects. She calls for Lucy to look at the "little
dolls," "tiny dishes," "tiny airplanes," and a "tiny fire engine." Ironically,
Lucy herself is too tiny to see any of these toys, and she is left to stare at
the front paneling of the counter. Thus while Lucy stands in a store that
displays and sells child-sized objects, the store itself is not designed for
a child of her size. In the last panel, a frustrated Lucy tells Patty that she
will likely enjoy another visit to the store after four years have passed,

acknowledging that her status as a young person is an obstacle to her participation in the market. Yet while Lucy's age limits her level of participation, the episode also reveals her precocity: she displays knowledge of the craft of carpentry, a subject that is not typically seen as part of a "child-sized" world. Left to stare at the counter's front panels, Lucy observes and evaluates the woodwork, praising the quality of wood, the attention to sanding, the use of screws instead of nails.

Indeed, Lucy appears to be a particularly discerning consumer. In a later episode, published on May 24, 1953, Charlie Brown refers to Lucy as a "real authority on jumping ropes." She demonstrates her knowledge as she examines Violet's new purchase:

> It doesn't look too bad . . . of course, I prefer the lightweight aluminum grips, but then, the wooden grips are better than the leather ones . . . especially in the rain . . . but then, who jumps rope in the rain? Ha ha.
>
> I hear the new "reminder" grips are pretty good . . . of course, a lot also depends on the rope itself . . . the quality of the weave, etc.

The figure of Lucy thus calls attention to the irony of the child who is typically excluded from practices of consumption but who nonetheless has a keen eye for practices of production.

While the February 1, 1953, episode illustrates the limitations placed on children's consumption habits—and the ways children respond to such limitations—it is worth noting that the title *Peanuts* itself indicates recognition of children as active participants in consumer culture. When United Feature Syndicate picked up Schulz's strip, the syndicate decided to rename it, as its original title, *Li'l Folks*, was too similar to that of two contemporary strips—*Li'l Abner* by Al Capp and *Little Folks* by Tack Knight. The syndicate's editors retitled Schulz's strip *Peanuts*, alluding to the "peanut gallery" in the popular postwar television show *Howdy Doody*. Although *Howdy Doody*'s peanut gallery was itself a reference to vaudeville's rowdy, heckling, peanut-throwing crowd, it was certainly a sanitized version, an in-studio audience composed of children who sang the opening song and laughed at the show's gags. The young audience members served as model viewers for children watching at home, their presence meant to encourage home viewers to sing and laugh along, to observe "Howdy Doody time," to intently watch the screen while products were advertised on the show. Spigel notes that *Howdy Doody* and its contemporary children's programs specifically "taught children the art of persuasion, advising them how to tell their parents about the wondrous items advertised on the show."[9] In the *Peanuts* strip, there was no similar overt effort to sell merchandising to children or instruct them how to exercise their "nagging power" to influence their parents' purchasing choices. But in choosing to reference the participatory child audience of *Howdy Doody*, United Feature Syndicate acknowledged the expanding role of children in consumer culture and, more pointedly, expressed its desire to tap the child market.

Schulz's resentment of the title has been widely documented. In a 1987 interview with Richard Marschall and Gary Groth, Schulz railed against the label *Peanuts*, which he described as "totally ridiculous," having "no meaning, . . . simply confusing—and [having] no dignity."[10] As Ben Schwartz suggests, Schulz's umbrage was rooted in his intention to address an audience of adults.[11] The cartoonist appeared to have an ambivalent stance toward his strip as it became associated with child readers. As Charles Hatfield claims, "in keeping with dismissive attitudes toward children's culture, [Schulz] often adopted a diminutive rhetoric when discussing his work (though he was in fact stubbornly proud of it at the same time)."[12]

Perhaps Schulz did not consider young people to be discriminating readers and consumers. He occasionally used *Peanuts* to poke fun at the image of young consumers, calling attention to how children lacked sensibility in their consumption practices. The July 20, 1952, episode features Charlie Brown standing in the middle of a store, debating whether he should spend his money on a balloon or a gumball. He thinks about whether he prefers something that would "taste mighty good" or something that "would be a lot more fun." He eventually settles on a white balloon, and takes pride in his ability to arrive at a rational choice, declaring that "sooner or later in life a person has to learn to make decisions." Yet the moment he sees Patty walk by with a red balloon, he experiences buyer's remorse.

The episode offers a critique of postwar prosperity, pointing out how the wide variety and availability of goods could lead to a constant sense of dissatisfaction among consumers, whether young or old. But the episode arguably represents the child as a particularly vulnerable consumer. The store that Charlie Brown visits conspicuously exhibits its abundance of goods: there is a display case full of toys, a rack stuffed with comic books and magazines, pictures of floats and sundaes. A pennant hanging in

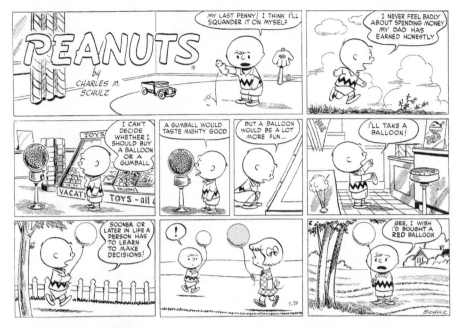

Fig. 4.2: Charles Schulz, *Peanuts*, July 20, 1952. PEANUTS © 1952 Peanuts Worldwide LLC. Dist. by UNIVERSAL UCLICK. Reprinted with permission. All rights reserved.

the background serves to announce a sale. Although Charlie Brown is pleased with his ability to make a rational decision, the episode's top tier shows that he still lacks the ability to exercise care and prudence in his purchases. As he shakes out the last coin from his piggy bank, he looks forward to "squander[ing] it." He eagerly runs to the store, declaring that he "never feel[s] badly about spending money" that his dad "earned honestly." This image of Charlie Brown implies how the offspring of the so-called Greatest Generation remain blind to the sacrifices endured by their parents and have consequently approached consumption as an inherent right.

Other episodes also call attention to the excessiveness of toys and diversions in children's lives. The June 6, 1954, episode at first appears to be a celebration of children's play, particularly outdoor play. Each panel provides a snapshot of children engaged in what appears to be a joyful activity: Violet, Patty, and Lucy play jump rope; Shermy is out for a run with Snoopy; Charlie Brown flies a kite; Schroeder runs with a balloon. But the children's games end in chaos, as the episode concludes with an image of the children entangled in ropes and strings. Although Schulz

shows only the aftermath, omitting the scene in which the children col-
lide into one another, the final panel suggests that the very objects that
are meant to enable children's play can actually violently disrupt it.

The April 2, 1951, installment offers a similar commentary on the
surplus of toys and other "child-sized" objects in the lives of children.
As Lucy prepares for bed, she throws a variety of objects into her crib,
including dolls, stuffed toys, blocks, a purse, books, and a ball. The crib
is so jam packed that there appears to be no room for Lucy, and she ends
up sleeping on top of a little mountain of toys. The last panel nudges the
reader toward feeling discomfited over Lucy's overreliance on toys for
comfort and security. Moreover, the crib no longer serves its purpose
to protect Lucy as she sleeps. Readers may also notice the lack of adult
supervision as Lucy prepares for bed. This episode implies that a child,
when left to her own devices, can end up endangering herself.

Yet the last panel also shows Lucy sleeping *soundly*. The image calls
attention to the incongruity between adult beliefs about childhood and
the actual experiences of children. While the image may reinforce adult
anxieties that children can be harmed by a lifestyle that is "overflowing"
with toys and other objects, it also offers that such anxiety may be un-
founded, as children appear to find pleasure and security in possessing
and using goods in abundance. In short, the episode signals that children
are not necessarily victims of an expanding culture of consumption.

In a sense, Schulz's strip seemed to mirror the function of the postwar
popular press, which "championed American consumerism [while] also
present[ing] parents with a stream of contradictory advice against 'over-
indulgence' in the 'synthetic pleasures' of consumer culture."[13] In fact,
even as the episodes I discuss above point to the fraught relationship that
children have with consumer goods, overall *Peanuts* tends to naturalize
rather than condemn the presence of material and commercial goods in
the lives of children. Many of the day-to-day activities of Charlie Brown
and his friends are intertwined with objects such as jumping ropes,
marbles, balls, wagons, dolls, toy soldiers, and toy guns. *Peanuts*, then,
suggests that the performance of innocent childhood in the postwar era
was inescapably tied to the act of consumption.

In some instances, the strip also illustrates the usefulness, even the
necessity, of toys in nurturing children's imagination and play. Linus
particularly serves as a character who demonstrates the creative use
of toys. As the younger sibling of Lucy (and, in these early episodes, a
preverbal toddler), Linus often finds himself excluded from the activities

that his sister and her friends engage in. In a series of episodes published in March 1954, Linus uses his building blocks to make a claim for inclusion. After seeing Charlie Brown and Lucy sitting on chairs as they watch television, Linus drags his bag of blocks in front of the television and builds an armchair and ottoman. In another episode, Linus attempts to play with his sister in a sandbox. But Lucy yells at Linus to "get away from here . . . ! This is *my* sandbox!" (emphasis in original). The disgruntled toddler then constructs his own sandbox using his blocks.

In both episodes, the older children regard Linus with surprise. Their astonishment indicates that Linus's constructions are unexpected and unusual for a child his age. In an earlier episode, Charlie Brown calls attention to Linus's precocity. When the toddler stacks the blocks in the shape of a staircase, Charlie Brown remarks: "That can't be done, Linus . . . They're going to fall right away. Watch." But the blocks do not fall over. As the puzzled Charlie Brown walks away, he states: "That kid is getting too smart-alecky." Thus, as the blocks defy the laws of gravity, Linus seems to defy the laws of childhood. But even as these episodes insist that Linus is an unusual, precocious child, they also point to how young people can sometimes use objects in unanticipated ways in order to assert themselves and participate in a culture that tends to exclude them.

PEANUTS AS INNOCENT ENTERTAINMENT

Despite the possibilities offered by toys and other cultural goods in enabling children to exercise creativity, resourcefulness, and autonomy, many adults were troubled by their own inability to constantly monitor their children's activities and consumption practices. Undoubtedly, one of the most powerful expressions of adult apprehension over children's expanding consumer culture and growing purchasing power was in the crusade against comic books in the early 1950s. Adult critics claimed that comic books were crass and overtly commercial texts that impeded the proper acquisition of literacy skills and encouraged delinquency and deviance through violent and sexual content. But these anticomics campaigns was also fueled by adults' belief that their role as mediators between children and consumer goods was being undermined. Comic books, as Bradford Wright puts it, became a "source of entertainment that spoke directly to young people as 'independent consumers.'"[14] The inability to supervise children's consumption practices thus caused unease among many adults. Joe Sutliff Sanders states that "comics traditionally have been seen as a threat to the power of adults . . . because comics are for solitary, unmonitored readers who are making meaning without the immediate involvement of adults."[15] Thus the anticomics campaigns were attempts by adults to "regain much of the consumer power behind choosing what youngsters would read."[16]

Adults also waged a similar battle against postwar television programming for children. Television was blamed for the "disruption of generational roles, particularly with regard to power struggles over what constituted proper children's entertainment."[17] Much like comic books, television was understood as sullying the innocence of the child viewer: it gave children access to programs that were purportedly unsuitable for the young and prematurely inducted children into consumer culture.[18]

What sort of commentary did *Peanuts* offer on these contemporary forms of consumer culture that figured prominently in the lives of many American children? In a few episodes, Schulz calls attention to the violent content of comic books. The July 22, 1952, episode shows a shelf marked "For the Kiddies" as full of comic books bearing titles such as *Mangle, Terror, Gouge,* and *Stab!* Charlie Brown exclaims: "What a beautiful gory layout!" Schulz appears to provide some assurance to readers by showing Charlie Brown settling for a comic book with an indistinct title, perhaps the cartoonist's way of signifying that his character was not necessarily reading a comic book full of violent images. In a later episode, in which Charlie Brown purchases a comic book for Schroeder's birthday, the magazine rack that he peruses is filled with similar titles, including *War, Hate, Killer Komix,* and *Slaughter.* Charlie Brown settles on a magazine that bears the rather innocent title *Comix* (Schulz used the term before it became associated with the "adult-themed" work produced by underground and alternative comix artists). He tells Patty that this particular comic book is a "good one"—good, perhaps not simply in terms of quality but also in terms of restraint and appropriateness. But what are we to make of Charlie Brown and Patty's apparent obliviousness to the violent comics displayed before them? On the one hand, their lack of comment indicates they are blind to, and thus unsullied by, the violence that is being peddled to them. On the other hand, they may also live in a culture so saturated with commercialized images and narratives of aggression that they have become desensitized.

Television was less of a target of criticism in *Peanuts*. For the most part, the strip depicts television viewing as a normal pastime of children.

One episode, published on December 11, 1952, does allude to adult worries that television viewing was ruining children's vision. Lucy tells Linus that he "can't watch television from way back here . . . move up where you can see." She then places him just mere inches from the screen, and the resulting cartoonish whorls in place of Linus's eyes suggest that he ends up with blurred vision. More broadly, the episode implies the role that children play in inducting one another into consumer culture. In this case, the interaction between the unsupervised Van Pelt children results in unhealthy viewing habits.

In general, however, *Peanuts* avoided a direct and explicit attack on television and comic books. Schulz's lack of commentary is in sharp contrast to the anticonsumerist stance expressed in a popular kid strip that debuted in the late twentieth century: Bill Watterson's *Calvin and Hobbes*. In a speech delivered at the 1989 Festival of Cartoon Art, Watterson railed against "business interests [that] in the name of efficiency, mass marketability, and profit, profit, profit . . . [keep the comic strip] art form from growing."[19] He often used his strips to not-so-subtly attack the effects of commercialization and mass media on children. In one episode, Calvin sits and criticizes "rotten" television programs. "There isn't an ounce of imagination in the whole bunch," he complains. "What bilge."[20] The television bounces on the TV stand, a visual representation of the amount of noise (and presumably violence) emanating from the so-called idiot box. But when Calvin poses the question, "Who do they think is stupid enough to sit and watch this trash?," Hobbes replies, "You." Calvin defends himself, saying, "If there was something *better* on, I'd watch *that*." Thus even while Calvin appears able to discriminate between "rotten" shows and "better" ones, he seems incapable of resisting the allure of television.

Another series of episodes shows how Calvin is easy prey to producers and marketers. He decides to consume several boxes of sugary cereal in order to save enough proofs of purchase to acquire "an official Chocolate Frosted Sugar Bombs beanie."[21] Watterson calls attention not only to the unhealthful cereal peddled to children but also to the marketing ploys designed to keep consumers consuming. Calvin, who patiently eats bowl after bowl of cereal, claims that he is "*earning*" the beanie, expressing how in a consumer capitalist society, the act of consumption is seen as work that deserves to be rewarded.[22]

The biting criticism of commercialism in *Calvin and Hobbes* is largely absent in *Peanuts*. But one can say that Schulz's strip censures *through*

absence: instead of offering an overt and constant assault on consumerism, *Peanuts* celebrates how childhood flourishes when the presence of
commercialization and popular cultural forms is minimal. The lives of
the *Peanuts* children do not revolve around television and comic book
reading. Their play is balanced between indoor play and outdoor games,
and toys enable the children to create a sense of community rather than
isolating them from one another. In some cases, the children use "child-
size" objects to demonstrate precocity, as in Linus's use of toy blocks and
Schroeder's ability to play Beethoven's compositions on a toy piano with
painted black keys.

More broadly, *Peanuts* positioned itself as a wholesome alternative
to more troubling entertainments such as television shows and comic
books. One way it did so was to feature characters who were far removed
from alarming images of juvenile delinquents. Certainly Charlie Brown
and his friends squabbled, misbehaved, and sometimes bullied one another. Yet there was very little indication that they were bad seeds on the
path of crime and deviance. As Geraldine DeLuca puts it, the "world of
Peanuts is a suburban pastoral where none of the characters has reached
puberty."[23] The images of white, suburban, preschool-aged children were
an antidote to what Jason Barnosky describes as the popular image of
nonwhite adolescent delinquents who purportedly roamed and made
trouble on city streets.[24]

Moreover, *Peanuts* provided assurance that children's autonomy was
limited. As discussed above, postwar adults often worried that their role
as mediator between children and the goods and entertainments they
consumed was being diminished. But Schulz's strip suggests that adults
had the ability to always monitor their children. He makes this explicit
in the January 29, 1953, episode: when one character sits in front of the
television, the words "Why aren't you in school?" appear on the screen.
Thus, the medium that supposedly weakened parental authority is being
used—presumably by adults—to monitor the child. But the strip itself
maintains that adults are omniscient figures who not only constantly
observe and scrutinize the young but also take delight in watching them.
Although *Peanuts* is a fictional world, the strip implies that the adult
cartoonist possesses the ability to open a window to childhood, providing
other adults with a glimpse of the lives of children.

Hatfield suggests that for many adult readers, the strip had a nostalgic
function.[25] *Peanuts* arguably conjured images of past childhoods by creating a world that was largely unsullied by the ravages of consumer culture.

Thus, the commodification and merchandising of *Peanuts* in the decades that followed disappointed many observers. As one critic, writing in the late 1960s, put it:

> Schulz first took a part of Charlie Brown away from me when he used his *Peanuts* characters in a series of ads for Falcon cars. I was hurt and puzzled to open a grown-up magazine and see my small friend touting a grown-up automobile. And why shouldn't I be? If there is one quality that particularly binds him to us as a character, it is his own hurt and puzzlement when innocence is betrayed.[26]

It is striking that the critic takes the advertisement as a personal slight, expressing pain at seeing the image of Charlie Brown shilling for a car. For the critic, this image disrupts the innocence of both *Peanuts* and childhood. But *Peanuts*, even in its earliest episodes, never claimed to separate childhood from consumerism. The fact is, the comic strip form has always been a commercial medium, a narrative meant to sell newspapers and often developed into various forms of merchandising. Although *Peanuts* sometimes mocked commercialization, it did not offer a direct, overt repudiation of it. Instead, Schulz's strip demonstrates that conceptualizations and experiences of childhood in the postwar era were deeply intertwined with consumer culture, naturalizing the presence of goods and mass entertainments in the lives of the young.

NOTES

1. Steven Mintz, *Huck's Raft: A History of American Childhood* (Cambridge, MA: Belknap Press of Harvard University Press, 2004), 276.

2. See Karin Calvert, *Children in the House: The Material Culture of Early Childhood, 1600–1900* (Boston: Northeastern University Press, 1992).

3. Lynn Spigel, *Welcome to the Dreamhouse: Popular Media and Postwar Suburbs* (Durham, NC: Duke University Press, 2001), 187.

4. Amy F. Ogata, "Building Imagination in Postwar American Children's Rooms," *Studies in the Decorative Arts* 16, no. 1 (Fall–Winter 2008–2009): 126.

5. Amy F. Ogata, "Creative Playthings: Educational Toys and Postwar American Culture," *Winterthur Portfolio* 39, nos. 2–3 (Summer–Autumn 2004): 129–30.

6. Ogata, "Building Imagination," 127.

7. Gary Cross, *The Cute and the Cool: Wondrous Innocence and Modern American Children's Culture* (New York: Oxford University Press, 2004), 124–25.

8. Mintz, *Huck's Raft*, 4.

9. Spigel, *Welcome to the Dreamhouse*, 204.

10. Quoted in Heather McKinnon, "Seattle's Fantagraphics Books Will Release 'The Complete Peanuts,'" *Seattle Times*, February 15, 2004.

11. Ben Schwartz, "I Hold a Grudge, Boy: Charles Schulz in Postwar America, 1946–1950," *Comic Art* 4 (2003): 11.

12. Charles Hatfield, "Redrawing the Comic Strip Child: Charles M. Schulz's *Peanuts* as Cross-Writing," in *The Oxford Handbook of Children's Literature*, ed. Julia L. Mickenberg and Lynne Vallone (New York: Oxford University Press, 2011), 182.

13. Spigel, *Welcome to the Dreamhouse*, 247.

14. Bradford Wright, *Comic Book Nation: The Transformation of Youth Culture in America* (Baltimore: Johns Hopkins University Press, 2003), 29.

15. Joe Sutliff Sanders, "Chaperoning Words: Meaning-Making in Comics and Picture Books," *Children's Literature* 41 (2013): 75.

16. Susan Honeyman, "Escaping the Prison-House: Visualcy and Prelanguage in Sheldon Mayer's *Sugar and Spike*," *Children's Literature Association Quarterly* 39, no. 2 (2014): 189.

17. Spigel, *Welcome to the Dreamhouse*, 195.

18. Ibid., 191–211.

19. Bill Watterson, "The Cheapening of Comics," paper delivered at the Festival of Cartoon Art, Ohio State University, Columbus, Ohio, October 27, 1989.

20. Bill Watterson, *The Indispensable Calvin and Hobbes: A Calvin and Hobbes Treasury* (Kansas City: Andrews McMeel, 1992), 38.

21. Ibid., 49.

22. Ibid., 50.

23. Geraldine DeLuca, "'I Felt a Funeral in My Brain': The Fragile Comedy of Charles Schulz," *The Lion and the Unicorn* 25, no. 2 (2001): 308.

24. Jason Barnosky, "The Violent Years: Responses to Juvenile Crime in the 1950s," *Polity* 38, no. 3 (2006): 316–17.

25. Hatfield, "Redrawing the Comic Strip Child," 185.

26. Quoted in Spigel, *Welcome to the Dreamhouse*, 246.

-5-

"HOW CAN WE LOSE WHEN WE'RE SO SINCERE?"

Varieties of Sincerity in *Peanuts*

LEONIE BRIALEY

In this strip from April 6, 1963, Charlie Brown is despairing over the loss of yet another baseball game. He can't understand it, and in the final panel, plodding along with his bat and mitt over his shoulder and looking vaguely distressed, he wonders: "How can we lose when we're so sincere?" The gag is that obviously sincerity has nothing to do with winning a baseball game, and as with most gags in *Peanuts* we may chuckle warmly while also feeling terribly sad at the same time. What do all our best intentions and warmest emotions count toward in a world that is often cruel or indifferent?

Along with the loneliness, anxiety, and other existential concerns of the strip, sincerity is a preoccupation throughout *Peanuts*. This chapter looks at the varieties of sincerity presented in the strip: Linus's religious sincerity regarding the Great Pumpkin, Lucy's lack of sincerity in continually promising then taking away the football, and Charlie Brown's vaguely absurd understanding of sincerity, as in the strip below.[1] This chapter also asks what it is that makes *Peanuts* sincere on the whole; if it indeed makes sense to talk about a comic strip (or any work of art for that matter) as being "sincere." Is it the ultimate sincerity of the artist, of Charles Schulz? Is it the fact that his characters are children, innocent and pure of heart? Is it Charlie Brown's loneliness and desperation, and our empathy for him? Is it the fact that the strip seems to speak to us on a deep, personal level, to reach out to the reader? The sincerity of the strip comes from a combination of all these. This chapter argues that the sincerity in *Peanuts* is mainly manifested in the gentle openness of the tone and register, expressed through Schulz's delicate line and timing,

Fig. 5.1: Charles Schulz, *Peanuts*, April 6, 1963. PEANUTS © 1963 Peanuts Worldwide LLC. Dist. by UNIVERSAL UCLICK. Reprinted with permission. All rights reserved.

along with the way "sincerity" as a concept is discussed within *Peanuts* itself. Through its sincerity and discussion of sincerity, *Peanuts* teaches us that sincerity is absurd and difficult but necessary, and best achieved with a gentle honesty and openness of heart.

IT DOESN'T MATTER WHAT YOU BELIEVE, JUST SO YOU'RE SINCERE

What is sincerity? It is, straightforwardly, the state of being sincere, of meaning what we say: the congruence of our inner, actual feelings and the expression of these feelings through our words and actions. This is how Lionel Trilling defines it in *Sincerity and Authenticity* (1971). But even this definition holds within it the seeds of confusion and complication. Our *actual* feelings? Not the pretend ones. How do we know and trust these feelings when they are constantly shifting? Especially when, throughout the past century, our ideas of truth and the self as stable, inner realities waiting to be found and expressed have been dismantled or pushed aside and replaced with a self that is fragmented and truth that is relative?

Before our ideas of truth and self shifted and slid away from our grasp, sincerity had a relatively concrete meaning. In the *Nicomachean Ethics*, Aristotle defined sincerity as the midway point between boastfulness and self-deprecation, and as a virtue. The same word (*eilikrineia*) defines any lover of truth for the sake of truth itself: "For the man who loves truth, and is truthful where nothing is at stake, will still be more truthful when something is at stake; . . . and such a man is worthy of praise" (IV.7, 1127b). The Latin *sincerus* denotes something whole, unadulterated, and pure; the word was used to describe physical objects such as wine, honey, and sculpture. One of the oft-mentioned (and sometimes dismissed) roots of the word "sincere" comes from the Latin cognate *sine-cera*: *sine* meaning "without" and *cera* meaning "wax," referring to the practice of fixing imperfect stone sculptures with wax. A sculpture *sine-cera* was as it was, hiding no imperfections.

The idea of sincerity applying to people appeared in the sixteenth century during the Reformation, when a turn toward inner conviction of faith took precedence over external ritual practices or empty worship. According to R. Jay Magill, the first usage of the word "sincerity" to mean "straightforward and honest" is attributed to John Frith, a Protestant reformer, in July 1533, in his testament to John Wycliffe (an Oxford Scholar who was a few months later burned at the stake for heresy).[2] Faith was now an intimately personal matter, between an individual and God, that only God could judge: no amount of sacrificial worship or payment of indulgences could make up for an insincere heart.

During this time, sincerity was still ascribed to things rather than persons, particularly to gospel and scripture that had not been altered or falsely presented. It was around this time when theater emerged as the dominant secular representation of the concerns and struggles of the human condition. When Shakespeare's Polonius says, "to thine own self be true," he is not telling us to look out for number one above all else.[3] He is highlighting that sincerity begins with self-knowledge, "and it doth follow, as the night the day, Thou canst not be false to any man." Sincerity is a state of being transparent before *ourselves* primarily, before being transparent before another.

Sincerity, in the latter sense—before another—is as much a rhetorical or performative mode as it is a state of being. This is perhaps closer to a modern or contemporary understanding of what sincerity is, and this is the view that Ernst van Alphen, Mieke Bal, and Carel Smith put forward in their collection *The Rhetoric of Sincerity* (2009). In recent decades, there has been a renewed emphasis on sincerity in various pockets of poetry, film, fine art, music, fiction, and nonfiction writing. Loose movements, critical writing, and manifestos in these fields have all, to varying degrees of seriousness, identified this renewed emphasis and enthusiasm as something called New Sincerity.[4] David Foster Wallace's essay "E Unibus Pluram" (1993) is often quoted as the ultimate articulation of the generational tiring of irony seen as the harbinger of New Sincerity in literature. It worth pointing out that, equally as often as the term "New Sincerity" is used, there is a critic cringing at the term, while recognizing its applicability. What generally characterizes this sincerity as "new" is its rejection of postmodern irony, cynical detachment, and any infinite deferral of meaning, recognizing at the same time the important work that poststructuralist theory did for our understanding of concepts such as the self or truth. While acknowledging the slipperiness of the self and the relativity of truth, artists working within this movement seem to maintain that concepts like the self or truth still hold essential relevance and importance for our existence as human beings. Jerry Saltz has said that these artists "not only see the distinction between earnestness and detachment as artificial; they grasp that they can be ironic and sincere at the same time."[5] This is the crux of New Sincerity: that it combines irony and sincerity, naïveté and knowingness, in work that seems ultimately sincere. Rather than thinking of irony and sincerity at opposite ends of a spectrum, they are entangled so tightly such that it would seem impossible to be completely sincere without a degree of irony, and such that any purposeful irony is always going to be, in some way, sincere.

Comparatively little writing has focused on sincerity in comics, and how this turn has manifested in graphic narratives and cartoons. Comics and cartoons themselves have a complicated history, at first glance at least, that focuses more on irony than sincerity. Gag cartoons often rely on the disjunction between image and text, showing and saying two different things to produce meaning and/or comedy. Satire in political cartoons shows the hypocrisy, the insincerity of politicians. But this could be said to be a sincere goal in which the aim is to shine light on hypocrisy, to make truth transparent. It is within autobiographical comics that sincerity is a more pressing issue. Critical writing on autobiographical comics has tended to focus more on *authenticity*, using sincerity only as a synonym: Bart Beaty, Charles Hatfield, and Elisabeth El Refaie have all written about authenticity and strategies of authentication in autobiographical comics. I would argue that there is a difference in tone and register between sincerity and authenticity in comics (autobiographical or otherwise) and that sincerity and authenticity have different goals and concerns. Authenticity has a more distant, indifferent tone, or is even more abrasive: the comics of R. Crumb and Joe Matt, for example, are more authentic than they are sincere. Sincerity has a much gentler tone: the comics of Gabrielle Bell and Jeffrey Brown, for example, feel sincere.

While not explicitly autobiographical, there is evidence, in David Michaelis's biography especially, that elements of *Peanuts* align with Schulz's life and beliefs and even that particular characters embody aspects of Schulz's personality. It is this intimacy and personal quality of *Peanuts* that enhances its sincerity. Looking at sincerity in *Peanuts*, it would seem that New Sincerity, as a combination of or oscillation between sincerity and irony toward an overall sincere purpose, is perhaps not so new after all. Within *Peanuts*, sincerity is almost always ironic, used as part of a punch line or to show the naïveté of a character while at the same time giving the strip an undeniable emotional weight. It is this emotional weight that give *Peanuts* its seriousness, and in turn its sincerity. The absurdity of the sincerity that Charlie Brown bestows upon playing baseball, or that Linus bestows upon a pumpkin patch, is not alienating or disorienting but rather seems to bring the reader closer to the heart of something: that sincerity is important, mysterious, and difficult.

THE GREAT PUMPKIN AND RELIGIOUS SINCERITY

The sincerity with which Linus believes in the Great Pumpkin and that he bestows upon the pumpkin patch in which The Great Pumpkin is foretold to appear aligns with the earliest understandings of sincerity in its religious context during the Reformation. The Great Pumpkin is first introduced in the strip on October 26, 1959. In this strip, Linus describes the Great Pumpkin as loving children and flying around the world delivering presents to them, and he is shown writing to the Great Pumpkin a list of all the toys he wants. Linus is arguably the most sensitive, spiritually inclined character in the strip, if also a little naïve. Schulz has described him as "bright but very innocent."[6] He has gotten ahead of himself with holidays, confusing Halloween and Christmas, and has thus invented the Great Pumpkin, whom he reveres with a religious fervor. In a strip from October 29, 1959, Charlie Brown tells Linus that he's crazy for believing in the Great Pumpkin. Linus replies: "The way I see it, it doesn't matter what you believe just so you're sincere!"

This sincerity is akin to religious or spiritual sincerity, sincerity as a Protestant virtue, and Linus is essentially a kind of Protestant reformer: in his heart, his belief in the Great Pumpkin is pure and unadulterated, and this is what the Great Pumpkin respects above all else. Schulz was frequently asked in interviews about his own religious beliefs. He was a member of the Church of God, even teaching Sunday School classes at a Methodist church for a number of years. But the appeal of the Church of God for Schulz was that it was nondenominational: that "by your belief

Fig. 5.2: Charles Schulz, *Peanuts,* October 29, 1964. PEANUTS © 1964 Peanuts Worldwide LLC. Dist. by UNIVERSAL UCLICK. Reprinted with permission. All rights reserved.

you were already a follower of the Way."[7] Schulz's beliefs were a great deal more liberal than might be expected; in an interview with Mary Harrington Hall, he said: "I think all God really requires of us is that we love one another. But it is hard to do. It is much easier to burn a sacrifice to God than to love someone."[8] What Schulz recognizes and expresses here is that sincerity is both necessary and difficult.

In strips from October 1964 leading up to Halloween, Linus is running for school president. His position is that "we're in the midst of a moral decline!!" and that he is going to "release us from spiritual Babylon." During his campaign, he mentions the Great Pumpkin, and this costs him the election: "Am I the first person ever to sacrifice political office because of belief? Of course not! I only spoke what I felt was the truth." One the more famous quotations from Linus is his revelation that there are three things never to discuss with people: "Religion, politics, and the Great Pumpkin." Linus may be sincere in belief, but this belief goes unappreciated.

Describing Linus waiting for the Great Pumpkin to appear, David Michaelis writes:

> The reader does not discern any radiance of certainty; the worshipper is not alight with enduring faith—he's hopelessly hyped up: enthusiasm is a more modulated and cheering emotion. . . . His willed mania demonstrates that people would rather live drunk on false belief than sober on nothing at all, at whatever cost in ridicule. Schulz is saying: be careful what you believe.[9]

With this in mind, *is* Linus actually sincere in his belief? That is, is he transparent about what he believes before himself, in his own heart, before anyone else? Let's remember that the sincerest pumpkin patch is of course Linus's own pumpkin patch, but also that the Great Pumpkin never appears. Does this mean that Linus and his pumpkin patch are ultimately insincere? Is this beside the point? The Great Pumpkin is a figment of Linus's own imagination, so of course it never appears, but that doesn't mean that Linus is insincere in his belief. But the fact that Linus is unable to admit to himself that the Great Pumpkin is his own invention begs the question that his sincerity is unexamined. The danger of this kind of religious sincerity is that it can be unthinking and alienating, and its adherent can tip over into fundamentalism.

Charlie Brown, although not immune to making fun of Linus for his beliefs, is (along with Sally and later Snoopy) the most patient and indulgent with Linus's beliefs, and the most acutely aware of their delicate absurdity. In the strip shown in figure 5.2, Linus is again explaining to Charlie Brown the precise conditions that make way for the arrival of the Great Pumpkin. He insists: "It's the sincerity that counts! The Great Pumpkin will appear in whichever pumpkin patch he decides is the most sincere!!" Charlie Brown answers, again looking vaguely distressed, that he would hate to have to make such a decision. On another occasion, Linus asks Charlie Brown if he thinks a particular pumpkin patch is sincere. Charlie Brown answers, "Oh, yes," it is "very sincere." In the final panel, walking away, he clarifies: "Well, it didn't look *insincere*."

In the way Charlie Brown looks to the reader in the final panel, we sense we've caught him in his own insincerity regarding his assessment of the sincerity of the pumpkin patch. Only it isn't so much Charlie Brown's *insincerity* we are catching but his uncertainty and his recognition of the absurdity of sincerity. Is certainty necessary for sincerity? Do we need to be completely clear in our feelings before professing them, and is this even possible? This is perhaps the ultimate irony inherent in every sincere act. Jonathan Lear, writing in defense of irony, particularly a Socratic understanding of it, notes that irony is "a form of not being perfectly sure—an insecurity about being human that is . . . constitutive of becoming human." The inherent irony of existence is that being human is not as easy as simply being born human; being human means constantly "becoming human."[10] "Being a human being" is a strange double act of sincerity and irony whereby we have to sincerely act like the thing we already ironically are. Schulz has said himself, "it took me a long time to become a human being."[11]

It makes no sense to us now to think of anything incapable of self-reflection as being sincere, and thus it seems absurd to talk about the sincerity of a pumpkin patch. At the same time, how can a pumpkin patch be anything *but* sincere? It can't be insincere, because it is incapable of being anything but itself. Its simplicity of existence makes its sincerity so easy, it is irrelevant; no effort has been made. This shows us that sincerity is necessitated by the ability to look inward in search of some ultimately true feeling and then expressing that true feeling as accurately as possible, in the face of uncertainty and the irony of being a human being.

THE OPPOSITE OF SINCERITY

The humor in *Peanuts* is deeply ironic, "stemming from the contrast of the speakers and what they said."[12] The irony is that mere babes are as neurotic and lost and flailing at life as adults (who are never seen). As tender and heartfelt as *Peanuts* is, the strip itself is parody, often sarcastic, and frequently cruel to its characters, a cruelty epitomized by Lucy's cruelty to Charlie Brown. In a strip from March 1964, Charlie Brown has "little leaguer's elbow." When Lucy suggests that this diagnosis was the doctor's way of saying he is a lousy pitcher, Charlie Brown admonishes her for having no sympathy and making only sarcastic remarks. Sarcasm, the lowest form of wit, is also perhaps the laziest opposite of sincerity. About sarcasm, Schulz himself has said,

> I don't think it's a good quality to possess. I'm not proud of it. I have had a few incidents down through the years, you know, when I was younger, and said things that I never should have said to people. I don't think it's a good trait to have. But it's good for creativity. That's why it's nice to have a comic strip where you can have an outlet for these feelings that you have.[13]

Even the very first strip in 1950 presents Shermy's sarcasm toward Charlie Brown. In each panel leading up to the last, he regards Charlie Brown warmly, or familiarly: "Good ol' Charlie Brown . . . yes sir!" Then, in the final panel: "How I hate him!" In the first few panels, it feels like Shermy is being sincere in his warm, familiar regarding of Charlie Brown, but the final reveal of his true feelings casts his previous sincerity into doubt. Was he being sarcastic in those first few panels? Was he being sincere, then changed his mind, realizing and expressing his true feelings? Sincerity and sarcasm are so flimsy here; the passing of time, mere moments, can change one into the other and vice versa. The joke relies on the reader's initial perception of Shermy's words as sincere, and it works because of the tone of sincerity that Schulz's lines and dialogue evoke.

Lucy's lack of sincerity, always pulling the football away no matter how many times she assures Charlie Brown that she won't, is the most obvious outlet for Schulz's demonstration of sincerity's limits. On September 1, 1963, she tells Charlie Brown: "Look . . . we'll shake on it, okay? Let's shake on it . . . this proves my sincerity." Charlie Brown shakes her hand and walks away saying, "What could I do? If someone is willing to shake on something, you have to trust her." Of course, she pulls the football away, saying: "A woman's handshake is not legally binding," which is cruel to both Charlie Brown and feminine reputation.

There is a painful existential inevitability to the setting up of the football gag and an absurdity to the trust that Charlie Brown continues to place in Lucy. But what is absurdity? To do something without meaning, or to understand that an action has no meaning, no end point—but to do it anyway? It is absurd that Linus believes in the Great Pumpkin, which he has invented and which will never appear, just as it is absurd that Charlie Brown will continue to run at the football even when it is forever being pulled away. What is it that unites these actions? It is their hope and sincerity in the face of indifference and cruelty.

Hope and trust are necessary if we are to read sincerity into a sincere act. It is, of course, entirely possible to be sincere and for one's sincerity to go unnoticed or unappreciated, just as it is entirely possible to be insincere and for that to be read as sincere. Does this take away from the sincerity of the act? If a sincere word is spoken and no one is around to hear it, is it really sincere? Of course. The ultimate sincerity is before ourselves (at least according to the post-Reformation model), and this is the ultimate difficulty and absurdity of sincerity. There is no guarantee of success, no material reward for our sincerity. It is purely an immaterial, spiritual knowledge for ourselves.

It is significant, in the strip from April 6, 1963, in which Charlie Brown asks, "How can we lose when we're so sincere?," that he is all alone. Charlie Brown is a generally warm and optimistic manager of his team—he's patient with Schroeder's and Lucy's inattention—but here he is alone; there are no witnesses (aside from the reader) to his sincerity, to his anguish. He doesn't even reach out to the reader with his pleading, beady eyes in the final panel. He looks straight ahead to where he is walking, into an uncertain future.

What does sincerity count for? Is it important or even relevant that we play baseball, or do anything sincerely? It's absurd to imagine playing baseball insincerely, or sarcastically, perhaps more so than to imagine playing it sincerely. It's still absurd, but somehow necessary, that Charlie Brown plays baseball sincerely, and that we do whatever it is we do in life (that matters to us) sincerely. It is necessary for our relationships with others, but also just for ourselves; there is something spiritually, personally significant, if absurd, in our most sincere acts.

Charlie Brown is not alone in his sincerity here, however. We are reading and appreciating the sincerity with which he plays baseball and the absurdity he recognizes in its futility toward winning a baseball game. The sincerity that counts toward something here is Charlie Brown's personal sincerity, which we have access to through the sincerity with which Charles Schulz drew him. As Umberto Eco has said: "In the next strip he will continue to show us, in the face of Charlie Brown, with two strokes of his pencil, his version of the human condition."[14]

SINCERITY IN LITERATURE, SINCERITY IN LIFE

What does it mean to talk about sincerity in literature? More specifically, sincerity in comics? To call a work of literature or art "sincere" can seem like a polite dismissal of its merit: in Trilling's words, "although it need be given no aesthetic or intellectual admiration, it was at least conceived in innocence of heart."[15] But is this always the case? Can a body of work be considered worthy of merit and be conceived with innocence of heart at the same time? *Peanuts* is a clear example of this in comics, if its merit can be measured by the success the strip brought Schulz and the extent to which it has infiltrated not only our culture but also our hearts. Intuitively, it feels right to call *Peanuts* sincere, but what does that mean? What are the markers that lead to this feeling that *Peanuts* is honest, straightforward, yearning to connect with its readers?

There are a few approaches to answering this question. One approach is to look at *Peanuts* aesthetically: what is it about *Peanuts* visually that gives it this air of sincerity? What is it that makes a cartoon drawing cut straight to our hearts? Elisabeth El Refaie differentiates between signs "given" and "given off" as ways of signifying authenticity in autobiographical comics.[16] Signs "given" would be those that are explicit claims to fidelity: artifacts, photographs, verbal statements of veracity. Signs "given off" are gestural cues to authenticity or sincerity: the style of drawing; the pace, the tone, and the voice the story is told in. Signs "given off" are less easy to control, as with body language. Ernst van Alphen and Mieke Bal hold that sincerity is

> fundamentally corporeal rather than textual. Within such logic, truth is enacted through the body and imagined as an integrated semiotic field. Beyond the truth that is stated, this field includes the unwittingly emitted signs of the body.[17]

Insofar as comics are marks on paper of movements the body has made in space, comics—especially those with emotional honesty that foreground the relationship between the body of the cartoonist and the page—could be said to be working toward a sincere exchange between the reader and the cartoonist.

The emotion that Schulz is able to portray with only a few lines on the enormous and simplified heads of his characters is simultaneously heartbreaking and heart-expanding. Gary Groth has pointed this out in an interview with Schulz, that his art "has life to it. It has spontaneity."[18] Spontaneity has a close and complex relationship with sincerity. To a certain degree, and certainly for Romantic poets and artists, the "spontaneous overflow of emotion" was crucial to art, and a sign of its sincerity. But there must be a balance between spontaneity and reflection. In the same interview with Groth, Schulz describes his drawing technique: "I block it in, so that I'll get them in the right place, and the right size, but I draw that face with the pen when I'm doing it. Because you want that spontaneity."[19] Schulz maintains this spontaneity, this raw emotion, while at the same time being deliberate and considered. It is this balance that touches our hearts and speaks to us as sincerity.

Groth also points out that Schulz's drawing, and perhaps cartooning in general, is a kind of handwriting.[20] It is intimately personal, and inimitably unique to Schulz. Chris Ware, writing about Schulz's preliminary drawings in *McSweeney's Quarterly Concern*, finds a similar parallel in Schulz's cartooning, stating that "every day, for half a century, millions of people learned to read Charles Schulz's handwriting."[21] Schulz's preliminary drawings included with Ware's article are shaky, light pencil sketches and notes on crumpled scrap or legal paper; they are the visual equivalent of a soft-spoken person attempting to articulate himself. Ware notes: "There's a strange sensation to these drawings, because in their expressiveness they look not unlike 'art,' yet one still tries to read the familiar feeling of the *Peanuts* characters and their personalities."[22] There is something inherently tender, and sincere, in these preliminary drawings; they remind us that *Peanuts* is the work of one person attempting to find truth and beauty in a harsh and complex world.

The final inked faces of course lose none of this sincerity in the inking but take on extra life and solidity, and in one line both irony and sincerity exist simultaneously. In a strip from July 18, 1963, Lucy and Charlie Brown are discussing the dangers of looking directly at an eclipse. Lucy doesn't want to do any harm to her self-proclaimed "beautiful eyes," and she asks Charlie Brown is he thinks her eyes are beautiful. He says, "Yes, they look like little round dots of India ink." They literally are little round dots of India ink. Lucy looks taken aback. Charlie Brown (or Charles Schulz himself) is being both sincere and ironic at the same time.

The simplicity of a look is frequently used as a punch line in *Peanuts*. Sometimes, Charlie Brown looks directly, pleadingly, into the eyes of the reader. In these moments, Charlie Brown is bemused, looking for reassurance and recognition at the absurdity or cruelty of life as he is witnessing it within the comic. It's a moment of connection between Charlie Brown and the reader. Ware writes of Charlie Brown: "He wasn't a picture of someone, he was the thing itself, and your heart went out to him."[23] It is this interpretation, that what we as readers are connecting with is "the thing itself" and not just a picture of someone, that presents this precise line of connection between the reader and Charlie Brown that sincerity can travel across.

The other approach to examining the sincerity of *Peanuts* is to look at how closely the strip aligns with Schulz's own life and beliefs and preoccupations. We have already looked at the parallels between Schulz's religious beliefs and the spiritual sincerity that comes through in the strip. In an interview with Jim Phelan for *Penthouse* in 1971, Schulz says:

> I've been doing this now for 21 years and if you're going to survive on a daily schedule you survive only by being able to draw on every experience and thought that you've ever had. That is, if you are going to do anything with any meaning. Of course, you can grind out daily gags but I'm not interested in simply doing gags. I'm interested in doing a strip that says something and makes some comment on the important things of life. I'm probably a little bit of Charlie Brown and a little of Lucy and Linus and all the characters. It would be impossible in this kind of strip to create any character and not be part of it yourself.[24]

Certainly the way David Michaelis has written his biography of Schulz, *Schulz and Peanuts*, weaving in and out of talking about Schulz's life and talking about the strip itself, draws an intimate connection between the two. We see here another meaning of sincerity in which the concept is applied to art: that there is no distinction between the life of the artist and the art itself. It is this kind of intimacy that we gain through reading *Peanuts* that adds to its sincerity. In an interview with Charlie Rose, Schulz said that to sit down and read and study *Peanuts* every day would be to know him. Rose comments, "To read your characters is to know you." Schulz answers, "Isn't that depressing?"[25]

When we read *Peanuts*, we learn about being human: about failure, loneliness, and the acute mental anguish caused by a consciousness that is trying to solve the ethical dilemmas of life, to live honestly and actively, but that is profoundly hindered by uncertainty and indecision. Uncertainty, even about the very bare facts of existence, about what our true and reliable feelings are and whether and how we share them with others, is a necessary and unavoidable state that we must accept; we must face our inherently absurd and ironic existence, being human beings, and aim for sincerity anyway. Sincerity is both an antidote for loneliness and one of the loneliest states to be in. In being sincere before another person, we attempt to fill this emptiness with the understanding and sympathy of another, yet we also risk being misunderstood, continuing our lives alone, perhaps even lonelier than before. But we have to try anyway. R. Jay Magill writes, "the ideal of sincerity, born five hundred years ago as a moral imperative, abides in us in ways silent and compelling, drawing the secular mind inward like a strange magnetic north."[26] Charles Schulz understands this and articulates with soft, gentle clarity that sincerity is important, mysterious, and difficult. And, truly, how can he lose when he's so sincere?

NOTES

1. This essay focuses primarily on strips from *Peanuts'* "peak" period, the late fifties through the early sixties, mainly because this is when the Great Pumpkin first appears but also because it would seem that this is the strip's most alternately cruel and sweet period. Schulz himself has said that the strip softened in the later years, and this transformation could be an interesting topic for follow-up to this paper.

2. R. Jay Magill Jr., *Sincerity: How a Moral Ideal Born Five Hundred Years Ago Inspired Religious Wars / Modern Art / Hipster Chic / and the Curious Notion That We ALL Have Something to Say (No Matter How Dull)* (New York: W.W. Norton, 2012), 23.

3. Lionel Trilling, *Sincerity and Authenticity* (Cambridge, MA: Harvard University Press, 1971), 3.

4. The first mention of New Sincerity emerged in the mid-1980s in post-Soviet Russian poetry through critic Mikhail Epstein and poet Dimitri Prigov. In American poetry, the term emerged around 2005 in relation to the blog-driven poetry of Joseph Massey, Andrew Mister, Rob Livingston, and Anthony Robinson, extending to include poets such as David Berman, Matt Hart, Catherine Wagner, Tao Lin, and Ellen Kennedy. In music criticism, the term emerged specific to bands in Austin, Texas, in the mid- to late 1980s but extended to the earnest, lo-fi folk music of Daniel Johnston, Will Oldham, Joanna Newsom, and Okkervil River. In film criticism, the term appeared in the early 1990s, used by Jim Collins to describe the purity and nostalgia in films such as *Field of Dreams* (1989) and *Dances with Wolves* (1990). More recently, the term has been associated with the films of Wes Anderson and Miranda July, in which the line between irony and sincerity is less clear.

5. Jerry Saltz, "Sincerity and Irony Hug It Out," *New York Magazine*, May 27, 2010, at http://nymag.com/arts/art/reviews/66277/.

6. M. Thomas Inge, *Charles M. Schulz: Conversations* (Jackson: University Press of Mississippi, 2000), 60.

7. Ibid., 207.

8. Ibid., 60.

9. David Michaelis, *Schulz and Peanuts: A Biography* (New York: HarperCollins, 2007), 354.

10. Jonathan Lear, *A Case for Irony* (Cambridge, MA: Harvard University Press, 2011), 6, 9.

11. Inge, *Charles M. Schulz: Conversations*, 168.

12. Robert C. Harvey, *Children of the Yellow Kid: The Evolution of the American Comic Strip* (Seattle: University of Washington Press, 1998), 123.

13. Inge, *Charles M. Schulz: Conversations*, 243.

14. Umberto Eco, "On 'Krazy Kat' and 'Peanuts,'" trans. William Weaver, *New York Review of Books*, June 13, 1985, at http://www.nybooks.com/articles/archives/1985/jun/13/on-krazy-kat-and-peanuts/.

15. Trilling, *Sincerity and Authenticity*, 6.

16. Elisabeth El Refaie, *Autobiographical Comics: Life Writing in Pictures* (Jackson: University Press of Mississippi, 2012), 144.

17. Ernst van Alphen, Mieke Bal, and Carel Smith, eds., *The Rhetoric of Sincerity* (Stanford, CA: Stanford University Press, 2009), 1.

18. Inge, *Charles M. Schulz: Conversations*, 192.

19. Ibid.

20. Ibid., 195.

21. Chris Ware, "Charles Schulz's Preliminary Drawings," *McSweeney's Quarterly Concern* 13 (Spring 2004): 66.

22. Ibid., 68.

23. Ibid., 66.

24. Inge, *Charles M. Schulz: Conversations*, 66.

25. "Charles M. Schulz Interview on Charlie Rose (1997)," YouTube, uploaded July 23, 2016, at https://www.youtube.com/watch?v=pQBBt_PR9VE.

26. Magill, *Sincerity*, 22.

-6-

"I THOUGHT I WAS WINNING IN THE GAME OF LIFE . . . BUT THERE WAS A FLAG ON THE PLAY"

Sport in Charles Schulz's *Peanuts*

JEFFREY O. SEGRAVE

The final installment of *Peanuts*, which appeared on February 13, 2000, included a signed farewell from Charles Schulz and a collage of a dozen vignettes, three of which showcased sport: Woodstock driving a Zamboni on his frozen birdbath, a baseball bouncing off Lucy's head ("Bonk!"), and Lucy, famously, pulling the football away from Charlie Brown ("AAUGH!"). That sports should figure so prominently in Schulz's tragicomic portrait of life is hardly surprising. In his hometown of Saint Paul, Minnesota, Schulz grew up playing a wide variety of sports, including football, skating, golf, hockey, and baseball, many of which made their way into his comic strip. He also coached the women's softball team at the art school where he taught in the late 1940s, and he remained active in sports, especially golf and hockey, throughout his life.[1]

References to sports serve a particular purpose in *Peanuts*; sports allow Schulz to move freely from childhood games to adult issues, to access and depict his characters' heroic attempts to make sense of the adversities and complexities that torment their everyday lives and to interrogate the daydreams and philosophical musings that render intolerable experiences more acceptable and even explicable. A powerful, albeit ersatz, representation of the ideology of a culture, sport appeals to the sensibilities of a contemporary audience; it also serves as an expressive vehicle for exploring the existential and social predicaments that constitute the inner life of *Peanuts*. As Schulz once acknowledged, "the challenges to be faced in sports work marvelously as a caricature of the challenges we face in the more serious aspects of our lives."[2]

Although sport has been an ongoing feature in a variety of contemporary and historical comics from *Frank Merriwell* to *Andy Capp* to *Doonesbury*, nowhere has it been more delicately and subtly used than in *Peanuts*. As Schulz puts it, "when Charlie Brown has tried to analyze his own difficulties in life, he has always been able to express them in sports."[3] For all the highly idiosyncratic personalities that populate the nameless American suburb of Schulz's imagination, sport, games, and athletic pursuits become an essential feature of daily life and illuminate the ontological tensions that constitute the basic substratum of our intellectual, emotional, and social lives—anxiety over our neurotic behavior, the drive to establish our identity and buttress the edifice of our self-esteem, the relationship of self to others and to society, and, ultimately, the overwhelming desire to gain control over our destiny and derive purpose, meaning, and satisfaction in our daily existence.[4]

The purpose of this chapter is to examine the role that sport plays in *Peanuts*. More specifically, I would like to explore the ways in which Schulz uses sport in the development of character, to address various social issues in contemporary sport, to elucidate significant ontological themes that constitute the human condition, and to champion the positive Olympian notion that nobility resides not in the winning but in the trying. Ultimately, I wish to argue that sport operates most powerfully in *Peanuts* as a thinly veiled mechanism that allows Schulz to make manifest what Robert Short calls the "hearts and minds of men."[5] Sport in *Peanuts* may well be about losing, losing again, and losing some more—or, as Lucy puts it in reference to the strip's hapless baseball team: "This team will never amount to anything! It's just going to lose, lose, lose, lose!!" (August 2, 1962)—but it is also about the recurrent possibility of redemption. Despite its tragedies and setbacks, sport in *Peanuts*, as in life, offers a unique sense of optimism whereby little folks with big dreams can trudge one more time to the mound.

SPORT IN THE DEVELOPMENT OF CHARACTER

Nowhere does Schulz more deftly, delicately, or commonly employ sport than in the portrayal of Charlie Brown, the strip's round-faced, angst-ridden protagonist, "the postmodern abstraction of Everyboy," as reporter Dan Hulbert calls him.[6] What distinguishes Charlie Brown is not that he succeeds but rather the opposite, that he fails, at everything, dismally. At

one point, he loses ten thousand games of checkers in a row to Lucy. His
baseball team gets pounded 40–0, 123–0, and even 200–0. "Our hits can
be measured quite adequately," he muses, "with an 18-inch ruler" (July 7,
1964). Tired of losing, he runs a classified ad looking for a new managerial
job; he only receives one reply—from his own team. As a relief pitcher
called in at the bottom of the ninth, he blows a 50–0 lead, and his team
loses 51–50—even the mound tells him he can't pitch. His favorite player,
Joe Shlabotnik, once gets demoted to Stumptown of the Green Grass
League after hitting .004. Doomed to failure, Charlie Brown's triumphs
are few, his tragedies many. He remains, as Lucy reminds him, the "desig-
nated goat" (March 13, 1977); she even advises him, "Don't let your team
down by showing up" (April 16, 1963). "Nothing," Schultz's biographer
Rheta Grimsley Johnson writes, "has come to typify *Peanuts* more than
Charlie Brown going down in flames on his pitcher's mound one more
time."[7] "You know what really bothers me most," Charlie Brown confides
in Schroeder after yet another loss on the neighborhood diamond; "I feel
I've let down you players who had faith in me as a manager." "Oh well,
if that's what's bothering you, Charlie Brown, just forget it," Schroeder
replies; "we never had faith in you" (April 26, 1957). Lucy, predictably, is
much more direct: "Manager! HA!" (April 25, 1957).

Not only a long-suffering, although lovable, loser, Charlie Brown is
also gullible and credulous, his abject cluelessness derivative of a sublime
admixture of blithe neuroticism, striking ineffectuality, and innocence of
spirit. The kite-eating tree remains the eternal symbol of his utter inept-
ness as well as the pretext for a wide variety of sardonic observations
from his diminutive peers. At one point, Marcie visits Charlie Brown
"to watch Charles fly a kite," as only she could put it. "It's something
I've always wanted to see," she proclaims. In the end, hanging upside
down with Charlie Brown in a classic pose of tree and tangled kite string,
Marcie reports: "It was an experience" (March 16, 1986).

Snoopy, the personification—or rather dogification—of the strip's
enduringly quaint optimism, is an extroverted beagle with an incred-
ibly active, indeed overactive, even if oddball, inner life. He is driven
by a vivid imagination that offers us a portal into a charming fantasy
universe. Adept in a vast array of sports, his inner newsreel transports
him to Wimbledon, the North American Figure Skating Championships
in Oakland, the Stanley Cup, the Masters in Augusta, the summer Olympics for chariot racing, and the winter Olympics for figure skating and
the "downhill supper dish" (January 25, 1984). A one-man show atop his

doghouse, his personal amphitheater, Snoopy is powered by a superior intelligence and an egotistical virtuosity. He doesn't just fly planes any more than he just plays hockey; rather, he skirmishes none other than the Red Baron, and when he scores in hockey, he proudly proclaims: "They're not sleeping well in Montreal tonight" (October 8, 1968). He also skates with Peggy Fleming, plays doubles with Billie Jean King, breaks Babe Ruth's home run record before Hank Aaron, and serves as Peppermint Patty's world-class figure skating pro. He is so good at pool that even Minnesota Fats won't play him. Snoopy also surfs, skateboards, fishes, plays football and basketball, drives a Zamboni, deftly catches baseballs in his mouth, and swims the backstroke—the dog-paddle is predictably beneath him.

Lucy Van Pelt is the comic strip's perennial grouch, a chronic complainer, "the crab grass in the lawn of life" (June 17, 1961), as her brother, Linus, aptly describes her. She can be bossy, vain, and tart tongued. With the exception of her beloved Schroeder, Lucy spares no one her biting sarcasm, especially Charlie Brown, who is forced to endure her barbs and denigrations on the baseball diamond. Feeling absolutely no sympathy for an ailing Charlie Brown, who fears the onset of pitcher's elbow, she proclaims, "What? A lousy pitcher like you?" (March 6, 1964). Terminally mean-spirited, she once tells Charlie Brown that good pitchers have nicknames. "You should be Catfish, or Babe, or Doc, or something," she says. Back in center field, she calls out, "Throw it in there, Cementhead!" (May 25, 1975). Dismissive of the conventions of baseball and more than willing to trample on inviolate values, she constantly infuriates the purist Charlie Brown with her belittling comments and attitudes; she calls the pitcher's mound a "mud pile" (March 13, 1978), uses her glove for potato chips and cracker sandwiches, denounces sliding into base because "it's wearing out the earth" (April 4, 1976), and finds more excuses for dropping the ball than any self-respecting manager can bear—"I was having my quiet time" (July 25, 1961), "toxic substances coming from my glove made me dizzy" (May 24, 1981), "the moons of Saturn got in my eyes" (July 15, 1977). Even the "air" gets in her eyes! (July 3, 1989).

Lucy's scholarly younger brother, Linus, is the intellectual of the gang, a profound thinker and philosopher who routinely expounds on the meaning of life. "I got it," he shouts on a pop-fly. "At least, I think I've got it! Who knows? Actually, who cares? When you've lost at love you've lost at everything. Nothing matters! Who's got it? That's a good question! I've got it! You've got it! Nobody's got it! We all lose in the end" (April 19,

1975). Woodstock, a lovable and cute if unintelligible bird and the smallest of the *Peanuts* characters, constantly falls prey to life's crushing enormity and unfathomable complexity; he stumbles into golf holes, catches his head in his football locker, and falls prey to footballs, basketballs, tennis balls, and baseballs. At one point, he even musters a "three-inch kick off" (November 22, 1973). And, one should never forget Pig-Pen, a perennial walking cloud of dust who blends in superbly with the dirt in the infield.

If, as philosopher Peter Heinegg claims, sport fashions a world of stasis, a separate universe that stands apart from the flow of time,[8] then sport operates in *Peanuts* as a salient proving ground for the construction of the ageless and timeless characters whose antics make up the strip's on-going parable of modern American culture. Moments in sports become the quintessential examples of what the writer Samuel Hayes calls "deep American ordinariness,"[9] seemingly mundane yet, in fact, profound, personally meaningful incidents that not only allow Schulz to travel from the comic to the cosmic but also serve as an entrée into the psychological.

One of the great charms of sport in *Peanuts*, in fact, is that it allows Schulz to portray the profound, angst-ridden interior problems that constitute the enduring tensions of daily life. Charlie Brown in particular reminds us, as Schulz biographer David Michaelis points out, what it is like "to be vulnerable, to be small and alone in the universe, to be human—both little and big at the same time."[10] Charlie Brown's solitude is an abyss, and his inferiority complex is deep seated and omnipresent. Flying a kite, kicking the unkickable pigskin, and winning baseball games become manias for Charlie Brown. His escapades and reflections are saturated with frustration, melancholy, fear, and self-doubt. Like Kafka's narratives, Schulz's strip blends the ordinary and the bizarre as they integrate issues of faith and existential dread.[11] Charlie Brown's nocturnal epiphanies about cosmic anxiety and apprehension are best expressed in a series of cartoons in which Charlie Brown hallucinates that the sun has transformed into a giant baseball and his own head becomes marked with a rash that resembles its stitches: "I think you'd better see your pediatrician," Linus soberly advises him (June 15, 1973).

Sport in *Peanuts* has the ability, to quote Shakespeare, "to hold . . . the mirror up to Nature—to show Virtue her own feature, scorn her own image, and the very age and body of the time his form and pressure."[12] Or, as Linus suggests: "Somebody said that sports are a sort of caricature of life"; to which Charlie Brown responds, "That's a relief. I was afraid it was life!" (May 24, 1979).

SPORT AND SOCIAL ISSUES

It is on the basis of the characters and their adventures in *Peanuts* that Schulz can explore a wide variety of contemporary issues in sport. In the same way that Schulz uses *Peanuts* to comment on currents and personalities in the real world—from nuclear testing and global overpopulation to Tiny Tim—so also he uses sport to comment on some of the social dimensions that contour modern sport. Let us examine, in turn, how the strip presents problems, including winning and losing in a philosophical context, sportsmanship and youth sport as they relate to community, and gender and race as social issues that bind *Peanuts* to its time.[13]

Losing is pathological in *Peanuts*, a running gag that allows Schulz to reverse the traditional pattern of winners and losers so that he can pass comment on some of the values and practices associated with sport. If we are, as political commentator George Will writes, a nation of failed baseball players, then Schulz was probably right when he noted: "Most of us are much more acquainted with losing than we are with winning."[14] Unlike winning, losing is also funny, and "nothing," as the playwright Samuel Beckett observes, "is funnier than unhappiness."[15] Schulz exaggerated losing to the point that Charlie Brown's kite does not just get stuck in a tree, it gets eaten by it; he does not just give up a line drive, he is disrobed and upended by it; his team is not just in last place on the Fourth of July but also on "Memorial Day and Mother's Day . . . Labor Day, Columbus Day, Thanksgiving, Christmas and [Lucy's] Birthday" (August 3, 1955). The team is so bad, they can't even "win enough games to have a slump!" (July 22, 1968).

On the other hand, the ultimate caricature of the widely held American belief that the only thing that matters is winning is Molly Volley, Snoopy's confrontational doubles partner, who freely bends the rules, overtly uses intimidation as a tactic, and accepts nothing less than complete victory, even if she is playing on some forlorn, windswept court in a no-name tournament that nobody cares about.[16] Deriding our cultural obsession with winning and at the same time acknowledging the developmental value of confronting adversity, Schulz celebrates the experiential, character-building model of sport: "I feel sorry for people who get so involved in sports that it makes them unhappy," Schulz said; "they get carried away with the winning and the losing of their team. With all these professional games, somehow we've lost the joy of the individual game."[17] Through *Peanuts*, Schulz promulgates the values of fair play and sportsmanship and celebrates the aesthetics, not the "win at all costs" mentality, of modern competitive sport: "It should be the plays," he writes, "great goals being scored, great baskets being made, great overhand shots hit. These are the things that count in sport."[18]

Predictably, Schulz also parodies the increasing bureaucratization and professionalization of youth sport programs. In particular, he laments the displacement of informal, unstructured, player-controlled physical activities in favor of formal, adult-dominated, specialized youth sports that have become valued community programs in neoliberal societies that prize individualism, material success, and high performance. "From now on," Linus tells Charlie Brown, "all snowmen have to be made under adult supervision" in "snow leagues" that have "rules and regulations . . . age brackets . . . and playoffs" (November 26, 1973). Sally rushes off to "snowman practice" as a member of the "Silver Flakes," who practice "every Tuesday with a coach" (November 27, 1973). Snowman leagues sport all the trappings of elite youth programs; as Lucy explains, "In adult-organized snow leagues, we have teams, and standings, and awards, and special fields . . . We even have a newsletter" (November 28, 1973). And the emphasis, of course, is predictably on winning: "It's very competitive," Linus tells Charlie Brown; "if your team builds the best snowman, you *win*! It's winning that counts! What's the sense of doing something if you can't win?" (November 29, 1973). Clearly, Schulz mourns the transition of childhood from an age of exploration and freedom to an age of preparation and controlled learning, the construction of what sport sociologist Jay Coakley calls an "uninformed childhood."[19] Speaking no doubt for Schulz, Charlie Brown lies in bed at night and ruefully wonders, "Why can't kids just do their own thing? Why does everything have to be organized? Why do we have to have trophies? Who cares who wins?" (December 5, 1973).

Given that Schulz worked in the second half of the twentieth century, an era that witnessed the struggle of women and minority groups to find legitimacy in the world of sport, it is perhaps not surprising that he addresses the important identity issues of race and gender. He is, though, clearly less political when it comes to the issue of race. Both the African American Franklin and the Hispanic José Peterson appear so briefly in the strip and on the baseball diamond that neither develops into much more than a token, and their dialogue is anything but a window into the complexity of race relations in American sport. In fact, Schulz consciously avoids racial humor: "What do I know what it's like to be black?" he once

Fig. 6.1: Charles Schulz, *Peanuts*, March 25, 1973. PEANUTS © 1973 Peanuts Worldwide LLC. Dist. by UNIVERSAL UCLICK. Reprinted with permission. All rights reserved.

remarked.[20] The only hint that Schulz recognizes the systematic marginalization and inferiorization of the minority athlete arises when Franklin tells Peppermint Patty that he is "practicing to become a great hockey player," to which Peppermint Patty duly responds, "How many black players in the NHL [National Hockey League], Franklin?" (November 6, 1974). Schulz may indeed have possessed that rare quality that Mort Walker, the creator of *Beetle Bailey*, identified as "never having offended anyone";[21] still, he did not attempt to sensitize his audience to the woeful plight of the minority athlete.[22] He was, however, more outspoken and progressive when it came to the matter of gender.

Throughout the life of *Peanuts*, relations between the genders were intense and hard edged. At one moment, the girls are forceful, belligerent, and independent, and at the next, mild and deferential, the epitome of traditional feminine deportment. At times, the girls are inexplicably hostile to the boys, the strip enacting what Robert C. Harvey characterizes as "every man's lurking anxiety about the opposite sex."[23] Peppermint Patty is more than willing to shove a hockey puck in a boy's mouth or force-feed a privileged hockey player a pair of goalie pads, and Lucy, the strip's sour-faced termagant, develops into a brutally sarcastic and caustic observer. "I wanted so much to be the hero," Charlie Brown pleads after losing yet another baseball game, but "I always end up being the *goat!*" To which Lucy bitingly replies, "BAAHHHHHH!" (June 17, 1958). The girls can be pugnacious and threatening: "Just one smart remark about my legs," Molly Volley tells her cowered doubles partner, Snoopy, "and you'll get a knock on the noggin!" (May 10, 1977). They are also rude and insulting: "Everybody knows you feel bad . . . about losing the championship," Lucy tells Charlie Brown, referring to a crucial misplay on his part, "and we know that you know it was the most dim-witted, cement-headed thing a pitcher could do no matter how many stupid blockhead things he may have done" (August 9, 1963).

Yet the girls also display all the qualities traditionally associated with a more genteel femininity. They are concerned about their looks and the impressions they make (assigned to the outfield, Frieda frets: "From that distance do you think people will be able to tell that I have naturally curly hair?" [April 3, 1961]), shamelessly flirt with the boys on the baseball field, routinely exercise their feminine guile, and worry about their clothes (Lucy refuses to slide in her "designer jeans" [April 21, 1981]). When necessary, they are more than willing to play the helpless girl act—"That's the worst kick I have ever seen," Charlie Brown tells Lucy; "Well, after all," she responds, "I am just a little girl, you know" (October 18, 1953). Furthermore, they decorate the baseball field with flowers, discuss the nuances of laundry, play coy ("I have a cute strike zone," Lucy says [September 2, 1983]), are fearful of bugs and spiders in the athletic equipment, and, perhaps worst of all, especially if one wants to irritate boys, trample on the sacred lore and conventions of sport—"I bet Ty Cobb had a cute arm, didn't she?" Lucy suggests to Charlie Brown (July 17, 1998).

In short, Schulz presents an ambivalent picture of gender in sport, often inverting the natural order of traditional gender relations by depicting the girls as meek and passive on the one hand and assertive and independent on the other. But, in the end, Schulz portrays a fully coeducational sports world. The girls in *Peanuts* play all the sports, from football to hockey to baseball, and share equally in the triumphs and tragedies. They also embrace the feminist agenda inscribed in Title IX, proselytizing the need to address the inequalities inherent in men's and women's sports that were so apparent in the 1960s and 1970s. Marcie and Peppermint Patty give voice to the differences in scholarship money, operating budgets, access, and opportunities. Lucy becomes a feminist:

"What am I, a 'new feminist,' doing standing out here in center field?" she wails. "This is a male dominated game . . . Why should I take orders from that stupid manager? . . . This is degrading and I resent it," she complains (April 8, 1970). Even Charlie Brown, in the half-hour television show *It's Spring Training Charlie Brown*, refuses sponsorship for his baseball team because the sponsor, Mr. Hennessey, will not supply uniforms to girls and dogs. Schulz's enlightened gender perspective led feminist activist and champion tennis player Billie Jean King to appoint him to the board of the Women's Sports Foundation: "He is so fair minded," she remarked, "with a basic belief that girls and women should have the same opportunities in sport as the males."[24] Ultimately, reporter Dana White was probably right when she concluded at the time of Schulz's death that "women's sports lost one of its most ardent and visible fans."[25]

CHARLIE BROWN AS THE ULTIMATE OLYMPIAN

In addition to his ongoing concern with the issues that confront and define the world of sport, Schulz also contemplated the mysteries of the human condition, especially the way in which we accept and confront the dehumanizing forces that we can neither control nor even barely comprehend; and how better to interrogate life's fundamental existential problems—fear, loneliness, frustration, isolation, despair, and, especially, failure—than through the medium of sport. And so, for nearly fifty years, Charlie Brown deludes himself into thinking that he can outwit Lucy and finally kick the football that Lucy temptingly holds, yet he never succeeds. For nearly half a century, he returns to the mound to claim his first baseball victory, yet one of the only times his team ever wins is by forfeit—"one more forfeit and we're in first place," he wistfully intones (April 25, 1969). For nearly a quarter of a century, he demonstrates a remarkable pertinacity of spirit as he seeks to foil the guiles of yet another kite-ivorous tree, but the tree always gets the better of him. No one confronts more failure than Charlie Brown, "pure, slink-back-home-with-your-back-dragging failure," as *New York Times* reporter Alan Schwartz puts it.[26] But, despite endless disappointments and adversities, despite embarrassment, mockery, humiliation, bewilderment, and frustration, Charlie Brown never quits; he never gives up. When the field is flooded in a downpour and only the pitcher's mound remains above water, he endures, ever ready to exhort his team

Fig. 6.2: Charles Schulz, *Peanuts*, August 8, 1982. PEANUTS © 1982 Peanuts Worldwide LLC. Dist. by UNIVERSAL UCLICK. Reprinted with permission. All rights reserved.

to practice. Unlike Ulysses, who goes off to seek or create a newer world, Charlie Brown remains, obdurate and resilient. To Schulz, Charlie Brown is anything but a failure: "How can you say that when he never stops trying?" Schulz asserts.[27]

Charlie Brown is not alone in his misery. Snoopy, too, knows failure. As Lucy wryly notes, man is born to suffer, and in the world of *Peanuts*, that means dogs, too. Snoopy's talent for self-delusion also makes him cruelly sarcastic, even mean. He constantly chastises Charlie Brown for his athletic incompetence, even to the point of being arrogantly patronizing. But he is also quick to exalt the humble, and despite his superiority complex, he is charitable and sensitive: he stops a baseball game to allow a bug to cross the infield, and he tenderly cares for his diminutive pal, the bohemian-looking, fluffy-topped Woodstock, whom he teaches hockey, tennis, basketball, and football. Although Snoopy endures anxieties and setbacks, like Charlie Brown he remains a perpetual bon vivant, an Epicurean who finds joy even in humility and failure. Foiled again on the tennis court, he simply shrugs it off: "Billie Jean still loves me," he consoles himself (March 29, 1986). Snoopy refuses to bemoan his fantasies and problems; he embraces them and lives them, whether as hipster and Legionnaire or surfer and golfer. Like Woodstock, he embraces the positive philosophy that "small is beautiful," and he dances his way through life with an incurable joie de vivre.

Ultimately, Charlie Brown and the gang actually enjoy success. On March 30, 1993, Charlie Brown hits a home run to win a baseball game, thus ending one of the longest losing streaks in history: his team had not won a game in more than forty-two years. The team had actually won a game once before, but the win was taken away because one of the players was caught betting on it. The player, it turns out, was Snoopy. But winning is not the point for Schulz: "Victories are fleeting," he duly notes, "but losses we always live with."[28] It is the losses that inform the *Peanuts* universe; it is the trying that matters; and Charlie Brown never stops trying. On the occasion of a 184–0 squeaker, he asks, "How can we lose when we're so sincere?" (April 6, 1963).

The ultimate tragedy is not that Charlie Brown is inferior but that he is completely normal. The message encoded in Charlie Brown's athletic tribulations is that while life may well be futile, perhaps even absurd, and certainly comic; while defeat is inevitable and fame ephemeral; and while the heaviness of Weltschmerz is inescapable, nobility lies not in the victory but in the challenge. As the founder of the modern Olympic Games, Pierre de Coubertin, memorably proclaimed: "The important thing in the Olympic Games is not to win but to take part, the important thing in life is not the triumph but the struggle. The essential thing is not to have conquered but to have fought well."[29] Like Charlie Chaplin's Tramp and George Herriman's Krazy Kat, Charles Schulz's Charlie Brown remains the classic embodiment of human courage and fortitude in the face of insuperable odds, the quintessential Olympian for whom another day on the mound always dawns and for whom the ongoing Sisyphean struggle constitutes the dignity and purpose of life. "It's not the winning that counts," Charlie Brown avers; "the fun is in the playing" (August 1, 1962). Or, as Charlie Brown's creator, sounding remarkably like Coubertin, said: "Losing is hard. But I think the best thing is to enjoy what you're doing for the moment. Remember. The joy is really in the doing."[30] In the miniature world of sport, Schulz's philosophy emphasizes that failure and the way we confront it constitute human success.

CONCLUSION

Driven to exile in America by Hitler's regime, German-born Harvard sociology professor Eugen Rosenstock-Huessy found over the course of his career that the best way to illuminate the points he was trying to make to his students was to reference the world of sport. "The only world in which the American student who comes to me at about twenty years of age really has confidence in is the world of sport. This world encompasses all of his virtues and experiences, affection and interests; therefore, I have built my entire sociology around the experiences an American has in athletics and games," he wrote.[31] When Rosenstock-Huessy wanted to talk about discipline, contingency, spirit, the recognition of limits, asceticism, mysticism, and the relationship between body and emotion and intelligence, he summoned the world of sports. Similarly, when Schulz wants to discuss teleology, grace, love, suffering, hope, solitude, and despair, even life and death, he invokes sport. The power of sport in the strip is perhaps best expressed in Art Spiegelman's extended meditation on the significance of *Peanuts* in which he employs three main visual symbols in the first panel of his comics essay to mourn Schulz's retirement—the football, the kite in the tree, and, juxtaposing them, the essay's first word, "Sigh."[32] Sport constitutes one of the fundamentally lived experiences of Schulz's world of *Peanuts*.

Of course, just when Charlie Brown and his sidekicks think they may have solved life's problems, they invariably find a flag on the play. So, if there is a "rage against the dying of the light" ending, it is predictably located on the field of sport—in this case, the gridiron, on the occasion of Peppermint Patty's final appearance. It's pouring rain and Peppermint Patty is kneeling in the middle of a muddy field yelling for Charlie Brown: "What are you going to do, Chuck? You gonna run or pass?" she inquires. "Everyone's gone home, sir," Marcie notes; "you should go home too . . . It's getting dark." "We had fun, didn't we Marcie?" "Yes, sir . . . We had fun." Alone and on her knees in the midst of a torrential downpour, the epitome of loneliness, Peppermint Patty soulfully reflects: "Nobody shook hands and said 'good game'" (January 2, 2000).

But of all the sports that capture and depict the primary themes that animate *Peanuts*, none of them approach the communicative and cultural salience of baseball.[33] As Charlie Brown rightly observes after losing his 999th game in a row: "The game of baseball and the game of life are very similar" (March 6, 1963).[34] Or, as Schulz himself acknowledged: "Baseball sort of reflects the problems we have in our own lives—fear, loneliness, despair, losing—and all these things can be talked about through the medium of baseball."[35] In Schulz's hands, baseball becomes a postmodern parody of life, a theater of the absurd whose deliberate pace as a sport renders it ideally suited to stage the profound discussions and exchanges that characterize the strip's inner life; or, as Charlie Brown comments as the gang collects on the pitcher's mound to pontificate on the nature of suffering—"I don't have a ball team . . . I have a theological seminary" (September 17, 1967). If, as both Al Capp and Charles Schulz argue, the basis of humor is pain, suffering, and humiliation, no sport is better suited to deliver the message than baseball, a sport of inches laced with heartbreak and disappointment, in which the difference between winning and losing hangs on one swing of the bat, one throw, one pitch, one error. In no other sport is luck so routinely the harbinger of success and failure. No wonder the Major League Baseball season consists of 162 games. How else to determine whether a team's success is grounded in talent or luck? But, like all sport, baseball also offers hope and the opportunity for redemption. So, Schulz's little folks traipse undaunted, one more time, to the mound to take on life's enormous trials and tribulations.

NOTES

1. Between 1957 and 1959, Schulz even wrote a series of sport-themed cartoons published under the title *It's Only a Game* that was specifically dedicated to what can best be described as leisure activities, which ranged from golf and fishing to Monopoly and bridge. See Charles M. Schulz and Jim Sasseville, *It's Only a Game: The Complete Color Collection* (San Bernardino, CA: About Comics, 2004).

2. Charles Schulz, *Peanuts Jubilee: My Life and Art with Charlie Brown and Others* (New York: Holt, Rinehart and Winston, 1975), 8.

3. Ibid.

4. M. Thomas Inge, *Comics as Culture* (Jackson: University Press of Mississippi, 1990), 105.

5. Robert L. Short, *The Parables of Peanuts* (New York: Harper and Row, 1968), 34.

6. Dan Hulbert, "Why Fans Love the Comics and Charles Schulz," *Atlanta Journal and Constitution*, February 3, 2000, A1.

7. Rheta Grimsley Johnson, *Good Grief: The Story of Charles M. Schulz* (New York: Pharos Books, 1989), 82.

8. Peter Heinegg, "Philosopher in the Playground: Notes on the Meaning of Sport," *Southern Humanities Review* 10 (1976): 153–56.

9. Quoted in David Michaelis, *Schulz and Peanuts: A Biography* (New York: Harper-Collins, 2007), 394.

10. Ibid., 247.

11. Gene Kannenberg, "Chips Off the Ol' Block: Evidence of Influence in *Peanuts* Parodies," *Studies in American Humor* 3 (2006): 94.

12. William Shakespeare, *Hamlet*, 3.2.18–19.

13. Schulz does consider other social issues in sport such as aging, salary negotiations, and violence, but he does so only briefly.

14. George Will, "George F. Will on Drugs and Sports," *Newsweek*, May 20, 2007; and Schulz, *Peanuts Jubilee*, 84.

15. Samuel Beckett, *End Game* (New York: Grove Press, 1958), 18.

16. See Charles M. Schulz, "What Do You Do with a Dog That Can't Talk?," *TV Guide*, February 23, 1980, 22–24.

17. Johnson, *Good Grief*, 229.

18. Quoted in Charles Maher, "You're a Good Sport, Charlie Schulz," *Los Angeles Times*, August 28, 1973, Sports Section, 7.

19. Jay Coakley, *Sports in Society: Issues and Controversies* (New York: McGraw-Hill, 2009), 139.

20. Quoted in Stan Isaacs, "Charles Schulz: Comic Strips Aren't Out," *Newsday*, August 28, 1977, 38.

21. Quoted in Johnson, *Good Grief*, 245.

22. In fact, Schulz's near-total ignoring of race is particularly noticeable at a time when comic strips were taking stands or at least commenting on big social questions, and at a time when the issue of race in sport was clearly in the national eye in the form of what sociologist Harry Edwards refers to as "the revolt of the black athlete." One of the most significant images of the era with reference to the issue of race was the black power salute of African American athletes Tommie Smith and John Carlos during a medal ceremony at the 1968 Mexico City Olympics. See Harry Edwards, *The Revolt of the Black Athlete* (New York: Free Press, 1969).

23. Robert C. Harvey, "The Pagliacci Bit," *Comics Journal* 24 (2008): 87.

24. Johnson, *Good Grief*, 228–29.

25. Dana White, "Playing Our 'Toon," *Women's Sports and Fitness*, July–August 2000, 61.

26. Alan Schwartz, "A 50-Year Old Streak in a Game of Failure," *New York Times*, December 19, 1999, 4.

27. Quoted in Hulbert, "Why Fans Love the Comics," A1.

28. Quoted in Schwartz, "A 50-Year Old Streak," 5.

29. Quoted in Bill Henry, *An Approved History of the Olympic Games* (New York: G. P. Putnam's Sons, 1976), ix.

30. Quoted in Neil Cohen, "Charlie Brown: A Winner at Last!," *Sports Illustrated for Kids*, June 5, 1993, 14.

31. Quoted in Clinton C. Gardner, ed., *Life Lines: Quotations from the Work of Eugen Rosenstock-Huessy* (Norwich, VT: Argo Books, 1988), 133.

32. Art Spiegelman, "Abstract Thought Is a Warm Puppy," *New Yorker*, February 14, 2000, 61–63.

33. According to United Feature Syndicate, which distributes *Peanuts*, about 10 percent of more than eighteen thousand strips deal with baseball. See Jack McCallum and

Richard O'Brien, "Good Grief! Sparky Hangs 'em Up," *Sports Illustrated*, December 27, 1999, 56.

34. Jon Borgzinner, "A Leaf, a Lemon Drop, a Cartoon Is Born," *Life*, March 17, 1967, 80.

35. Charlie Brown [Charles M. Schulz], "The Fan: Baseball Is Life, I'm Afraid," *Inside Sports*, May 1985, 82.

PEANUTS AND HISTORY

FOOTBALLS AND OTTIM LIFFS

Charlie Brown in Coconino

MICHAEL TISSERAND

There's something about *Peanuts* that reminds me of *Krazy Kat*.
CARL SANDBURG[1]

Officer Pupp sees the football on the ground, but he doesn't notice a string attached to one end. Pupp takes off running. His foot goes out; the string tightens and the ball pulls away. Pupp flies in the air, throwing one leg skyward. He lands hard.

Ignatz emerges from behind a brick wall, blowing smoke rings from a tiny cigar. "Lost your equilibrium, Officer Pupp?" he asks slyly.

This scene from George Herriman's comic strip *Krazy Kat* first appeared in newspapers on the day after Christmas, 1932. At the time, ten-year-old Charles "Sparky" Schulz was a comics-loving student at Richards Gordon Elementary School in Saint Paul, Minnesota. Yet Schulz didn't read this strip or follow *Krazy Kat* at all. The *Minneapolis Tribune* had once carried Herriman's comics, but by 1932, Schulz later recalled, William Randolph Hearst's King Features Syndicate had no *Krazy Kat* customers in the Twin Cities. Possibly, young Schulz knew the name "Krazy Kat" from early-1930s animations that screened at the nearby Park Theatre, but those weren't Herriman's works.

Unseen by Schulz, then, Herriman's football gag stretched over the final week of 1932. On one day, Krazy tries and fails to kick the ball, and goes flying. On another, Pupp gives the ball a kick and discovers it's made of stone. The series ends as do many of Herriman's tales, with a modernist acknowledgment that it's all a comic strip. This time, Pupp hits the ball with his billy club and makes it explode in a splash of printer's ink.

Fig. 7.1: George Herriman, *Krazy Kat*, December 28, 1932.

Fig. 7.2: George Herriman, *Krazy Kat*, December 29, 1932.

Fig. 7.3: George Herriman, *Krazy Kat*, December 30, 1932.

With that, Herriman's football gags were complete. It would take the kid from Saint Paul to one day expand them into a comic epic of one child's villainy and another's undimmed optimism.

Is the story of Lucy, Charlie Brown, and the football an homage to George Herriman? As it turns out, kicking a football might be an elusive pursuit, but so too is attempting to trace a clear pathway of influence from one cartoonist to another.

"A cartoonist is someone who has to draw the same thing day after day after day without repeating himself," Charles Schulz once said. Few approached Herriman's ability to draw and write these same things so wondrously. As critic Gilbert Seldes wrote in 1922, in *Krazy Kat*, the "variations are innumerable, the ingenuity never flags."[2]

The story structure of *Krazy Kat* might seem simple enough. Krazy Kat loves Ignatz. Ignatz is obsessed with beaning Krazy Kat with a brick. Officer Pupp is duty-bound to jail Ignatz and also harbors his own affection for the Kat. Yet Herriman's *Krazy Kat* is also a meditation on love and fate, good and evil, and even language and reality. It was uniquely nuanced, even for a golden era of newspapers when there was more page space for nuance.

Herriman was typically modest, telling others that his job amounted to turning out comical pictures to amuse Hearst's readers over their morning eggs and coffee. Yet the depth of purpose and clarity of vision in Herriman's work indicate that he believed otherwise. With *Krazy Kat*, Herriman brought all he had to the comics page, creating a deeply personal work that pushed open door after door for any artist hoping to test the limits.

It was also a work that reflected a unique biography. George Joseph Herriman was born to a mixed-race family in New Orleans in 1880. When George was ten years old, the Herrimans fled the Jim Crow South for Los Angeles, choosing to improve their economic chances by the controversial practice of "passing" as white. It's not completely clear how much the Herriman children were informed about their family, but George Herriman would live out the rest of his life as a white man. He married a white woman and lived in neighborhoods restricted to whites. He also worked in an industry that did not yet include African Americans, laughing along with friends and coworkers when they called him "George the Greek."

Around Herriman's twentieth birthday, he set off to New York to join a small legion of ambitious young artists inventing the American newspaper comic. He got hired by Hearst, fired by Hearst, found a job with Joseph Pulitzer, and then found his way back to Hearst's pages. After a few more stints at various newspapers and newspaper syndicates, he was back in California and on staff at Hearst's *Los Angeles Examiner*. He never again left Hearst's employment. Wrote Herriman in a 1943 cartoon for Hearst's birthday: "Could be our boss. Could be our chief. Could be our friend."

Herriman's best-known character, Krazy Kat, developed in appearance and personality over the span of fifteen years. When Herriman was still a teenage office boy at the *Los Angeles Herald*, he added a small, mute cat to a cartoon that the newspaper published in the classified advertisement pages. The cat found a voice in 1902 when it appeared as part of a tiny animal sideshow in a short-lived comic titled *Acrobatic Archie* and uttered to a bulldog: "T'was a mighty chase." Over the next decade, Herriman occasionally promoted household pets to starring roles while filling the margins of his "human" strips with tiny talking animals. An early version of Krazy Kat also showed up in Herriman's sports cartoons, in which he caricatured African American prizefighters as black cats.

Then, in 1910, in the margins of a comic strip about a family named the Dingbats and their troubles with some upstairs neighbors, Herriman added a tiny scene of a white mouse throwing a rock at a cat. An editor encouraged Herriman to expand his little stories of feuding animals, and *Krazy Kat* was born.

In short time, Herriman began to use his *Krazy Kat* stories to riff on the nature of identity and the slipperiness of language, reflecting the unique perspective of a New Orleans Creole finding his way in a black-and-white world. In 1915, he relocated the strip to Coconino County, a fertile and restless landscape he assembled from the buttes, mesas, and sandstone monuments of northern Arizona and southern Utah. The slapstick gag of throwing a brick propels the stories of *Krazy Kat*, but the strip also serves as a character study of a Kat whose love for a tormentor increases with each knock on the noggin. Told in a rich language that blends street slang and Elizabethan English, *Krazy Kat* lasted a full thirty-four years in Hearst's newspapers. Herriman's tales of Krazy, Ignatz, Officer Pupp, and an all-animal supporting cast are now well considered as some of the richest comic tales in American literature.

Yet *Krazy Kat* also perplexed Hearst's readers to no end. Even in the early 1920s, when *Krazy Kat* was at the height of its popularity, some editors had to wage battles with their business managers just to keep the strip in their paper. This happened in Cedar Rapids, Iowa, where the business office wanted to replace *Krazy Kat* with Billy DeBeck's more popular *Barney Google*. (The paper eventually found room for both strips.) Why the lack of popularity for the strip? The dense language and shifting desert landscapes were admittedly challenging, but what most confounded readers was Herriman's choice to make *Krazy Kat* both male and female.

Movie director Frank Capra came closest to getting an explanation for this decision. Capra encountered Herriman at Hal Roach Studios and asked him if Krazy Kat was a "he or a she." Herriman replied that he had tried making Krazy a female, but it just didn't seem to work. Capra recalled in his memoir what Herriman said next: "Then I realized Krazy was something like a sprite, an elf. They have no sex. So that Kat can't be a he or a she. The Kat's a sprite—a pixie—free to butt into anything."[3]

Soon after Charles Schulz's birth in 1922, he received a lifelong nickname: Sparky. Ironically, it came from the horse Spark Plug in DeBeck's *Barney Google*—the same strip that some Iowa newspaper bean counters had once tried to sub in for *Krazy Kat*.

Like many children growing up between the world wars, Schulz eagerly followed adventure comics such as *Tim Tyler's Luck* and *Buck Rogers in the 25th Century A.D.* He also read Walt Disney's funny animal stories and especially E. C. Segar's *Popeye*—both influenced by Herriman. During this time, however, Schulz remained unaware of Coconino County and of any love triangle involving Kat and Mouse and Pupp.

After high school—when he reached the age at which Herriman started to break into the New York newspapers—Schulz tried to interest Disney and others in his comics. Unlike Herriman, however, Schulz enjoyed no early luck. After jobbing around Minneapolis and Saint Paul, he was drafted into the US Army. By the time Herriman died in 1944, Schulz, nearly twenty-two, had risen to the rank of buck sergeant. Schulz returned home the following year and continued sending out his work, including to King Features. He finally found a job at Art Instruction, a training school, where he graded student submissions. In 1947, he placed *Li'l Folks*, a comic about children, in local newspapers. Three years later, the comic was picked up by United Feature Syndicate and retitled, against Schulz's wishes, to *Peanuts*.

Yet something besides a name change happened on the way from *Li'l Folks* to *Peanuts*. In 1944, when poet E. E. Cummings learned of Herriman's death, he convinced his publisher to release a book of *Krazy Kat* strips along with a Cummings essay that, clearly influenced by a still-raging world war, likened Krazy to democracy's "spiritual values of wisdom, love, and joy."[4]

The comic *Krazy Kat*, as Cummings saw it, was a work of optimism, a "meteoric burlesk melodrama, born of the immemorial adage love will find a way." Among those who read his words was Charles Schulz. "After World War II, I began to study the *Krazy Kat* strip for the first time," Schulz later recalled. "A book collection of *Krazy Kat* was published sometime in the late 1940s, which did much to inspire me to create a feature that went beyond the mere actions of ordinary children."[5]

Fig. 7.4: Charles Schulz, *Peanuts,* September 18, 1974. PEANUTS © 1974 Peanuts Worldwide LLC. Dist. by UNIVERSAL UCLICK. Reprinted with permission. All rights reserved.

In appearance, *Peanuts* and *Krazy Kat* might seem dissimilar, even polar opposites. Schulz, well aware that he had to effectively communicate his story no matter how large or small his comics might be reprinted, used a bold, fluid line to accomplish an elegant comics minimalism. The central images in *Peanuts* are large, expressive children's faces balanced on disproportionately small bodies. Where Herriman rendered darkly shadowed desert vistas, Schulz's backgrounds are either deceptively simple interiors of couches, lamps, rugs, and televisions, or Midwest-inspired landscapes of grass or snow, trees, sidewalks, and picket fences. Schulz usually limited his language to speech or thought balloons in the top third of a panel, except for an occasional "AAUGH." Instead of filling his margins with little animal sideshows, as Herriman did, Schulz nearly always presented his action on a single stage.

Yet Herriman's influence can be detected throughout *Peanuts*, visually as well as thematically. One of the most striking visual similarities is also the most iconic image of *Peanuts*. Herriman traveled extensively throughout northern Arizona, and among the many ideas he adapted from Navajo artists were bold zigzag stripes, symbols of lightning. Although Schulz's former girlfriend Donna Wold would recall the cartoonist wearing a gray shirt with a black zigzag pattern, Schulz himself subscribed to the idea that Herriman's drawings played a part. *Mutts* cartoonist Patrick McDonnell, a Herriman scholar as well as a friend of Schulz's, recalled a conversation in which they discussed Charlie Brown's shirt. Although Schulz said it hadn't been a conscious homage, he acknowledged that it appeared to be the kind of influence that results from one artist deeply admiring and studying another.

This was just the beginning of similarities, however. Under Schulz's pen, a placid midwestern landscape might at times spring to sudden Coconino life. Just as Herriman might show a cactus raising or shrugging

Fig. 7.5: Charles Schulz, *Peanuts*, October 12, 1965. PEANUTS © 1965 Peanuts Worldwide LLC. Dist. by UNIVERSAL UCLICK. Reprinted with permission. All rights reserved.

its branches to comment on the main action, so might Charlie Brown's fears suddenly animate a tree into a grinning destroyer of children's kites.

Not only flora and fauna become animated. In an occasional series that took place in September and October 1974, Sally, Charlie Brown's kid sister, begins talking to her school building. Sally's adoration of Linus is among the many cases of unrequited love that infect Schulz's pint-size population. When Sally tries to introduce Linus to her school as her "boy friend," Linus erupts in a storm of wild eyes and hair, shouting in bold type, "Waddya mean, boy friend?!" In an imitation of Ignatz, the school building drops a brick on Linus's head. "I'm the jealous type," says the building. Even more to the point, the school also dropped a brick on Lucy, telling her, "We're all a little crazy, kid!"

One of Schulz's most poignant and expressive uses of nature in *Peanuts* is his depiction of autumn leaves. In the Midwest of Schulz's childhood, a riotous flash of seasonal color prefaces winter's disintegrations. In *Peanuts*, leaves always have their stories to tell. Some are lighthearted: a pile of leaves provides an opportunity for an athletic leap (but preferably not while holding a sucker). In quieter moments, melancholic conversations might be accompanied by a single leaf blowing in the wind, not unlike the answer in a song by another Minnesotan poet, Bob Dylan.

Throughout his half-century with *Peanuts*, Schulz returned again and again to stories about falling leaves. Some starred Linus, who began talking with leaves. In the October 7, 1960, strip, he informs Lucy forthrightly: "Leaves need me! I help them through what is really the big emotional period of their lives!" Snoopy (arguably the most sprite-like creature in comics since Krazy Kat) joyfully dances along with a leaf as the wind blows it to the ground, then thanks it for the dance (October 9, 1967). Woodstock even suffers a "fear of falling leaves" (October 22, 1972). Lucy, not surprisingly, is most blunt about the leaf's fate. "Stay up there you fool!" she tells a single leaf on a tree, and, when it falls, she says bleakly: "Now, it'll be the rake and the burning pile" (October 12, 1965).

Schulz's recurring stories of autumn leaves echo a contemplative series of daily *Krazy Kat* strips published over six days in November 1934. The story begins with Krazy Kat noticing a single "ottim liff." Soon, Krazy is joined by Ignatz and Officer Pupp. The trio sits on a log, waiting for the leaf to drop. Ignatz's and Pupp's patience is soon exhausted, but Krazy keeps a moonlight vigil, saying that if the leaf doesn't fall this year, "they is always 'ottim' afta next." On the fourth day, just as Officer Pupp and Ignatz fall to their knees to beg Krazy to end the vigil, the leaf falls with a sudden "plip." In a coda, Ignatz ties a brick to a branch. "Wot a pleasing pleasure I'm gonna get, wen it falls," says Krazy, as Ignatz prepares to cut the cord.

"You know, I always thought if I could do something as good as Krazy Kat, I would be happy," Charles Schulz once said. "Krazy Kat was always my goal."[6]

Schulz had certainly read the "ottom liff" stories when he was just beginning *Peanuts*, for they were among the daily strips reprinted in Cummings's *Krazy Kat* collection. The football gags were not among the strips in Cummings's book. Yet such parallels probably shouldn't be considered direct borrowings or homages. Rather, the connections appear to exist because of important similarities between the artists themselves.

Charles Schulz and George Herriman were both deeply spiritual men, yet each grew iconoclastic in his beliefs. Schulz grew up a Protestant churchgoer and as an adult led Bible studies sessions at his local church, but he later considered his faith to be an intensely private matter. Herriman was raised in a family of devout Catholics and as a schoolboy learned catechism from Vincentian priests, yet his work is replete with references to séances, reincarnation, and especially Navajo beliefs. With the possible exception of Percy Crosby's *Skippy* (also a sizable influence on Schulz), no general-interest comics are filled with as many overtly spiritual ideas and quotations from the Bible as *Peanuts* and *Krazy Kat*.

Fans of *Peanuts* are well aware of the lengthy quotation from the book of Luke offered by Linus in the television special *A Charlie Brown Christmas*. Schulz frequently turned to Bible passages for his newspaper strip as well, as in the 1970 Sunday strip in which Charlie Brown, being offered yet another turn at kicking the football, cries in anguish, "How

Long, O Lord?" Says Lucy, holding the football: "Actually, there is a note of protest in the question as asked by Isaiah, for we might say he was unwilling to accept the finality of the Lord's judgment."

Such a meditation on fate is seen again and again in *Krazy Kat*. "It is the things we don't see which guide our course in life, 'Krazy,'" Ignatz says in a 1918 strip. Replies Krazy, "He what guides a brick to my bean each day aint so inwisibil y'betcha." Herriman might turn to the Bible (as he did to classic works of literature) for whimsical fun, as in a 1939 comic in which Krazy casts a "loafibread" in the water and a fish complains that it's not buttered. Yet the most consistent spiritual theme throughout the thirty-four-year life of *Krazy Kat* is its meditation on sin and the brick-obsessed Ignatz, who is, as Ignatz himself howls, "a bad wicked 'mouse.'"

Neither brick nor football can daunt the optimism of Krazy Kat and Charlie Brown. There is, however, one crucial difference in Schulz's and Herriman's spiritual slapsticks. "Happiness does not create humor," Schulz once said. "Sadness creates humor. Krazy Kat getting hit on the head by a brick from Ignatz Mouse is funny."[7] This might hold true for Charlie Brown, who lands in anguish after each attempted football kick, but not for Krazy Kat. With each brick, Krazy is literally love-struck, believing ever more deeply in Ignatz's devotion. There lies the greatest difference between Charlie Brown and Krazy Kat: when succumbing to fate, Krazy would never utter an "AAUGH," and Charlie Brown would never be seen swooning in bliss after a football prank. One knows only love; one is doomed to be forever denied it.

Umberto Eco, writing of both *Krazy Kat* and *Peanuts*, described "a constant seesaw of reactions" in which "we never know whether to despair or to heave a sigh of optimism."[8]

Herriman and Schulz achieved this effect, Eco said, by their "lyrical stubbornness." Both cartoonists inscribed rules for fantastical, self-enclosed worlds in which they could explore stunningly wide ranges of emotions and experiences. In Coconino County, it's not just that there are no human beings; it's that humans are unthinkable. In *Peanuts*, adults do live just off-frame, similar to the Dingbats' upstairs neighbors. But an adult strolling down a sidewalk in *Peanuts* would be as inconceivable as a human standing guard at Officer Pupp's jail.

Nowhere is the connection between creator and creation felt more deeply than at the end of each strip's run. In the final years of Herriman's life, arthritis and other ailments made the act of drawing increasingly painful. The changes can be traced right in the *Krazy Kat* strip itself, with characters and scenery being drawn in a scratchier line and emotions expressed in the most minimal number of dots and dashes. Schulz's late art reflects the effects of a worsening tremor, with wavy lines replacing the swooping curves of earlier years. For both, the resulting effect is the embedment of individual suffering directly in the art. This offers the sense of a full, complete life to both *Peanuts* and *Krazy Kat*, from their whimsical, gag-filled youth, through adult meditations, to a final unification of artist and work.

The syndicates retired both *Krazy Kat* and *Peanuts* after the deaths of their creators. Yet Schulz's and Herriman's works live on to inspire new generations, traversing those mysterious zigzag lines of influence that lead from cartoonist to cartoonist. For the final word on all the tossing of bricks and pranking of footballs, one need look no further than the original *Krazy Kat* comic that Schulz hung on the wall of his drawing studio. In the strip, which dates to 1916, Krazy Kat talks to a pair of hedgehogs who have just witnessed Ignatz throwing a brick.

Says Krazy: "You rilly must not mind 'Ignatz,' he's only got a great sense of 'fizzikill humor,'—thats all."

NOTES

1. Quoted in Gregory d'Alessio, "Cartoons? Yes! Says Carl Sandburg," *The Cartoonist*, Summer 1957; reprinted as "News of Yore: Carl Sandburg on Cartoons," *Stripper's Guide*, March 11, 2008, at http://strippersguide.blogspot.com/2008/03/news-of-yore-carl -sandburg-on-cartoons.html.

2. Gilbert Seldes, *The 7 Lively Arts* (New York: Harper and Brothers, 1924), 238.

3. Frank Capra, *The Name above the Title: An Autobiography* (New York: Macmillan, 1971), 40.

4. E. E. Cummings, "A Foreword to Krazy," in *Arguing Comics: Literary Masters on a Popular Medium*, ed. Jeet Heer and Kent Worcester (Jackson: University Press of Mississippi, 2009), 32.

5. Charles M. Schulz, *My Life with Charlie Brown* (Jackson: University Press of Mississippi, 2010), 6.

6. Charles Schulz, interview with Mary Harrington Hall, in *Charles M. Schulz: Conversations*, ed. M. Thomas Inge (Jackson: University Press of Mississippi, 2000), 55.

7. Quoted in M. Thomas Inge, *Comics as Culture* (Jackson: University Press of Mississippi, 1990), 65.

8. Umberto Eco, "On 'Krazy Kat' and 'Peanuts,'" trans. William Weaver, *New York Review of Books*, June 13, 1985.

-8-

SCHULZ AND THE LATE SIXTIES

Snoopy's Signs of the Times

JOSEPH J. DAROWSKI

Any discussion of the 1960s in American history seemingly must include an evocative adjective. Preferably one that starts with the letter *T*. "Turbulent." "Tumultuous." "Troubled." Perhaps even "Topsy-turvy." Needless to say, there were many high-impact events in that decade that shaped American culture. With the Cold War, the Vietnam War, social movements, campus demonstrations, marches, counterculture, the space race, protests, and other social upheavals, all the adjectives listed above and more can accurately be applied to the sixties. This was a noted departure from the 1950s, which, while not as simple and homogeneous as sometimes presented in popular culture,[1] did indeed witness a consensus culture built around America's role and identity on the world stage. In the 1960s, this consensus culture would be fractured by domestic issues (the civil rights movement, the feminist movement, a presidential assassination) and foreign events (the Bay of Pigs fiasco, the Cuban Missile Crisis, the Vietnam War).

The impact of these social and historical events can be seen in music, film, television, comic books, and on the comic strip pages of newspapers produced in the period. Even *Peanuts*, a quintessentially child-friendly property, was not immune to the culture-shaking movements and defining historical moments of the 1960s. As Hal Hartley explains:

> Perhaps it's the very sparseness of the *Peanuts* world—the anywhere at anytime simplicity—that allows us to see the world we ourselves actually move through. . . . When I read these strips now, I sense the times in which they were written and drawn. I sense the characters have been shaped by an awareness of the real world that Charles Schulz moved through as well.[2]

Sometimes, as with Snoopy's trip to the moon, which was produced in anticipation of America's successful effort to win the space race, the connections are obvious and unavoidable. Other instances, such as echoes of the Vietnam War that can be seen through Snoopy's World War I flying ace, are not as overt or explicit as what can be found in other cultural artifacts of the era. Whether plain or subtle, though, the fingerprints of the 1960s can clearly be detected on the content of Schulz's work from that period.

THE FIRST BEAGLE ON THE MOON

The space race between the United States and the USSR began shortly after World War II and remained a constant facet of the Cold War until its conclusion. The competition began with America's first supersonic flight in 1947 but gained a heightened urgency with Russia's launch of *Sputnik*, the first orbiting satellite. Subsequently, the moon became the primary focus of the space race, and the effort to successfully land a man on the lunar surface was a defining goal of the dueling world powers during the 1960s.

Because the producers of entertainment are often members of the same communities that will enjoy their productions, it is only natural that "reflections of leading preoccupations in society" find their way into popular entertainment.[3] Of course, the truth is much more complex than simply seeing reflections of a society in the pop culture of the time, because, simultaneously, the media is shaping the concerns, attitudes, and hopes of consumers. The reflection goes both ways. With the space race acting as a technological measuring stick between the two Cold War superpowers, such reflections can be seen in cinema, where space-themed sci-fi movies gained popularity in the 1950s and 1960s; in television, where space heroes replaced the frontier protagonists of the 1950s; in comic books, where Superman suddenly gained an extraterrestrial rogues' gallery after he had largely been limited previously to earthbound villains; and even in *Peanuts* comic strips, where Snoopy imagines himself becoming the first beagle in space. Just as "the Cold War extended its reach beyond Earth" in the 1960s, Snoopy would leave Earth's atmosphere for a nine-day series of *Peanuts* comic strips.[4]

In 1961, while delivering his "Special Message to Congress on Urgent National Needs," President John F. Kennedy famously declared a national

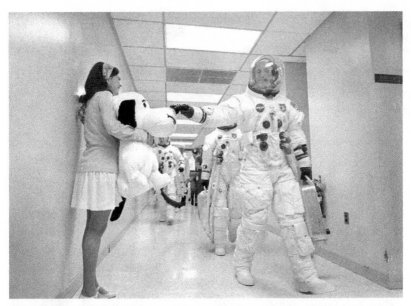

Fig. 8.1: "A Touch of Luck": As the Apollo 10 crew walks along a corridor on the way to Launch Complex 39B, mission commander Thomas P. Stafford pats the nose of Snoopy, the mission's mascot, held by Jamye Flowers, astronaut Gordon Cooper's secretary. © Copyright NASA.

goal of landing a man on the moon before the decade's close. This was one of the rare instances in which an American president used Article II, Section 3, of the Constitution to deliver an address other than the traditional, annual State of the Union. During this address, Kennedy stated:

> I believe that this nation should commit itself to achieving the goal, before this decade is out, of landing a man on the moon and returning him safely to the earth. No single space project in this period will be more impressive to mankind, or more important for the long-range exploration of space; and none will be so difficult or expensive to accomplish. We propose to accelerate the development of the appropriate lunar space craft. . . . But in a very real sense, it will not be one man going to the moon—if we make this judgment affirmatively, it will be an entire nation. For all of us must work to put him there.[5]

NASA became a beacon of hope, as American citizens sought evidence of their nation's superiority over the USSR. Even before Schulz would

Fig. 8.2: Charles Schulz, *Peanuts,* March 14, 1969. PEANUTS © 1969 Peanuts Worldwide LLC. Dist. by UNIVERSAL UCLICK. Reprinted with permission. All rights reserved.

depict Snoopy's quest to become the first beagle on the moon, *Peanuts* would have a role with NASA.

NASA requested Schulz's permission to use Snoopy as the organization's "safety mascot," and the famous beagle was employed in that role beginning in 1968.[6] Additionally, the command and lunar modules of Apollo 10 were named *Charlie Brown* and *Snoopy,* respectively. As the Apollo 10 mission was the dress rehearsal for the successful Apollo 11 lunar landing, the *Snoopy* module was launched, and a part of the craft did land on the moon, so Snoopy touched the moon's surface in the real world as well as in the comic strip. The other portion of the *Snoopy* module remains in outer space, where it was propelled to settle into an orbit around the sun.[7] During the journey to the moon, Captain Eugene A. Cernan held up a picture of Snoopy to the television camera that was on board the spacecraft providing footage for newscasts on Earth. "NASA estimated that more than a billion viewers all over the world saw Snoopy at that moment."[8]

In anticipation of the successful moon landing of Apollo 11 that would occur in July 1969, Schulz produced six daily strips that ran in March of that year. These strips depicted Snoopy, wearing his World War I flying ace costume as well as an additional bubblehead helmet, traveling to the moon and back. In all of the strips to the moon, Snoopy is facing the right-hand side of the panels, but in the final strip he is facing the left side, slyly noting: "You can tell I'm returning because I'm facing the other way" (March 15, 1969), a playful metacommentary about the way comic strips are read in the West.

The strips have Schulz's characteristic simple but pleasing humor, with the last panel providing a punch line that varies between a self-aware winking at the audience, absurd demands from Snoopy, self-doubt, and a subversive contrast of the grand with the trivial. In one strip, after Snoopy imagines that he has walked around the surface of the moon, he

declares: "I did it! I'm the first beagle on the moon! I beat the Russians
... I beat everybody ... I even beat that stupid cat who lives next door!"
(March 14, 1969). In one panel, Schulz makes mention of the Russians,
the enemy America was racing to the moon, and in the next a smirking
Snoopy gloats in his triumph over the cat next door. It is an innocent
enough final panel but one that carries an indictment of the geopolitical
climate at the time. Were the United States and the Soviet Union simply
fighting like cats and dogs, with no real purpose behind the barking and
yowling? Was a triumphant moment in human history being overshadowed by political rivalries? While not overtly asking those questions,
the series of comics portraying the first beagle on the moon invites the
thoughtful reader to ponder the matter in the gutter between the panels.

FROM WORLD WAR I TO VIETNAM

While it is difficult in any era to say that only one issue mattered—a
truth even more applicable when discussing a period as fractured as the
1960s in America—it is safe to contend that in the latter half of the1960s
the war in Vietnam was a defining element of American society. For the
most part, Charles Schulz avoided explicit mention of the topic in his
Peanuts comic strip. This is not surprising considering the general nature
and tone the series presented to readers. As Robert C. Harvey writes:

> The principals of its cast include a chronic loser, a cranky fussbud-
> get, a precocious genius beyond the aspirations of us all, and an aca-
> demically impotent pupil. But Charlie Brown always comes back; he
> is never defeated. Likewise his cohorts; they persist. And so the strip
> is also about human resilience and hope, hope that rises again like a
> phoenix from the ashes from each and every disappointment. Against
> this somewhat ordinary and certainly unglamorous assessment of the
> human condition, Schulz balanced the fantasy life of Snoopy, a blithe
> beagle whose seeming brilliant success at every endeavor reassures us
> that life is not only about disappointment and endurance: it is also
> about dreams and the sustaining power of imagination.[9]

Of particular note is the summation of Snoopy's role in the series: he
is a dreamer whose fantasies inject optimism into the sometimes dour
philosophies of the human characters. However, this otherwise accurate

summation of the series omits Snoopy's most notable and unavoidable disappointment: his imagined role as the World War I flying ace, a role that inevitably ended in frustration and failure. If so many of Snoopy's fantasies are about success and fulfillment, the World War I flying ace who is constantly bested by the Red Baron is an intriguing exception to this rule. Examining the timing of the introduction of this incarnation of Snoopy to the series is illuminating as to why the otherwise triumphant dog is doomed to be bested by the cursed Red Baron.

The World War I flying ace made his first appearance in 1965, an introduction that seems timed, through the safety of fantasy, to comment on a dispiriting and divisive issue in America: the Vietnam War. A close reading of the comics of the era reveals that Schulz addressed many of the issues surrounding the controversial war through Snoopy's imaginary adventures as a World War I flying ace. While explicit references to Vietnam are rare—though not entirely absent—in *Peanuts*, the imagination of a beagle provided a safe window through which Schulz could acknowledge some of the social issues percolating within American culture. The allegorical rendering of a historical war was an innocuous place for commentary that lessened the risk of alienating readers with strong opinions regarding the conflict.

As fans of *Peanuts* via the comic strips, television specials, or even merchandising are aware, Snoopy possesses a rich internal life. In his head, Snoopy can perfectly imitate a menagerie of animals (shark, wolf, vulture, etc.) and enjoy a plethora of "world famous" occupations (attorney, surgeon, disco dancer, etc.). Schulz explained that in the 1960s, after a decade of publishing, his strip experienced "a turning point when Snoopy began thinking his own thoughts and began getting up on his hind feet and walking around."[10] Schulz concluded that "the best thing I ever thought of was Snoopy using his own imagination,"[11] arguing elsewhere that a daily comic strip afforded the kind of long-term character development that readers can find in a novel because "even though it takes only 16 seconds a day to read, cumulatively it goes on forever."[12] Although not a part of the original conceit of the series, through the slow and natural evolution of a daily comic strip, one of the most iconic aspects of Snoopy developed and allowed for stealthy commentary about controversial subjects.

While Snoopy's imaginary roles became a more prominent part of the strip in the 1960s, undoubtedly one of the most famous flights of fancy Snoopy enjoyed was pretending to be the World War I flying ace who constantly battles his archfoe, the Red Baron. Schulz recalls that his son, Monte, was building plastic models of World War I airplanes and showed one to him. That day he first drew Snoopy atop his doghouse as a fighter pilot.[13] Donning a pair of aviator goggles and climbing on top of his doghouse, which was transformed into a Sopwith Camel in his imagination, Snoopy duels with the Red Baron in the skies above World War I battlefields. Inevitably, bullet holes riddle the side of his doghouse, and Snoopy curses the Red Baron for defeating him once again. Often, after crashing his plane, Snoopy imagines that he is behind enemy lines, where he makes his way to a French café and flirts with a waitress while drowning his troubles in root beer. No doubt one reason this alter ego has become so famous is that it was very quickly adapted into the television specials. Just over a year after the World War I flying ace's first appearance in the comic strip, the character had significant screen time in the third animated special based on the *Peanuts* gang, *It's the Great Pumpkin, Charlie Brown* (1966).

Like so many of the human characters in *Peanuts*, the World War I flying ace doesn't have it easy and carries his own set of issues and emotional baggage. But, rather than abstract existential angst, this character's suffering is reminiscent of the issues facing many Vietnam soldiers and veterans. And, instead of the successes that defined many of Snoopy's "world famous" flights of fancy, from the beginning the flying ace fails to accomplish his goals. In the first strip in which he appears, Snoopy is startled by Linus and falls off his doghouse (October 10, 1965). In his second appearance, Snoopy imagines that his plane catches fire, forcing him to parachute behind enemy lines, where he has a meltdown imagining that he'll be captured and shot at dawn (November 7, 1965).

The trend continued in the next year. Snoopy is shot down and walks away muttering "I hate the Red Baron!" (January 9, 1966), bails out after being shot (January 23, 1966), crawls behind enemy lines and through barbed wire (really two girls' jump rope) (February 6, 1966), and so on. In each adventure, the Red Baron bests the World War I flying ace. The futility of the warfare is evident, even if the flying ace's willingness to get up again has a certain romantic heroism to it. Besides the general sense of repetitive failure that permeates these war-themed strips, some strips demonstrate more pointed commentaries that are applicable to the Vietnam War.

Consider the Sunday comic strip from January 1, 1967. While in the throwaway title-card panel Snoopy appears in his classic

flying-his-doghouse pose while wearing a New Year's hat, in each narrative panel Snoopy wears the telltale aviator goggles of his flying ace persona. Only in the final panel does another character—Charlie Brown—appear. And what does this comic strip, the first of a new year, address for comedy? Imperialism—"Alone in a strange country" (panel 3); the interminable nature of war—"How much longer can this war go on?" (panel 4); the mental health of soldiers—"I think I shall go mad!" (panel 4); alcoholism—"Garçon, another root beer please" (panel 5); the horrors of war—"How many root beers can a man drink? How many does it take to drive the agony from your brain? Curse this war!" (panel 6); hatred—"And curse you Red Baron, wherever you are! I'm going to get you yet! I'm going to shoot you down!" (panels 7 and 8); belligerent soldiers—"Disturbance? Who's creating a disturbance? I'm a pilot with the Allies! I'm going to save the world!" (panels 9 and 10); and the treatment of soldiers—"You can't do this to a flying-ace! You'll be sorry!" (panel 12). This is dramatic material for a so-called comic strip, but that was not unusual for *Peanuts*. Because it features a cartoony-looking beagle in old-style goggles and scarf, it's easy to smirk at, but despite the disguise it's hard not to recognize that the issues being raised in this strip are applicable to America's relationship with the Vietnam War and its veterans.

Clearly, this does not have to be simply allegorical, as the horrors of war that were seen in Vietnam are not exclusive to that theater of war. The struggles of soldiers and civilians alike in wartime have parallels across all the battles of history. But Schulz introduced Snoopy's World War I flying ace in the mid-1960s as the Vietnam War was dragging on and, for a time, Snoopy's fantasy character became a mainstay of the series. The character was introduced late in 1965, on October 10, and only appeared in one more strip that year, on November 7. In 1966, this version of Snoopy appeared forty times, or in 10.9 percent of the strips from that year. In 1967, *Peanuts* strips featured the flying ace thirty-three times, or in 9 percent of the strips. From this point on, the character appears much less frequently. In 1968, he is depicted in twelve strips (3.3 percent); in 1969, eight strips (2.1 percent); and in 1970, seven strips (1.9 percent). Schulz acknowledged his growing discomfort in drawing this version of Snoopy during the 1960s, and he made a direct connection with America's involvement in the Vietnam War. When asked if he felt that drawing Snoopy as a war character during the Vietnam War was inappropriate, he responded affirmatively and explained:

> Well, because . . . war . . . we were suddenly realizing just everybody that . . . this was such a monstrous war and everything. It just didn't seem funny. So I just stopped doing it. Then going into bookstores and seeing the revival of war books, mostly World War II, Korea, World War I books, . . . I thought, "It's coming back again," so then I started doing some more. But I didn't do him fighting the Red Baron. Mostly, it was just sitting in the French café flirting with the waitress.[14]

The change in attitude Schulz cites was one that was growing in the mid- to late sixties as the horrors of the war became more undeniable. In part, this was because of President Lyndon Johnson's escalation of troop deployments in Vietnam, which resulted in greater loss of life. When Johnson became president in 1963, there were 21,000 troops in Vietnam, but "by June 1965 there were 75,000 men. Two months later there were 125,000 . . . on the way to a peak of 540,000 by the time Richard M. Nixon replaced Johnson in January 1969." The death toll similarly rose. There were 246 American soldiers killed in 1964–1965, but "during the first year of full-scale conflict 1,363 Americans were slain. Before it ended there were 58,003 U.S. troops dead and 303,704 wounded."[15]

Notably, the flying ace version of Snoopy first appeared in the same year as the first Vietnam War protests on college campuses. The character was used more consistently as the Vietnam War dragged on but then tailed off as the debates around the war became more fiery. While America's involvement in both World War I and World War II was ultimately seen as necessary and the soldiers fighting in those wars generally valorized, such was not the case with Vietnam. The picture painted of war by Snoopy is not of romantic nostalgia but of drudgery, futility, and horror, suggesting that the latter conflict is indeed the true referent.

Even though he can be read as a criticism of the Vietnam War, Snoopy's World War I flying ace became a symbol used by some within the armed forces during the Vietnam War, with Schulz's permission. David Michaelis provides a list of the figure's adoption:

in Vietnam as a talisman on American fighter planes and on the short-range Sidewinder air-to-air "dogfight" missile; in California, as an emblem emblazoned on aircraft spearheading the flight test program of the GAM-77 Hound Dog strategic missile; and in Germany, as a flight shield for the "Able Aces" of the Air Force's 6911th Radio Group Mobile, patrolling the skies over Darmstadt.[16]

This was not the only explicit Vietnam connection that would arise in connection with the character.

A band called the Royal Guardsmen released a song titled "Snoopy vs. the Red Baron," without the knowledge or consent of Schulz or his syndicate. Schulz relates that after a friend complimented the song, he "checked with [his] lawyer the next day and [they] put a stop to that right away. Or rather [they] threatened to put a stop to it" until licensing and royalties were sorted out.[17] The song was very popular, reaching #2 on the charts, and the Royal Guardsmen, now with permission, released several other songs that referenced Snoopy and the Red Baron (including "The Smallest Astronaut," which told a story of Snoopy preventing the Red Baron from landing on the moon before American astronauts). Another of these songs, "Snoopy's Christmas," sees Snoopy and the Red Baron call a Christmas truce and share a toast. While likely inspired by the Christmas truce of World War I, the single was intended by the band "basically [to] expose the futility of never-ending conflict," and it specifically address the pointlessness of the Vietnam War.[18]

SCHULZ AND THE LATE SIXTIES

Although drawing the same round-headed children that he had been depicting for over a decade, Schulz was still a part of an American society that was experiencing growing pains and revolutionary changes. As the creator of a multimedia and merchandising empire that was already achieving significant cultural penetration in the 1960s, it would have been unwise to take extreme political positions during the tumultuous decade. Even without any economic motive, it simply would not have fit with the tone of the apolitical series that Schulz had created and that was so beloved for him to actively court controversy by addressing issues that inherently poked at a divided American populace. A series of strips tying in with a national and global event, such as the moon landing, was a safe subject and a shrewd bit of publicity. But, through subtle punch lines about the space race and through the allegory of a struggling World War I flying ace, Schulz did publish commentary about the larger political landscape of the time. He also simultaneously created one of the most popular versions of Snoopy, a soldier engaged in a never-ending and futile mission.

NOTES

1. Thomas Doherty, writing about the television show *I Love Lucy*, described the disconnect between the cultural memory of the 1950s and that most popular show of the era: "In a decade misremembered as all whitebread homogeneity, male dominance, and stately decorum, the first breakout television show was multicultural, emphatically female-driven, and loopily anarchic." Thomas Doherty, *Cold War, Cool Medium: Television, McCarthyism, and American Culture* (New York: Columbia University Press, 2003), 49.

2. Hal Hartley, foreword to *The Complete Peanuts: 1965–1966*, ed. Gary Groth (Seattle: Fantagraphics, 2007), xi–xii.

3. Lori Maguire, "Supervillains and the Cold War Tensions in the 1950s," in *The Ages of Superman: Essays on the Man of Steel in Changing Times*, ed. Joseph J. Darowski (Jefferson, NC: McFarland, 2012), 23.

4. Matthew J. Costello, *Secret Identity Crisis: Comic Books and the Unmasking of Cold War America* (New York: Continuum, 2009), 60.

5. John F. Kennedy, "Special Message to Congress on Urgent National Needs," May 25, 1961, American Presidency Project, at http://www.presidency.ucsb.edu/ws/?pid=8151.

6. Susan Hodara, "When Snoopy Landed on the Moon," *New York Times*, June 17, 2011.

7. Robert Z. Pearlman, "The Search for 'Snoopy': Astronomers and Students Hunt for NASA's Lost Apollo 10 Module," Space.com, September 20, 2011, at http://www.space.com/13010-snoopy-nasa-lost-apollo-10-lunar-module-search.html. A group of astrologists are attempting to find the orbiting *Snoopy* module, which was not tracked after its mission was completed and has not been identified since it launched away from the moon.

8. David Michaelis, *Schulz and Peanuts: A Biography* (New York: HarperCollins, 2007), 400.

9. Robert C. Harvey, "Charles Schulz and Mort Walker," in *Cartoon America: Comic Art in the Library of Congress*, ed. Harry Katz (New York: Abrams, 2006), 214.

10. Charles M. Schulz, *Peanuts: A Golden Celebration*, ed. David Larkin (New York: HarperCollins, 1999), 39.

11. Ibid.

12. Charles M. Schulz, "What Do You Do with a Dog That Doesn't Talk?," in *Charles M. Schulz: My Life with Charlie Brown*, ed. M. Thomas Inge (Jackson: University Press of Mississippi, 2010), 172.

13. Schulz, *Peanuts*, 62.

14. Charles M. Schulz, "Schulz at 3 O'Clock in the Morning," interview with Gary Groth, in *Charles M. Schulz: Conversations*, ed. M. Thomas Inge (Jackson: University Press of Mississippi, 2000), 219.

15. Fred J. MacDonald, *Television and the Red Menace: The Video Road to Vietnam* (New York: Praeger, 1985), 220.

16. Michaelis, *Schulz and Peanuts*, 387.

17. Charles M. Schulz, "You're a Good Man, Charlie Schulz," interview with Barnaby Conrad, in *Charles M. Schulz: Conversations*, ed. M. Thomas Inge (Jackson: University Press of Mississippi, 2000), 18.

18. Quoted in Michaelis, *Schulz and Peanuts*, 399.

-9-

FRANKLIN AND THE EARLY 1970S

CHRISTOPHER P. LEHMAN

By 1973, Charles M. Schulz had developed one of the most durable and widely seen African American comic strip characters in the history of the industry. Five years earlier, he had added an African American boy named Franklin to his comic strip *Peanuts*, which featured a cast of European American boys and girls (and a beagle, Snoopy). Schulz created him in response to a letter from a concerned reader, who had convinced the artist to add an African American to the cast in the wake of the national unrest following civil rights leader Martin Luther King Jr.'s assassination in April 1968. However, Franklin soon provided stability to *Peanuts* itself, for Schulz used the character to help older figures like the friendless loser Charlie Brown to evolve and newer figures like the tomboy Peppermint Patty to establish their personalities. Schulz did not early on develop Franklin into a strong character, but Franklin's frequent appearances with the major characters in the early 1970s legitimized Schulz's promotion of him as a major character himself at the end of 1973.

Franklin's birth as a result of King's death was not an isolated incident in American popular culture; television networks, for example, increased the number of series featuring African American stars in the first television season after the killing. Moreover, *Peanuts* was not the only strip affected by King's death. An African American cartoonist named Morrie Turner initially experienced low newspaper circulation of his comic strip *Wee Pals*, but he noticed a dramatic uptick in circulation after April 1968. Similarly, John Saunders and Al McWilliams began a new, integrated comic strip named *Dateline Danger* that year.[1]

Schulz conceived of Franklin as a conservative African American. His curly hair more closely resembled a short, traditional cut instead of an Afro. He wore the shirts and pants of mainstream America—not dashikis or bell-bottoms. Also, Schulz refrained from illustrating concerns for civil rights and other topical issues through Franklin. Nevertheless, an African American character's emergence after King's death made the debut political as well as topical. Schulz added to Franklin's topicality by making the character's father a soldier overseas in Vietnam. By doing so, the artist showed that Franklin came from a politically mainstream family instead of African Americans who advocated militant revolution. Also, the wartime service allowed Franklin to bond with Charlie Brown, whose father had also served in a military conflict.

On July 31, 1968, the strip introduced Franklin to readers by placing him at a beach where Charlie Brown played. The venue was perfect for Schulz's goal of making *Peanuts* more inclusive through the new character, because it allowed for Franklin and Charlie Brown to share a public space. *Peanuts* did not go into detail about where Franklin lived, but the absence of other African Americans from the strip suggested that his family had integrated a previously all-white neighborhood. Three months earlier, Congress had passed the Civil Rights Act of 1968, which desegregated public housing, but Schulz chose not to risk losing readership by showing Franklin moving into the neighborhood. On the other hand, a public beach was open to everyone, and Schulz's beach setting for Franklin's debut symbolized that *Peanuts* was now open to everyone, too.

The two characters became fast friends, and their relationship provided a major turning point for Charlie Brown. Ever since the debut of *Peanuts* in 1950, Schulz had portrayed him as a hapless character who suffered constant teasing and bullying from his neighborhood peers. Franklin, on the other hand, was the first character to maintain a consistent friendship with Charlie Brown and to refrain from calling him names or hurting his feelings. Schulz relied on Franklin to start the process of moving the strip's focus away from Charlie Brown's faults, a transition that necessitated a new direction for *Peanuts*.

Franklin's residence in a different neighborhood limited Schulz's ability to redefine *Peanuts* through the boy's friendship with Charlie Brown. *Peanuts* was a clannish strip because its characters lived in the same neighborhood and rarely ventured from it. On occasion, Schulz placed Franklin in the same movie theater as the other characters, but he had nothing to say besides "One, please" at the ticket booth. In order to feature Franklin more prominently and continue with the strip's overall transition from Charlie Brown's "loser" identity, Schulz placed Franklin in the same neighborhood as another relatively new "outsider" character—Peppermint Patty. He also put them in the same school, and in November 1969 they sat next to each other in the same class for the first time.[2]

At the time, school desegregation was a hot political topic. Only one month earlier, the Supreme Court ruled that states resisting the integration of public schools through *Brown v. Board of Education* (1954) could no longer delay compliance, and the state of Mississippi refused to air *Sesame Street* because of its scenes of children in integrated settings. Likewise, the image of Franklin and Peppermint Patty in class together was too radical for some readers. Nevertheless, Schulz kept him in that setting, and most of his episodes in all his years in the strip were in integrated classrooms.[3]

The novelty of Franklin's presence at the school overshadowed the means by which Schulz shaped Peppermint Patty as an academic underachiever. Franklin regularly outperformed her on assignments and tests, and he beamed about his B grade on an assignment while she bemoaned her much lower grade. While there is no evidence that this depiction of an African American as academically superior to a European American caused a stir among readers, such depictions were far from standard in American media.

Other comic strips introduced African American characters throughout the early 1970s, but those figures were often the means by which the strips employed ethnic humor. During this period, militant characters populated some strips, such as Garry Trudeau's *Doonesbury*, in which a Black Panther named Calvin and an intimidating teenage boy named Thor first appeared in 1971. Franklin outlasted these characters primarily because of the lack of self-conscious topicality that Schulz gave to him. On the other hand, Franklin was a weakly developed character, but Schulz remained consistent in the roles he gave to the figure. As long as *Peanuts* needed diversity, Charlie Brown needed a friend, or Peppermint Patty needed a smarter second banana, Franklin was there.

In the midst of ethnic turmoil in 1970, Franklin had a chance to shine in his integrated classroom. Peppermint Patty cried when she learned that the school forbade her to wear sandals to school. The normally emotionless boy instead became stern, and he said to himself, "All I know is, any rule that makes a little girl cry has to be a bad rule" (February 2, 1970). At the time, the American media rarely presented people of different skin colors expressing compassion and empathy toward one another. African Americans in movies and television shows were coworkers with European Americans, but *Julia* (1968–1971) was one of the few weekly television series in which members of both groups were friends. Meanwhile, in December 1969, the Federal Bureau of Investigation worked with the Chicago police to invade a Black Panther Party member's home and kill him, and in May 1970 police in Mississippi fired into a dormitory at the predominantly African American Jackson State College.[4]

Franklin's statement also allowed Schulz to slyly dig at Vice President Spiro Agnew. Nixon's second-in-command had little tolerance for public expressions of dissent, and he stated that private citizens did not have the right to decide which laws were wrong. Franklin's line also marked a turning point in how Schulz addressed politics. Previously, characters had focused predominantly on their own identities—for example, Snoopy advocated for "paw power" (July 8, 1968), and Lucy called herself a "new feminist" (March 30, 1970). In contrast, Franklin challenged the status quo by questioning law and order as it might apply to someone other than himself.[5]

The sandal strip began a progression of bolder statements on current social and political issues in *Peanuts*, but Franklin was not involved in those to follow. That same year, Schulz showed willingness to embrace elements of the counterculture by naming a new major character—a small, yellow bird befriended by Snoopy—after the previous year's hippie music festival, Woodstock (June 22, 1970). In addition, Schulz countered the negative imagery of student protests by giving Snoopy the alter ego of the sunglasses-donning, popular college student Joe Cool. Meanwhile, Franklin merely stayed at his desk at school, listening to Peppermint Patty's woes. Still, his continued appearances at that school remained tacitly political, because a girl was shot and killed in Mississippi hours after having been the first African American to graduate from her small town's high school in 1971.[6]

Franklin's ethnicity saved him from becoming obsolete in the strip. Schulz frequently experimented with new characters in the late 1960s and early 1970s. While Peppermint Patty, Woodstock, and Franklin survived, others like Snoopy's original owner Lila and Peppermint Patty's baseball teammate Thibault quickly came and went. Meanwhile, the successful new characters also crowded out older characters who had appeared in the strip from the beginning in 1950. Charlie Brown's original peers (and detractors) like Violet and another girl named Patty all but vanished in the early 1970s, for the strip had moved away from featuring antagonists who ridiculed Charlie Brown's shortcomings. As with Franklin, the

Fig. 9.1: Charles Schulz, *Peanuts*, November 16, 1973. PEANUTS © 1973 Peanuts Worldwide LLC. Dist. by UNIVERSAL UCLICK. Reprinted with permission. All rights reserved.

aforementioned older characters did not have complex personalities that endeared them to readers; the girls existed to tease and bully Charlie Brown. In contrast, Franklin's skin color allowed Schulz to continue to provide diversity to the strip.[7]

Moreover, Franklin survived because Schulz needed to place him with other characters in order to illustrate *Peanuts* as integrationist. However, this function stifled the development of the character as an individual, while newer additions to the strip developed stronger personalities in less time. Franklin did not carry a single daily episode alone, and he was not even in an individual panel by himself until his fourth year in the strip. Rather, Schulz placed him walking, sitting, or standing next to at least one of his costars. A new baby character named Rerun Van Pelt often appeared in entire episodes by himself after his debut in the spring of 1973, filling each of the four-panel installments with thought bubbles of his musings on life as a newborn or toddler. Marcie usually engaged in dialogue with Peppermint Patty but occasionally delivered a line or a punch line in a panel by herself. Even the little bird Woodstock appeared solo in panels, despite his inability to talk or think in English.

Schulz's constant pairings of Franklin with others allowed the artist to avoid the challenge of developing the character beyond his role as a reactive figure. To show Franklin alone in a panel meant imagining an African American character solely on the character's own terms. The lack of a solo Franklin showed the artist's discomfort with focusing only on another ethnic group. He placed female characters in episodes without boys because of his comfort in depicting girls as children, and Snoopy's solo appearances showed his effervescent humanity despite his existence as a dog. In contrast, Schulz failed to develop Franklin beyond his skin color, and color was central to Franklin's functionality in the strip as a diversifying figure. In addition, Franklin's persona as a middle-class conversation partner for European Americans made him an assimilationist figure. Thus, Schulz opted against giving the character soliloquies from the point of view of an African American boy. The artist had no way of knowing that viewpoint firsthand, and he did not even try to present it and risk exhibiting his ignorance in an embarrassing, public manner.

Peanuts also distinguished Franklin from the other characters by having him refrain from anger and violence. By doing so, Schulz avoided having the character conform to the stereotype of the "angry black man," but Franklin had a limited emotional range as a result. His costars often physically assaulted one another. Lucy hit Linus and Snoopy. Linus assaulted Snoopy as retribution for the dog's stealing the boy's blanket. Marcie fought with Peppermint Patty to try to drag her to school. Peppermint Patty beat up boys who taunted her. Even Snoopy (accidentally) struck Charlie Brown in the nose. Franklin proved a challenge for Schulz, because the artist had to make him a popular character with readers based on words alone and not with the crutch of slapstick, physical humor. The durability of the character testifies to the skill with which Schulz handled the challenge.

Franklin's color and blandness were among the few reliable fixtures of the strip in its transition from the 1960s to the 1970s. Snoopy stopped his happy dances, and the winding down of the Vietnam War meant fewer appearances of Schulz's outlet for war commentary—Snoopy's fantasies as a World War I flying ace. In 1973, Schulz divorced and remarried, and, according to Schulz biographer David Michaelis, his happier second marriage resulted in fewer visits by Charlie Brown to Lucy's "psychiatric help" booth. Charlie Brown's "loser" persona was toned down, and he experienced fewer stress-induced stomachaches.[8]

The end of the Vietnam War also necessitated a fundamental change in Franklin's biography. With the withdrawal of the last US troops from the war in March 1973, the narrative of Franklin's father as overseas in Vietnam became obsolete. Schulz never reconciled the father to the end of the war, neglecting to illustrate whether the character stayed overseas in another country or left the service and came home to his son. Then again, Franklin rarely mentioned his father after telling Charlie Brown about Vietnam during their first meeting. Still, other comic strips made references to the war's conclusion. In October 1973, George Lichty's *Grin and Bear It* joked about the "secret Cambodian bombings," and the following month *Doonesbury* devoted multiple episodes to a storyline about Cambodians testifying to Congress about the bombings.[9]

The loose end regarding the wartime service of Franklin's father was also part of the strip's shift away from exploring the characters' relationships with their parents. In *Peanuts'* early years, the children often talked about their parents, and some of the episodes featured speech bubbles of parents. By the 1960s, Schulz had stopped giving lines to parents, but he showed how Violet enjoyed bragging about her father's possessions, how proud Charlie Brown was that his father always made time for him while working at his barbershop, and how Peppermint Patty liked hearing her father call her a "rare gem." In the following decade, the decreasing frequency of parental references paralleled the developing "parental" roles of the characters themselves. Snoopy became a father figure to the small bird Woodstock, and Lucy served as a motherly figure to her toddler brother Rerun.[10]

In other media, Schulz struggled to give Franklin a prominent place. The character's primary role as Peppermint Patty's classmate in the strips did not serve him well when Schulz made *Peanuts* television specials. Ever since 1965, Schulz had written the programs for animation producer Bill Melendez, and at least one new special was broadcast each year on CBS. The animated episodes were half-hour narratives about the core group, and they reflected the clannishness of the pre-1968 strips. Starting in 1968, Peppermint Patty made appearances in the specials, but Franklin did not. Scenes of noncore characters in a distant neighborhood compromised the clannish narratives. As a result, Franklin did not make his television debut until 1973.

By waiting so long to animate Franklin, Schulz missed an opportunity to contribute to the integrationist era for television—the same era he had pioneered for comic strips. Television sitcom *The Bill Cosby Show* (1969–1971) and the comedy-drama *Room 222* (1969–1974) were set in integrated schools, and their characters included African American instructors who shared Franklin's conservative appearance. The settings for both series were similar to the integrated classrooms that Franklin and Peppermint Patty attended, except of course that the teachers had no visible presence in *Peanuts*. Meanwhile, African American comedian Flip Wilson applied Schulz's integrationist approach to hosting a weekly variety show in which he mixed ethnic humor with performances from people across the color line. He likened his guest rosters to salad, because he tried to cast a collection of people who would attract as broad a demographic range as possible each week.[11]

Franklin made his first television appearance in *There's No Time for Love, Charlie Brown* in March 1973, at the tail end of the golden age of African American animated images. Even Morrie Turner had the brought comic strip integration of *Wee Pals* to television before Franklin's animated debut, with Turner's weekly series—rechristened *Kid Power*—beginning six months earlier. In the previous four years, the number of African American characters in television cartoon series had increased, and some figures were the stars of their shows. In the peak season of 1972–1973, African Americans headlined three cartoon series (*Harlem Globetrotters, The Jackson 5ive,* and *Fat Albert and the Cosby Kids*) and integrated the casts of two others (*Josie and the Pussycats in Outer Space* and *Kid Power*). When the next television season started, only *Fat Albert* starred African American principals.[12]

Schulz largely stuck within the parameters of Franklin's strip appearances when adapting him for television. The character's only scenes in *There's No Time for Love, Charlie Brown* were in classrooms, and he only spoke when interacting with either Peppermint Patty or Linus. He wore the same conservative clothes as in the strip, and he was either mildly happy or expressionless when conversing with his costars. Just as Schulz only occasionally drew episodes of Franklin in any given year, the character's scenes in the special were confined to the first fifteen minutes and were a small portion of the program's content. In addition, as if to suggest Franklin's role in *Peanuts* as assimilationist, a European American boy named Todd Barbee provided Franklin's voice for the special.

Although the March 1973 special introduced Franklin to television viewers, it did not provide background information about him. Instead, he simply appears with his costars as if he had always been a part of the cast. The program's plot centers on Peppermint Patty's feelings for Charlie Brown, and Franklin's role as her classmate in the strip provides a natural rationale for his appearance in the special. Schulz saw no need to have the program explain how Franklin entered the animated world of *Peanuts* or how the character came to know Peppermint Patty and Linus. In a sense, Schulz assumed the audience's familiarity with the characters based on previous appearances in the strip, but his special also suggested that the means by which an African American suddenly integrated a school were unimportant. Franklin was there and belonged there, according to the special. Also, Schulz did not bother justifying Franklin's presence with any references to his father in Vietnam; Franklin's clothes and his comfortable interactions with his schoolmates demonstrated his middle-class assimilation.

In November 1973, Schulz took two major steps to present Franklin more fully as part of the main *Peanuts* group. The character appeared in the television special *A Charlie Brown Thanksgiving*, which aired on November 20. In his first scene, Franklin reinforces his role as a pioneer in integrationist imagery by standing next to Peppermint Patty at her house; African American boys rarely visited European American girls' homes in films and movies at the time. In a later scene, Peppermint Patty and Franklin stand with Marcie at Charlie Brown's front door, and what follows is some cultural context for Franklin. Franklin walks in and greets Charlie Brown with two ethnic hand gestures—the "soul handshake" and the slapping of each other's palms (giving "five"). Interestingly, Charlie Brown is not ignorant of the gestures but readily engages in them with him, suggesting their long friendship if not Charlie Brown's familiarity with popular African American cultural expressions of the day. Also, this time an African American named Robin Reed voiced Franklin, and Todd Barbee—Franklin's voice in the first special—now provided Charlie Brown's voice.

Schulz seemed more at ease with Franklin on television than in the strip, and the character's appearance in *A Charlie Brown Thanksgiving* gave him a complexity that eluded him in print. For example, in both television specials Franklin briefly appeared on camera by himself, in contrast to his appearances only with others in the strip panels. Also, the strip had not yet shown Franklin and Peppermint Patty inside each other's homes, and Franklin never demonstrated popular African American cultural expressions to his costars in the strip. In *A Charlie Brown Thanksgiving*, Franklin even had more time on screen than Lucy, who appeared only in the first minute of the special to pull a football away from Charlie Brown. A half-hour of animation provided more leeway for Schulz to explore Franklin than a four-panel strip with limited space for text did. The majority of Franklin's scenes in both specials were with the rest of the cast, but the few seconds of solo time and African American representation hardly dented the integrationist content of the telecasts as a whole.

Five days after the airing of *A Charlie Brown Thanksgiving*, in the Sunday strip of November 25, 1973, Franklin joins all the major *Peanuts* characters as the players and officials of a hockey game, suggesting his ascension to major-character status. The episode completely overlooks Franklin's residence in a neighborhood apart from that of the other principals. Instead, the dog Snoopy and the bird Woodstock play against each other on a frozen birdbath, and Franklin shares space with all of the others on the tiny makeshift rink. Schulz takes the physical closeness of Franklin to the European American girls Lucy, Marcie, Peppermint Patty, and Sally for granted, preferring to focus on the lack of space for everyone on the bath. "Where do we put the organ for the national anthem?" Snoopy asks himself.

The year 1973 marked the peak of Franklin's visibility in *Peanuts*, and his diminishing appearances in the newspaper strips and on television the following year dovetailed with the end of integrationism in entertainment media. He remained a staple of the *Peanuts* comic strip, but he did not appear in the next three *Peanuts* specials after *A Charlie Brown Thanksgiving*. Television shows with African American leads were common by 1974, and the concept of African American presence merely for diversity's sake lost its novelty and edginess. *Flip Wilson* and *Room 222* were canceled that year, and *Sanford and Son* and *Good Times* became top-rated series with exclusively African American principals. Similarly, the comic strip *Dateline Danger* disappeared in the wake of the new African American–led comic strips *Quincy* and *Friday Foster*.[13]

By the mid-1970s, more of the established comic strips diversified their casts. Artists still used African American characters for ethnic humor, but their strips moved beyond the simplistic militaristic caricatures of the early 1970s. In 1974, *Doonesbury*'s Thor was less militant, using his real name Rufus more frequently, and a new African American character appeared, a law school student named Virginia. Meanwhile, a soldier with an Afro appeared in *Beetle Bailey*, thus allowing for countercultural and decidedly ethnic symbolism for a government officer. Through the character, the strip showed that an Afro or any other ethnic expression did not mean the absence of patriotism or sense of national duty.

For the most part, ethnicity remained a tacit subject in *Peanuts*. When Schulz finally tackled racism in the second week of August 1973, he based a series of episodes on Hank Aaron's real-life struggle with death threats from bigots during his pursuit of Babe Ruth's home run record. Schulz, however, still shied away from using Franklin to openly discuss discrimination. Instead, Snoopy was cast as the home run chaser, and his detractors threatened him because he was a dog—not because of his skin color. Franklin, in fact, did not appear in *Peanuts* that week at all.[14]

Franklin was even displaced by Snoopy in terms of relevance to the Vietnam War. The strip's only reference to the war after Franklin's mention of his father was in the July 10, 1970, strip, in which Snoopy falls in love with another dog. Snoopy is an innocent bystander at an antiwar rally, in which activists protest against "dogs being sent to Viet Nam and then not getting back," according to Linus. The reference to the war has nothing to do with Snoopy's characterization, and Schulz never revisited either the demonstration or the war. Meanwhile, the episode was a lost opportunity for Schulz to connect the war to Franklin's father.

Soon thereafter, Franklin no longer served as Peppermint Patty's main "straight man" partner at school, as that role fell to a new character. Schulz added a bespectacled girl named Marcie to the school in 1971, and he immediately gave her a depth that Franklin still lacked at the time. Marcie, like Franklin, was another voice of reason to counter Peppermint Patty's outlandish statements, but she showed deference to her tougher and taller friend by calling her "sir." She also displayed vulnerability by secretly pining for Charlie Brown. She soon won over readers and became part of the main *Peanuts* cast by 1973.

As an African American character, Franklin could do neither of the things that made Marcie a hit. After the Black Power era of the late 1960s, African American characters no longer called European American characters "sir" or other titles that signified deference. Diahann Carroll gained notoriety in the fall of 1968 as the first African American woman to star in a television series and not play a domestic servant. Even television's most famous African American servant-playing actor, Eddie "Rochester" Anderson, appeared with his fictional employer, Jack Benny, on a reunion special that same fall, just to say that he was not Benny's valet anymore. In addition, with Franklin's integrated schoolroom scenes causing alarm among readers, he would have generated a greater stir by secretly longing for one of the European American girls in *Peanuts*.

Schulz significantly broadened Franklin's characterization for the last time in 1974. The artist became a grandfather that year, and Franklin was the first character he chose to convey his feelings about the transition. Over the strip's next twenty-six years, Schulz's characters talked about their grandparents whenever the artist wanted to muse about being a grandfather, but Franklin established the format. In the first such episode, Franklin talks with Peppermint Patty about his grandfather's zest for life and quotes from him: "Once you're over the hill, you begin to pick up speed" (May 3, 1974). It is one of the rare occasions in which

Franklin delivers the punch line, suggesting the artist's growing trust in the character to play more than a "straight man" role to major characters. Also, Schulz's decision to cast Franklin to articulate feelings on becoming a grandfather allowed the artist another approach besides the integrated classroom to demonstrate the common humanity that transcends skin color. The episode was another high point among Franklin's appearances, but it was soon followed by a new low.[15]

After years of resisting broad jokes that addressed color, Schulz himself attempted to extract ethnic humor from Franklin negatively on November 6, 1974. Franklin and Peppermint Patty argue over the use of a frozen pond. He wants to practice hockey there, but Patty responds, "How many black players in the NHL?" She draws attention to his color and uses the privilege of her skin color's long access to ice-related sports to legitimize the continued restriction of his color's access. Schulz demonstrated that integrationism had its limits. Peppermint Patty could welcome Franklin as a classmate and a dinner guest, and she could tolerate Franklin's superior academic performance to hers. But she drew the line on public space to which she felt an entitlement by virtue of her color.

The episode's timing was unfortunate, because it appeared as Boston was experiencing violence over school busing, in late 1974. A federal district judge ordered the busing of African Americans to schools in European American neighborhoods and vice-versa in order for Boston to fully integrate its schools. Peppermint Patty used only words to keep Franklin in his "place," but Bostonians threw rocks, bricks, and other items at each other when fighting over integration. The skating strip reinforced the limits of integrationism that Boston seemed to suffer at the time.

The imagery of the skating strip is ironic, because it shows the polarized opposite of Franklin's debut in multiple ways. Charlie Brown and Franklin got along in 1968, but Peppermint Patty and Franklin quarreled in 1974. The sunny public beach was the setting for the hope of integration when Charlie Brown and Franklin met, but the frigid pond symbolized the cooling of the friendship between Peppermint Patty and Franklin. Also, Franklin was all smiles in his debut, but he became angry at one of his costars for the first time in 1974. Peppermint Patty's winning of the argument negated whatever threat Franklin's anger posed, because he saw that he had no power to refute her statement.

The innocence of Franklin's integrationism was destroyed forever, as was the illusion of tolerance in *Peanuts*. Moreover, the argument about the pond suggests that Peppermint Patty conveniently forgot about the hockey game that she and Franklin shared on a small frozen birdbath with a dozen other people the previous year. They had, in fact, walked to the birdbath together. They continued to appear in the classroom together after 1974 but less often, and Schulz rarely found other uses for Franklin. The character's golden age was over, but he had helped usher in a new era of *Peanuts* while setting standards for integrated imagery in American media.

NOTES

1. Lynn Spigel, *Welcome to the Dreamhouse: Popular Media and Postwar Suburbs* (Durham, NC: Duke University Press, 2001), 243; and Christopher P. Lehman, *American Animated Cartoons of the Vietnam Era* (Jefferson, NC: McFarland, 2006), 163.

2. See the *Peanuts* episodes of October 20, 1968; November 12, 1969; and June 20, 1970.

3. *Peanuts*, November 12, 1969; Christopher P. Lehman, *Power, Politics, and the Decline of the Civil Rights Movement: A Fragile Coalition* (Santa Barbara, CA: Praeger, 2014), 126; and Michael Davis, *Street Gang: The Complete History of Sesame Street* (New York: Viking 2008), 201–2.

4. Lehman, *Power, Politics, and the Decline*, 127, 146–48.

5. Ibid., 80.

6. Ibid., 193–94.

7. David Michaelis, *Schulz and Peanuts: A Biography* (New York: HarperCollins, 2007), 214, 223, 271–72.

8. Ibid., 395, 482, 501–2.

9. George Lichty, *Grin and Bear It*, October 14, 1973; Garry Trudeau, *Doonesbury*, November 5–December 8, 1973.

10. Michaelis, *Schulz and Peanuts*, 509.

11. Kevin Cook, *Flip: The Inside Story of TV's First Black Superstar* (New York: Viking, 2013), 124–27.

12. Lehman, *American Animated Cartoons*, 163.

13. Cook, *Flip: The Inside Story*, 164, 179.

14. Howard Bryant, *The Last Hero: A Life of Henry Aaron* (New York: Random House, 2010), 361.

15. Michaelis, *Schulz and Peanuts*, 537–38.

TRANSMEDIAL *PEANUTS*

-10-

MAKING A WORLD
FOR ALL OF GOD'S CHILDREN

A Charlie Brown Christmas and the Aesthetics of Doubt and Faith

BEN NOVOTNY OWEN

According to the standard story told by its creators, *A Charlie Brown Christmas*, one of the most familiar and well-loved American animated films, was expected to be a flop. Lee Mendelson, the producer, recalls that before the special aired the filmmakers were unsure whether they had made something good, and, worse, "the two top executives at CBS" were decidedly negative, seeing the film as "a little flat . . . a little slow."[1] The program of course went on to be very successful, both critically and commercially, taking the number two spot in the Nielsen ratings for the night it first aired on December 9, 1965, with an estimated fifteen million viewers (second only to the ratings juggernaut *Bonanza*), winning an Emmy and a Peabody Award, and inaugurating a series of more than forty television specials (as well as four theatrical movies, a Saturday morning cartoon series, and a television miniseries about US history). It still airs twice a year on ABC, and the soundtrack album by the Vince Guaraldi Trio has sold more than three million copies.

While there is no reason to doubt the version told by Mendelson and his partner Bill Melendez, who animated and directed *A Charlie Brown Christmas* (and all of the subsequent *Peanuts* specials until 2006), the story of near-failure works as a perfect origin myth. After all, the special's emblematic story is about Charlie Brown choosing a small, misshapen Christmas tree among the painted aluminum trees to feature in his Christmas pageant, then being mocked by the other children for his blockheaded choice, until Linus reminds everyone of "what Christmas is all about," at which point everyone learns to love the tree. The cartoon's message about the tree is the same as the filmmakers' message about

Fig. 10.1: Still from *Rooty Toot Toot,* dir. John Hubley (UPA, 1951).

the cartoon; although the animation had, in Melendez's words, "so many warts and bumps and lumps and things," the imperfections "seem to make it even more endearing to a lot of people."[2] Indeed, the special's lack of polish, including its use of real children's voices for the characters rather than adult actors, contributed to what Richard Burgheim, the reviewer for *Time,* called its "refreshingly low-key tone."[3] And the story that CBS executives were doubtful about its popular appeal potentially complements its anticommercial stance, even while broadcasts in the 1960s included plugs for Coca-Cola, which commissioned the special.

Still, the success of *A Charlie Brown Christmas* poses several questions. If the special was successful as much because of its flaws as in spite of them, what elements resonated with the public, and why? One answer is simply that some of the things that made the special at best a modestly accomplished cartoon—the flatness of the characters and backgrounds, the recycling of sequences at different points in the film—allowed it to be a faithful rendition of the *Peanuts* comic strip, which was hugely popular at the time. Not only are the jokes and scenarios familiar to readers of the strip but the characters look very similar to Charles Schulz's drawings, and this visual similarity was a relatively rare phenomenon in the history of animated adaptations of comic strips. For example, while *Krazy Kat* animated shorts followed the plot of the comic strip with varying degrees of faithfulness, even in the most similar, none of the characters ever looked much like George Herriman's drawings.

On the production side, the directness of the visual adaptation was a matter of deliberate choices on Melendez's and Schulz's part, and on the reception side it was enabled by an audience taste for a flat, graphic style in animation. Viewers of *A Charlie Brown Christmas* were already familiar with the style of "limited animation" pioneered by artists working in and around the United Productions of America (UPA) animation studio from the late 1940s through the 1950s, a style deployed by many different studios by the mid-sixties. The flatness of this style allowed for a relatively straightforward transition from newspaper page to television screen, preserving the characteristic lines of Schulz's world without warping them to accommodate the rounded volume of an animated body in the Disney or Warner Bros. mold. But where UPA made limited animation a sign of modernist sophistication, *A Charlie Brown Christmas* uses it to create a sketchy or unfinished appearance, thereby engendering a sense that the special was, as Burgheim described it, "unpretentious." Melendez wished to make limited animation—an artistic style born of economic necessity—seem like a deliberate choice rather than a failure of quality.

In the best UPA cartoons, the artists involved accomplished this by employing art styles that included nods to various postimpressionist painters as well as to the sophisticated *New Yorker* illustrations of Saul Steinberg (which themselves assumed modernism as an established idiom, available for use, citation, and parody). Not merely derivative, however, UPA artists were also experimental in their techniques, as when background designer Paul Julian used a corroded gelatin roller to produce the distressed-looking backgrounds for director John Hubley's masterpiece *Rooty Toot Toot* (1951) (fig. 10.1). Despite limited animation's origins in economic considerations, a cartoon like *Rooty Toot Toot* drew on an enormous amount of labor and planning to produce its effects. For example, the studio hired the dancer Olga Lunick to choreograph the dance sequences.[4] By contrast, Melendez, up against a six-month deadline to produce a half-hour special, could not necessarily create the polished look of a UPA short and so needed to create an alternative aesthetic of directness and sincerity.

The special's soundtrack was key to creating this aesthetic. Taking his cue from the Maypo commercials made by John Hubley, Melendez directed the child actors who voiced the *Peanuts* characters to speak in a markedly unpolished, naturalistic manner. To some extent, the change in the connotations of limited animation—from modernist sophistication to unpolished "authenticity"—that we see on display in *A Charlie Brown Christmas* is characteristic of a shift in medium, as television rather than film became the primary focus of animation production, and budgets for animation shrank. Despite its origins in the 1940s as a cost-cutting measure, the virtuoso graphic design necessary for the sophisticated appearance of early-1950s UPA animations was impossible to produce cheaply, and the voice of the performer consequently became more important in compensation for restrictions on compelling visuals.[5]

But the unpolished aesthetic also goes some way to explaining the success of the program with a mid-1960s American audience (and audiences since). Both vocals and visuals continually remind us of their manufactured nature, and yet the effect is to strengthen rather than weaken the special's claim to a form of spiritual truth. *A Charlie Brown Christmas* regularly oscillates between two contradictory kinds of truth claim—a naturalistic investment in presenting kids as they are, and a stylistic breaking of the "the illusion of life" produced by Disney-style realism.[6] But unlike avant-garde works in which the demystification of the illusion of life is an end in itself, in the *Charlie Brown* special, skepticism is a prerequisite for communicating certainty. The early *Peanuts* animations spoke to an audience who wanted trust to emerge from an openness to interpretation, and not from the overemphatic explanation of the hard sell.

This conception of truth is best exemplified by Linus's famous recitation of Luke 2:8–12 from the King James Version to an almost empty auditorium, a statement of Christian belief left without a settled explanation of meaning. The special's combination of unpolished simplicity and anti-illusionism fit well with the new idiom of advertising in the mid-1960s, which aimed to address an increasingly skeptical, media-savvy audience. As a television program commissioned by Coca-Cola, using animated characters originally created in 1959 to sell the Ford Falcon, *A Charlie Brown Christmas* countered its own status as an advertisement with a message of anticommercialism and an unfinished visual style that attempted to engage the viewer on terms of equality.

Bill Melendez created the look of the Peanuts specials, reworking Schulz's drawings for a new medium. Melendez started in animation at Disney in 1938, working on many shorts and several features including *Pinocchio* (1940), *Dumbo* (1941), and *Bambi* (1942). He took part in the animators' strike of 1941, after which he left Disney for Leon Schlesinger Cartoons, which later became Warner Bros.[7] He began working for UPA in 1948 and contributed to some of their best-known shorts, including the classic *Gerald McBoing-Boing* (1950). In the late 1950s and early 1960s, he worked at Playhouse Pictures producing animated commercials for various companies, including Ford. His collaboration with Schulz began in 1959, when he animated the first in a series of ads for the new Ford Falcon model of compact cars featuring the *Peanuts* characters.[8] He and Schulz continued to work together for the next forty-one years.

Melendez's principle challenge in creating the *Peanuts* commercials was to figure out how to animate "a cartoon design, a flat design," which he "had always wanted to do."[9] *Peanuts'* "flat design" meant, in this context, that in the newspaper strip the characters tended to exist in certain specific positions, mostly either in profile or in three-quarter view. They did not have the "roundness" of, say, a Warner Bros. character because, unlike Bugs Bunny, they were not understood as three-dimensional entities and so would never appear from a full range of angles. Because of this, Melendez became adept at animating Schulz's characters so that "you wouldn't see the turns," and they existed for almost all of their screen time in positions familiar from the comic strip. According to Melendez, this was actually something Schulz required, regarding views of the characters from other angles as bad drawings.[10] As David Michaelis writes, the former Disney animator Melendez "earned Schulz's respect by *not* Disneyfying the Peanuts gang when he made the Ford commercials," and that Schulz trusted Melendez "to place Charlie Brown and the others into animation without changing their essential qualities, either as 'flat' cartoon characters or as *his* cartoon characters."[11]

The limitations on the *Peanuts* characters' dimensionality and movement presented particular challenges for Melendez.[12] The characters couldn't reach above their heads, for example, and so in moments when this was required, such as during the decoration of Charlie Brown's tiny Christmas tree at the end of the film, he drew the characters facing away from the viewer in a clump. Their arms disassociate from their bodies in a flurry of activity to distract from the basic implausibility of the motion. By 1959, Melendez was very experienced in animating flat design. His former employer, UPA, was the pioneer of what came to be known, pejoratively, as limited animation, and with it a type of modern design that by the mid-1950s had become the critical "reference point" for new animation.[13] Best understood as a deliberate departure from Disney-style animation, which tended to function as the standard for the industry from the late 1920s onward, limited animation refers to a group of practices designed to limit the number of drawings and frames used in animation, thus reducing the cost of production. At UPA this meant, among other things, that animators supplied one drawing for every two frames of animation (as opposed to one drawing for every frame), and also that they departed from the traditional animation approach of using three parts for every on-screen action—anticipation, the action itself, and follow-through. UPA animators tended to cut the anticipation phase.[14]

Limited animation came to be associated with shoddy-looking television animation in the 1960s, as studios stopped producing the theatrical animated shorts that had been the industry standard since the earliest days of animation. But in its richest sense it also referred to an attempt to treat economic restriction as an enabling condition for artistic experiment. Understood in this way by animators at UPA in the late 1940s and early 1950s, limited animation meant a new emphasis on graphic design as a primary consideration of animation, ideally giving animated cartoons a sophisticated graphic logic. At its theoretical edges, the UPA approach to animation was an artistic expression of cofounder Zack Schwartz's observation that "[o]ur camera isn't a motion-picture camera. Our camera is closer to a printing press."[15] Animators at UPA, and others working in a similar idiom, self-consciously aligned their work with modern art, particularly with the sophisticated print graphics of illustrators like Saul Steinberg.

The *Peanuts* animations belong to this tradition. Besides the graphic flatness of its characters, *A Charlie Brown Christmas* shows its roots in midcentury limited animation in part through the choppiness of its animation, which emphasizes expressive poses rather than the smooth movement between those poses. We can see this in the repeated shots of the characters dancing and playing music on stage, while Guaraldi's "Linus and Lucy" plays. And the UPA style also appears in the use of abstracted backgrounds, which show brush marks and other signs of their manufacture, do not employ point perspective, and include objects that appear as geometric blocks of paint, without shading or other modeling (fig. 10.2).

By the end of the 1950s, financial troubles and a change in ownership ended UPA's reputation as an artistic innovator, but the look of design-centric, flat animation was already an integrated feature of work from other studios, including Disney. The style is evident in the short *Pigs Is*

Fig. 10.2: Still from *A Charlie Brown Christmas,* dir. Bill Melendez (1965).

Pigs (1954), and in the features *Sleeping Beauty* (1959) and *101 Dalmatians* (1961).[16] The familiarity of the flat aesthetic in animation by the late 1950s was a necessary condition for the creation of the *Peanuts* Ford commercials, and later the specials, since it enabled comics characters' transition from newspaper to television without them having to be reimagined as voluminous, spheroid bodies. This gave *Peanuts* a strong aesthetic identity across media. As Leon Morse wrote in his review for *Variety,* "the animation was intentionally uncomplicated so that the characters did not lose their basic comic strip identity."[17] Peanuts remained a coherent brand in which the newspaper strip served as the template for subsequent iterations. The visual similarity between strip and TV program reinforces other elements taken directly from the strip. The majority of jokes in the special are in fact from the newspaper strip. For example, Lucy's complaint that she never gets what she really wants for Christmas, "real estate," is a version of a gag from the September 18, 1961, strip. And when Charlie Brown yells "Don't you know sarcasm when you hear it!" after Violet, he's repeating a joke that originated in the December 27, 1962, strip.

But the aesthetic choices about the look and sound of *A Charlie Brown Christmas* did not simply produce a faithful adaptation. Morse concludes his review with the claim that what made the special "fascinating and haunting was its intentional sketchiness, an artifice that allowed each viewer to fill in the details to fit his own needs. A more elaborate show on the same simple subject would have been a cliché and a dud." In other words, Morse understood the style of the animation as producing a kind of interpretive space for the viewer around *A Charlie Brown Christmas*'s very direct Christian content. This is a complicated effect because that space for interpretation seems to work against, or at least complicate, what Morse sees as the special's "fundamentalist message" "that man can find certitude only in the word of God as revealed in the Bible." Linus's recitation of Luke 2:8–14, which describes the angel of the Lord's announcement of Jesus's birth to the shepherds in the field, and which Linus says is what "Christmas is all about," certainly does accord with a fundamentalist view. And yet the special's refusal to explicitly interpret that message appears to leave room for a kind of open interpretation anathema to the fundamentalist view of the Bible as meaning only one thing.[18] That is not to say that the special presents a direct challenge to a fundamentalist Christian view but rather that it leaves open an implicit space for interpretation without calling particular attention to that space. The emptiness of the auditorium Linus addresses, emphasized aurally by the echo of his voice, suggests that the adult, social world does not heed his message. And this lack of support reinforces the special's view— compatible with a fundamentalist worldview, although held by a broader swathe of American society—that the essentials of faith have been lost.[19] But the empty auditorium also proposes that the adult world has yet to form its opinion about what Linus says. It amounts to a refusal to model a reaction to the verses, placing the onus on the viewer to consider his or her own response.

This is, of course, characteristic of *Peanuts*, a strip that forever deferred the depiction of adults. When adults finally do speak in the animated specials (which doesn't happen in *A Charlie Brown Christmas*), they do so with trombone voices. The absence allows *Peanuts* to appear didactic without hectoring. It's possible to see the ostensibly fundamentalist stance of the Christmas special, which nevertheless refrains from naming exactly what the truth ought to mean, as in accordance with Schulz's own complicated relationship to Christianity, in which he publicly allowed his work to support an evangelical message while privately maintaining skepticism toward anyone claiming definitive knowledge of religious truth.[20]

The special tells a story of Charlie Brown's shift from doubt to faith, but the answer to his question about the real meaning of Christmas does not preclude ambiguity or interpretation. There is no stated moral, only a series of recuperative actions toward Charlie Brown and his tree, but the lack of a decisive answer connotes possibility rather than doubt. As Morse notes, the sketchy style of the special is central to the success of this transformation because it suits the idea that the special is imaginatively unfinished, allowing the viewer to fill in what's left out. The cartoon takes a midcentury modernist concern with exposing artifice and revealing the materiality of the artwork and repurposes it as sketch-like unpretentiousness. In doing so, *A Charlie Brown Christmas* helped change the rhetoric of limited animation for the television market, making it less a sign of sophisticated awareness about the medium-specific qualities of animation and more a handmade charm.

This shift in meaning is as apparent in the special's sound as in its visuals. The *Peanuts* animations are notable for their use of children rather than adults to voice the characters and for an unrehearsed-sounding style—"real rather than stage kids," Burgheim calls the performers in *A Charlie Brown Christmas*, although principal performers Peter Robbins, Christopher Shea, and Tracy Stratford (who voiced Charlie Brown, Linus, and Lucy, respectively) were all experienced actors.[21] The deliberate move toward vocal naturalism had at least one major precedent in the commercials the animator John Hubley created for Maypo cereal in 1956. Hubley had been forced to leave UPA in 1952 after refusing to cooperate with the House Un-American Activities Committee's hunt for communists. Blacklisted in Hollywood, he found advertising work in New York. The Maypo commercials, drawn in the flat style (although—characteristically for Hubley's work—not especially limited in terms of the number of intervals between poses, and the consequent fluidity of motion), featured the voice of Hubley's four-year-old son Mark, who sounds like he is not reading lines. Hubley and his wife, Faith Elliott, would use the style of improvised vocal performance again in their Oscar-winning cartoon *Moonbird*, which featured Mark and his younger brother, Ray, and appeared in 1959, the same year that Playhouse pictures produced the first *Peanuts* Ford Falcon commercial.

As in the Hubleys' films, the *Peanuts* style of naturalistic vocal performance uses its departure from a more polished approach to provide a feeling of authenticity—this is what kids *really* sound like. But, particularly in *A Charlie Brown Christmas*, the authenticity of the voices does not mean that the production attempts to create a realist illusion. Rather, the authenticity seems to rely, in part, on the fact that the voices are obviously edited recordings. In this foregrounding of recording technology, the Christmas special bears a surprising similarity to another cartoon about a misfit kid looking for understanding that Bill Melendez worked on fifteen years earlier, *Gerald McBoing-Boing*. On the face of it, the two ways in which the cartoons present children's voices seem to be opposed. *A Charlie Brown Christmas* features only children's voices (plus Snoopy's sped-up gibberish, a manipulation of Melendez's voice), while Gerald doesn't speak as we expect a child to speak at all—that's the premise of the story. Directed by Hubley's main creative rival at UPA, Robert "Bobe" Cannon, and based on a story by Dr. Seuss, the cartoon tells the story of a small boy who speaks only in sound-effect noises. A mystery to the family doctor, rejected by his school and his family, Gerald ultimately finds fame and recognition providing the sounds for radio shows.

The conceit of the cartoon calls attention to the artificiality of recorded sound in a couple of ways. There is clearly no natural correspondence between what Gerald appears to be and the sound he makes. And when he finally finds his niche in the production of sound effects for radio, the story emphasizes sound—in radio but also in films—as a manufactured artifact, suggesting the audience's general unawareness of what produces the sounds we hear in a story. Is the sound of a horse galloping produced by a horse galloping, a small boy, or a foley artist with two coconut shell halves? The animation's deliberate reference to its own status as a manufactured object is of a piece with its drawn-ness, whereby characters reveal themselves as lines rather than bodies by changing color with the background.

By contrast, *A Charlie Brown Christmas* emphasizes its use of real children as vocal performers. Yet, like *Gerald McBoing-Boing*, the children's voices in the *Peanuts* special are also a reminder of the recording process, albeit for less explicit, story-based reasons. Throughout *A Charlie Brown Christmas*, the weird emphasis in certain lines reveals the presence of the voice actor, separate from the drawn character, who is unable or unwilling to deliver the line "properly." This is particular apparent in some of Sally's lines, voiced by Kathy Steinberg, who was six at the time of production and who needed to be given her lines one by one because she couldn't read.[22] Sally's punch line, after she has dismayed her brother with her letter to Santa asking for cash, is: "All I want is what I have coming to me. All I want is my fair share." A slight shift in the quality of the sound recording between the two sentences suggests that it is the product of two separate recordings spliced together, and Steinberg pauses very slightly after the word "have," as though unsure of her words. We are momentarily aware that Sally's voice is not Sally's but rather a recording of a child actor, reciting a script rather than saying her own words. The awareness of the recording process doesn't register as a deliberate formalist gesture here but rather as a mistake. And yet Burgheim, in his review for *Time*, saw the mistake as adding to the special's appeal; the "occasionally amateurish" voices "contribute to the refreshingly low-key tone."[23]

The vocal performances in the first *Peanuts* special suggest authenticity in two opposing ways. On the one hand, the fact that the voices are those of "real rather than stage kids," "low-keyed at about the level that tykes talk when no grownups are around," supports the illusion created by Schulz's strip that the *Peanuts* characters are themselves real children—the voices are the way the characters really would sound. On the other hand, the traces of the recording and production of the soundtrack suggest a more formalist kind of truth claim, in line with *Gerald McBoing-Boing*—an artwork that proves that it's not fooling its audience by not attempting to conceal the signs of its manufacture.

But this oscillation between two kinds of truth claim does not make the production *feel* unstable. In terms of the emotions it elicits, *A Charlie Brown Christmas* is very far from the experience of watching a Bertolt Brecht play. The movement of the special's plot is from alienation to acceptance, from depression to comfort. It begins with Guaraldi's melancholy "Christmas Time Is Here" and ends with the more affirmative "Hark! The Herald Angels Sing." With its slow rhythms and lack of manic drama, it's not an anxious cartoon. For the most part, the conspicuous signs of the special's manufacture don't directly challenge the illusion of the story but rather inflect it, testifying to its *lack* of artifice or pretension. In this, the special draws not on the self-conscious sophistication of UPA but on some of the earliest connotations of the modern, pre-animated cartoon—a form that linked the idea of a preparatory drawing beneath the painted surface (the older meaning of cartoon) with the sense of honest directness in the depiction of society. The choppy sound and limited animation support the story, which performs the idea of an honesty beneath appearances by focusing on Charlie Brown's sense that Christmas has become too commercial—a phony ritual—and then moving toward a resolution in which noncommercial (handcrafted, rough-looking) values triumph. The nostalgic refraction through which subsequent viewers have watched the special amplifies the effect. *A Charlie Brown Christmas*'s success guaranteed its rebroadcast in the year following the original airing, establishing it as a tradition. And as a tradition, the special's artistic roughness could come to seem the token of a mythic simpler time.[24]

The special's oscillation between illusion and disenchantment fits with a shift in the rhetoric of advertising in the late 1950s and early 1960s, which spoke to a growing skepticism among Americans toward ads that seemed to speak with the voice of authority. As Hazel Warlaumont describes it, the emphasis on "creativity" as a cardinal virtue of 1960s advertising led to ads that "disarmed those groups justifiably concerned about deceit and subliminal trickery" through an "irreverent and at times self-deprecating approach."[25] One of the best-known icons of the new creativity (particularly since it featured in the third episode of the drama series *Mad Men*) is the Doyle Dane Bernbach agency's "Think Small" ads for Volkswagen, which first appeared in 1959. These were among the first American advertisements to incorporate self-deprecating humor about the featured product, in an approach that combined a comparatively honest directness about the qualities of the thing being sold (Volkswagens are small and weird looking compared to most other cars in America) with a reliance on the reader's imagination to bridge the disconnect between the abrupt and apparently negative slogan and the intended message of the ad.

While less obviously oppositional than the Volkswagen ads, the first *Peanuts* commercial for the Ford Falcon and Fairlane 500 exhibited some of the hallmarks of the new rhetoric of advertising, particularly a reliance on humor. For an advertising strategy this makes sense, since the economy Falcon was Ford's response to consumer demand for smaller cars such as the Volkswagen. Although several later *Peanuts* Ford ads pursued a traditional hard-sell style, having Schulz's characters list the virtues of the Falcon, the first commercial is notable for relying on a strip-style gag that eschews any direct discussion of the car. Linus explains to Lucy that Charlie Brown is handing out chocolate cigars celebrating the release of Ford's new "economy twins"; Lucy asks if he's handing them out to everybody, and—as Snoopy snaps his teeth and dances by with a cigar—Linus confirms, "Yes, everybody." As in Hubley's Maypo commercials, the ad uses children's voices and a situation that develops quasi-independently of the product itself.

In part, the market position of the Ford Falcon as an economy alternative to larger, more expensive cars dictated the need for an approach to advertising that emphasized smallness and a move away from the hard sell. *Peanuts* characters were ideally suited for this role, partly because the appeal of the strip lay so firmly in its focus on truths presented in an undogmatic manner by children, and partly because of the attractiveness of Schulz's minimalist lines even when reduced to the small scale required of strips in postwar comics pages. As the *Time* cover story on *Peanuts* from April 1965 argued: "Comics have espoused many causes; the strips have been crammed with all kinds of propaganda. But Peanuts is the leader of a refreshing new breed that takes an unprecedented interest in the basics of life. Love, hate, togetherness, solitude, the alienation in an age of anxiety—such topics are so deftly explored by Charlie Brown and the rest of the Peanuts crew that readers who would not sit still for a sermon readily devour the sermon-like cartoons."[26] *Peanuts* was a good fit for a new era in advertising because it seemed to manage the trick of imparting a message without registering as propaganda, at a moment when advertisers were attempting to figure out how to appear to share the values of a generation of consumers fundamentally skeptical of the corporate world.[27]

Confronting its own premise as a sponsored promotion for Coca-Cola, *A Charlie Brown Christmas* presents a paradoxical message of anticommercialism. And similarly, its message of Christian faith confronts a profound sense of loneliness and "alienation in an age of anxiety." Linus, the character most desirous of security, delivers his sermon in the voice of Christopher Shea, who lisps slightly. The lisp serves as a marker of authenticity, but it also connotes an intense vulnerability—again, Linus sounds like an actual kid, not a performer. In his speech particularly, the special seems to be replying not only to viewers' doubts about the voice of corporate authority but perhaps to a related but much more radical doubt about the security of the entire world. While the clearest animated precedent for use of unpolished kids' voices was the Maypo commercials, one of the clearest nonanimated precedents was a very different commercial that aired in September 1964, fourteen months before *A Charlie Brown Christmas*. This was the Doyle Dane Bernbach–produced ad for Lyndon Johnson, attacking (though never naming) Barry Goldwater's frighteningly aggressive stance on the use of nuclear weapons. In it, a young girl counts up as she pulls the petals off a flower, then looks up as a man's voiceover begins a countdown, followed by a zoom-in on her iris, followed by footage of a mushroom cloud.

The ad serves to make the threat of nuclear annihilation emotional and personal by freighting it with the ideology of childhood innocence and vulnerability. As Robert Mann shows in his comprehensive book on the commercial and its political effects and contexts, it was a watershed in American political advertising, marking the first use of fear as a dominant theme and the first reliance on viewers to create their own interpretive frame. Although it only aired officially once, the controversy it sparked meant that it was re-aired several times on the evening news, and in all as many as one hundred million people saw it.[28] The ad's sound recording was considered central to its success. Doyle Dane Bernbach recruited artist and ad man Tony Schwartz, who had "a reputation as a wizard of sound and sound effect" and who had made some of the earliest ads to feature a real child's voice. As in the *Peanuts* animations, the apparent flaws in the girl's—Monique Corzilius's—speech (she skips from five to seven in her count, then repeats six) create the sense of something unrehearsed, although the miscount was scripted and the final shot the end result of at least twenty takes.[29]

Heard in this context, Linus's recitation of Luke 2:8–14, with its concluding promise of "on earth peace," sounds like a reply. The fragment of Johnson's speech that concludes the "Daisy" ad outlines a choice: "to make a world in which all of God's children can live, or to go into the dark." Linus, spotlit on the stage, appears to stand in that world where "God's children can live." The "Daisy" ad uses an image of an innocent and vulnerable child to terrify its audience and equate a vote for Johnson with a vote to defend the defenseless. *A Charlie Brown Christmas* echoes this appeal but expands it, making the voice of the child signify not only what needs to be protected but what desperately needs to be heard. In this way, the special dramatizes the implicit nuclear anxiety that attends Schulz's anxious child characters. At a time when doubt about the trustworthiness of the establishment was taking on existential significance, Schulz and Melendez treated the words and feelings of children with a seriousness that made them seem a vital source of counsel.

NOTES

1. Lee Mendelson and Bill Melendez, *A Charlie Brown Christmas: The Making of a Tradition* (New York: HarperResource, 2000), 27.

2. Ibid., 61.

3. Richard Burgheim, "Security Is a Good Show," *Time*, December 19, 1965, 95.

4. Adam Abraham, *When Magoo Flew: The Rise and Fall of Animation Studio UPA* (Middletown, CT: Wesleyan University Press, 2012), 96.

5. J. Michael Barrier, *Hollywood Cartoons: American Animation in Its Golden Age* (New York: Oxford University Press, 1999), 523, 572.

6. *The Illusion of Life* is the title Frank Thomas and Ollie Johnston's 1981 book that codifies Disney house style as a set of "basic principles of animation." Frank Thomas and Ollie Johnston, *The Illusion of Life: Disney Animation* (New York: Disney Editions, 1981).

7. Melendez's full name was José Cuauhtémoc Meléndez. At Warner Bros. he was credited as J. C. Melendez and, at UPA, as Bill Melendez. I refer to him as Bill Melendez because that was the name he gave to his own production company.

8. David Michaelis, *Schulz and Peanuts: A Biography* (New York: HarperCollins, 2007), 320–21.

9. Mendelson and Melendez, *A Charlie Brown Christmas*, 55.

10. Ibid., 55, 57.

11. Michaelis, *Schulz and Peanuts*, 346.

12. At a screening of the most recent *Peanuts* feature film at Ohio State University's Wexner Center for the Arts in November 2015, director Steve Martino discussed confronting similar challenges and acknowledged his debt to Melendez in figuring out solutions.

13. Barrier, *Hollywood Cartoons*, 537. As Adam Abraham notes, two of UPA's best-known animators disliked the term: "Although John Hubley used the term 'stylized' animation and Bobe Cannon preferred to call it 'simplified,' *limited*, with its sense of the pejorative, is the name that stuck" (*When Magoo Flew*, 102). Leonard Maltin, whose *Of Mice and Magic* devotes an entire chapter to UPA, never refers to their cartoons as "limited animation" and instead uses the term only to refer to the television animation of the 1960s and 1970s, which he clearly detests (*Of Mice and Magic: A History of American Animated Cartoons* [New York: New American Library, 1987], 338). I do not use the term pejoratively but rather as a way of referring simply to a set of related techniques, no matter the quality of the cartoons produced.

14. Abraham, *When Magoo Flew*, 102–3.

15. Ibid., 32.

16. Amid Amidi catalogs the spread of the modern style to the point when it became ubiquitous in his book *Cartoon Modern* (San Francisco: Chronicle Books, 2006).

17. Leon Morse, review of *A Charlie Brown Christmas*, *Variety*, December 15, 1965, 46.

18. Luke 2:8–14 reads:

And there were in the same country shepherds abiding in the field, keeping watch over their flock by night. And, lo, the angel of the Lord came upon them, and the glory of the Lord shone round about them: and they were sore afraid. And the angel said unto them, Fear not: for, behold, I bring you good tidings of great joy, which shall be to all people. For unto you is born this day in the city of David a Saviour, which is Christ the Lord. And this shall be a sign unto you; Ye shall find the babe wrapped in swaddling clothes, lying in a manger. And suddenly there was with the angel a multitude of the heavenly host praising God, and saying, Glory to God in the highest, and on earth peace, good will toward men.

19. *Time* printed the question "Is God Dead?" on the cover of its April 8, 1966, edition, the first time they had used text without an accompanying image. The question was meant to provoke Americans concerned about the appeal of Christianity in what seemed an increasingly secular society.

20. Michaelis, *Schulz and Peanuts*, 350–52.

21. Mendelson and Melendez, *A Charlie Brown Christmas*, 20–23.

22. Ibid., 23.

23. Burgheim, "Security Is a Good Show."

24. Even the use of jazz in the special's score, a novel move for the time, could in a relatively small span of years come to seem traditional, as the various postwar jazz styles that Guaraldi synthesized in "Linus and Lucy" became safer and more familiar to large numbers white Americans.

25. Hazel G. Warlaumont, *Advertising in the 60s: Turncoats, Traditionalists, and Waste Makers in America's Turbulent Decade* (Westport, CT: Praeger, 2001), 163.

26. "Good Grief," *Time*, April 9, 1965, 82–84.

27. Warlaumont, *Advertising in the 60s*, xi–xii.

28. Robert Mann, *Daisy Petals and Mushroom Clouds: LBJ, Barry Goldwater, and the Ad That Changed American Politics* (Baton Rouge: Louisiana State University Press, 2011), 109–12.

29. Ibid., 55–60.

-11-

CHARLES SCHULZ, COMIC ART, AND PERSONAL VALUE

M. J. CLARKE

Charles Schulz used his own attitude toward traditional fine art as a recurring subject matter in his comic strip *Peanuts*. In a short series of strips appearing in January 1999, Schulz depicted Rerun's first trip to an art museum to examine his own complicated relationship to high art. After the young characters' brief outing, Rerun and his classmates return to their school to attempt their own paintings, an assignment that compels the junior artist to despairingly exclaim, "I'll never be Andrew Wyeth" (January 29, 1999). Here, Rerun is parroting Schulz's own self-deprecating attitude toward his own medium, comic art, which he reiterated in several interviews throughout his career. For example, in a 1977 conversation, Schulz flatly stated that "comic strips aren't art; they never will be. They are too transient, art is something which is so good it speaks to succeeding generations, not only as it speaks to the first generation but better, and I doubt my strip will hold up."[1]

But while Schulz frequently paid deference to legitimate, high art, the artist just as frequently made arguments for the unique pleasures of comic art. Earlier in that same sequence of strips following Rerun's trip to the art museum, Schulz depicts two artworks competing for the children's attention in one single, wordless panel (January 28, 1999). On the far left, a large group of kids huddle around the bottom edge of an elaborately rendered oil landscape; the picture, residing mostly off panel, is positioned both literally and figuratively above the heads of the children. And on the far right of the strip, Rerun stands alone, contemplating a simple line drawing of a small dog that looks very much Snoopy (but who is in fact Earl from Patrick McDonnell's *Mutts*, a strip Schulz admired by a younger cartoonist who was profoundly influenced by Schulz). The picture, both literally and figuratively approachable, hangs low enough for Rerun to observe it all at once. This entire strip reads like a mathematical formula wherein the acclaim and adherents for traditional fine art may be greater than or more numerous than those for comic art, captured here by the modest, Schulzian dog picture; however, comic art provides its own less celebrated but individually felt pleasure that speaks to its audience more directly and with a deeper personal resonance (remembering that Rerun, for a decade or more of real time, has been begging for a dog of his own). Putting this graphic argument into words in an earlier interview, Schulz reconsidered the balance between fine and comic art, declaring: "I think that the comic strip is better than a lot of things around that they call art, but I don't think that it's as good as anything Picasso did. I also don't think that Picasso could have drawn a comic strip."[2] With this strip as well as through these and similar comments, Schulz suggests that comic art is a sphere unto itself only circumstantially related to fine art, which places special demands on its artists, provides alternative forms of valuation to its critics, and grants unique forms of artistic appreciation for its viewers. Building from this fundamental insight, this essay will examine how the idiosyncratic features of comic art shade and color the unique features of the market for Schulz's own drawings as art objects themselves. Drawing on Howard Becker's "small world thesis" to describe and explain the institutional mechanics of art markets, I will attempt to describe first how the market for comic art, like Schulz's, both emulates and differs in practice from that of the traditional art world; how the market for Schulz draws upon and recruits entrepreneurial fans to manage its operations; and how Schulz collectors sacralize the artist's work through personal, affective, and nostalgic valuation, which both alleviates and exacerbates the endemic problem of price uncertainty that haunts all art.

Schulz's conflicted feelings toward comic art also inflected his attitude toward the fate of the physical artifacts of his own strips and the original drawings that were reproduced to create them. In his lifetime, Schulz leveraged and exploited his images, stories, and characters in myriad ancillary texts, licensed products, and advertising endorsements. However, the one economic activity that he seems to have been entirely disinterested in was the sale of his drawings themselves as artwork. In interviews, the artist frequently expressed disbelief that such a market could even exist, stating, in his typically self-deprecating tone, "we [comic artists] don't hang in art galleries . . . we're not good enough."[3] This dubiousness, however, has in no way discouraged the robust and

Fig. 11.1: Charles Schulz, *Peanuts*, January 28, 1999. PEANUTS © 1999 Peanuts Worldwide LLC. Dist. by UNIVERSAL UCLICK. Reprinted with permission. All rights reserved.

expanding market for Schulz's original strips, which has grown from an informal system based on gifts and acquaintance trading partners to a more formalized market of significant scale and consequent price ranges. For example, a *Peanuts* drawing from Sunday, April 10, 1955, depicting Charlie Brown playing baseball was auctioned by the firm Heritage Auctions in 2007 for $114,000. The same auction house routinely reports typical price levels between $20,000 and $30,000 for Schulz daily strips.

The market for Schulz's comic art has grown alongside interest in several other forms of reproduction art, objects that were part of a mass media process and thus potentially hold an iconic lure. Today there exist healthy markets for paperback illustrations (works by painter Frank Frazetta have sold for as high as $286,000), calendar pinups (works by painter Gil Elvgren have also sold for $286,000), recent magazine illustrations (works by artist Patrick Nagel have sold for $161,000), and animation cells (cells from Mickey Mouse cartoons have sold for $99,000).[4] Newfound interest in these and similar works has been extensively studied under what sociologists have called the omnivore thesis. Richard Peterson and his collaborators have astutely suggested that our contemporary, more open society has fundamentally altered the function of art with respect to social stratification.[5] Specifically, the elitism of connoisseurship is no longer guaranteed by familiarity with one strata of high art but instead is earned through a broad appreciation of different art forms, some of which had been neglected by former so-called elites. This seemingly plausible theory, however, unsurprisingly relies solely on the honorific worth that connoisseurs place on objects and, therefore, can never explain how and why certain objects are elected to the omnivore repertoire and the specificity of their appreciation.

In many ways, the market for Schulz's original works as well as other markets for comic art function in manner similar to more traditional art markets. Interested buyers and sellers meet to transact for drawings on paper and coordinate to resolve the fundamental price uncertainty that hovers around all art objects. And, as with traditional fine art, the market for comic art is a hybrid market that places objects we call "art" on a variable spectrum from a hypothetically pure commodity with perfect exchangeability to sacred, singular objects that exist outside and above everyday life and whose value could never be compared.[6] In other words, hybrid markets openly manage and negotiate what Richard Caves and many other authors have called the "art versus commerce dilemma" fundamental to all creative industries.[7] In pure commodity markets, actions would be guided by transparent and knowable values, participants would be perfectly informed of these established facts, and transactions would be conducted largely through formal relationships, uninfluenced by personal relations to objects or trading partners. However, this economic ideal-type is particularly disrupted by trade in art. In art markets, knowledge and understanding of value necessitate years of initiation and instruction. And these values frequently do not translate into other spheres; in other words, only within the enclosed art market will high prices be attached to its objects, while observers from the outside can only look on incredulously. Transactions in art markets typically occur through long-standing, embedded ties between artists and dealers as well as between dealers and collectors based on personal relations and trust. Because worth outside the sphere of the art market does not exist, it is these shared relations that act as the most determining factor in maintaining an object's worth. And lastly, in art markets the objects themselves are only intermittently available as salable commodities. Indeed, Igor Kopytoff has argued that art is not valued because of the structure of commodity exchange but because of its brief punctuated forays as a commodity, from which it subsequently retreats.[8] Trade in comic art and traditional art shares these features, making them hybrid markets that equally complicate our ideas of exchange and its relation to visual culture. However, in this essay I will suggest that collectors and dealers value Schulz's art in a fundamentally different way—in a way suggested by the artist himself—that marks it as a distinct art world particularly instructive in elucidating our shared relationship with mass mediated yet somehow still sacred images.

Unlike traditional art markets, the market for Schulz drawings retains a larger measure of what Ramon Lobato and Julian Thomas recently have termed "informal media activity."[9] These authors use informality to describe the unofficial, unsanctioned, and unremarked-upon qualities that encompass everyday media experience but are often neglected in media analysis because they are harder to track and harder to define. Art markets specifically rely upon informal practices to exchange tacit aesthetic standards, coordinate economic trading partners, and broadcast social prestige, but these practices are met with an equally formalizing impulse to more clearly establish prices, procedures, and industrial durability. For example Olav Velthuis has recently argued that the seemingly irrational practice of pricing fine art by size and demand in fact serves a strategic need to maintain both dealer and artist reputation and stabilize future values.[10] However, the market for comic art and Schulz drawings has not been formalized to the degree of fine art and, thus, relies on a idiosyncratic indicators of recruitment and value, as will be indicated through informant conversations with several actors with the market for Schulz originals.

Discussing a similarly overheated, bullish market, namely that for contemporary art in the 1980s and 1990s, Paul Ardene astutely remarked that what is sold in the art market are not objects but are better understood as "crystallizations."[11] The author elaborates: "[O]ver and above a particular form, a work of art possesses both its being and what the various actors in the cultural world are willing to invest in that thing, the quelling of an aesthetic desire but also, occasionally, much more: the materialized representation of acquired economic or political power, capital to be frozen, or even just spent purely and simply, a living sign of wealth."[12] For Ardene, art on the market then resides at the vertex of at least three values: the aesthetic, the economic, and the social. Aesthetic value appreciates artworks as cultural objects that inhabit some mixture of acknowledged artistry, novelty, or innovation that adds to or complements its medium broadly considered. Economic value considers artworks as objects of financial worth that can be used as a form of property to store currency or to advance capital through speculation and trade. And social value casts artworks as honorific symbols of power that give owners access to potent rituals of social stratification by acquiring, possessing, or donating these objects. The hybrid art market functions to negotiate and mediate the shifting balance of these intersecting values and occasionally meets at the complex term that we abbreviate as "price"; in the fine art world, these mechanisms have been formalized to a degree that marks its constituent works as either masterpieces or safe investments.

In another strip depicting the aforementioned trip to the art museum, Rerun asks his classmate about the collection (January 26, 1999). Sitting on the bus, Rerun innocently asks if the museum will include a picture of his mother, following up his own question with the matter-of-fact observation that his mother is very pretty. Here, Rerun misunderstands the mechanisms of art valuation, which leave no room for the personally significant or the intimately meaningful, such as a picture of one's mother or a picture of a longed-for puppy. I argue that collectors and dealers of Schulz and comic art in general operate under a similarly productive but informal misunderstanding and in so doing suggest another way to value art and visual culture.

Undoubtedly, such collectors and dealers activate aesthetic, economic, and social value in their coordinated actions; however, drawing on a small sample of interviews with actors in the market (eight collectors, two dealers, and one archivist), I argue that there is a fourth system of value that, while perhaps of minor importance in markets for traditional art, dominates the discussion of Schulz's work. Specifically, collectors and dealers cite a great personal value and affective devotion to the objects that goes well beyond the aesthetic, the economic, or the social, echoing Rerun's own misunderstanding. This deeper connection between the objects and the lives of their owners is evident, for example, in the actions of entrepreneurial fans who saved what was once considered the detritus of an industrial process, or worse, rubbish; in the tendency of collectors to hold onto their objects despite tenfold increases in price; in the boundary work conducted by collectors to parse out and segregate themselves from speculators; and in collectors' practice of trading objects among fellow collectors not to maximize price but to acquire pieces that are personally meaningful. In this I mean neither to suggest that these attitudes and feelings concerning personal value do not exist in other markets for collectibles or for other art objects nor to determine precisely the nature of the psychological link between art and connoisseur, but only to state that what distinguishes the market for Schulz and comic art as different from more traditional art markets is its skewed hierarchy in which collectors and dealers place personal value above all other concerns.

Using these observations, the remainder of this essay will briefly sketch the contours and operations of an alternative art world. The art world thesis draws from an aesthetic philosophy positing that art is actively defined not through anything inherent in the object but rather through the context of artistic theory itself and the institutional efforts of those operating within it, as well as from a sociology of art that casts art making as a vast communal and transactional effort extending well beyond artists and held together by shared conventions that coordinate motivation, meaning, and valuation.[13] Over the past thirty years, several sociologists have expanded upon these initial insights to explicate the functioning of alternative art worlds, namely art worlds that in their difference and separation from the legitimate field of high art offer complications to the theory, specifically offering insight in how art is valued in cases where the traditional stores of worth are complicated or altogether inaccessible. For example, Gary Alan Fine has extensively examined the market for outsider art and found that aesthetic value is linked less to an artist's place within established artistic traditions and more to his or her claims of authenticity and, specifically, socially marginal position.[14] Similarly, Michal McCall has investigated the resolutely regional art market of St. Louis, which lacks connections to New York City–based critics, dealers, and collectors and, therefore, the stores of value with which the New York art world has imbued its art objects. Instead, the small art world of St. Louis has organized itself around art schools, which function as the only source of social value that can be used to differentiate between aspiring high artists and local hobbyists and so-called picture painters.[15] Heather FitzGibbon likewise has examined the market for reproduced art—posters and prints—and found that galleries dealing in these media have also created their own mechanisms of valuation by crediting their own institutions (libraries, research centers, etc.), by educating customers, and by relying on fame and notoriety from outside the sphere of art.[16] In all these cases, the trade and practice of art exist largely without a relationship to the high art world and, as a result, have created entirely new conventions to accord, bestow, and maintain value. I argue that the market for Schulz's strips and comic art more broadly also functions as an alternative art world, which, with historically limited access to stores of aesthetic, economic, or social value, has centered itself around what I call personal value.

In her examination of the emergence of a robust market in contemporary fine art, the sociologist Raymonde Moulin described the importance of interested parties staking their reputations to create "technologies of consumption," or social mechanisms to promote and distribute new objects and new artists.[17] However, in the case of the Schulz art market, little promotion or seeding has been necessary, as collectors and dealers have predominately come not from the ranks of existing art connoisseurs but from a base of fans and professionals already deeply invested in the medium of comic art and the artist himself. Historically, the interest in comic art emerged with the modern phenomenon of fandom, the intensely felt, shared devotion for mass-media texts. Many collectors comment that their first or early experience with comic art objects occurred at conventions, at occasional social gatherings of fans to share, trade, and sell artifacts of their devotion, or through contacts made via the back pages of fan-centric periodicals, specifically the now-defunct *Comics Buyers Guide*. Regardless of the exact historical origins of the comic art market and the market for Schulz originals, its intense and expanding interest owes much to at least three recent factors. While comic strip artists have routinely received their original drawings back from their editor-syndicators, comic book artists, for the first several decades of their profession, rarely saw their work returned. This changed thanks to the efforts of artist-advocate Neal Adams and others, who secured policy changes such that by 1974 Marvel Comics had returned all pages to their artists.[18] This gave comic artists a chance to offer a tremendous volume of stock in original drawings to a nascent base of interested consumers. While the exact effect of digitally enabled sales on the comic art market is a matter of contentious debate, the use of the Internet beginning in the 1990s to facilitate contacts and transactions also expanded the number of available and interested buyers. Several collectors told me that it was only through the Internet that they first learned of the market and became involved in comic art collection; the Internet gave people without face-to-face access to conventions, including international collectors, a chance to acquire comic art. In the words of one collector: "Once the Internet hit . . . people around the world were seeing the stuff and then all of a sudden everybody started to realize that it's an important art form and it is interesting."[19] The sociologist Chandra Mukerji has discussed the complicated transition of industrial commodities into fine art, drawing namely on the example of the critical ascendency of film.[20] Mukerji specifically discusses efforts to embed film within preexisting artistic traditions, but more importantly she casts artification as only possible when the threat of potential scarcity emerges, in this case the supplanting of film by television and other media. Similarly, it is no coincidence that the market for Schulz's works has expanded in the wake of his retirement and passing. While it is typical for the death of an artist to raise the desirability of possessing his or her work, the end of *Peanuts* signified not only the end of Schulz's oeuvre but also the slow demise of the comic strip and comic books themselves, both suffering from drastically declining interest, syndication, and sales, as well as the demise of the craft tradition, as hand-drawn art in these media is being replaced with digitally native techniques. Thus, a nascent fan market supplemented by expanded volume, a broadened potential audience, and a perceived scarcity has resulted in what many informants have referred to as a booming market. For example, one dealer told me about Schulz pieces that sold for $300 to $400 only twenty-five years ago now selling routinely for $20,000 to $30,000, and another collector mentioned that prices had increased tenfold for desirable comic art like Schulz's over this same period. Rapid increases in price have left many early collectors unable to afford additional Schulz pieces, or hypothetically even the pieces in their own collection if they were on the market once again. In conversation, many collectors expressed regret concerning these inflated prices and look wistfully back at an earlier era when comic art could be more easily acquired. As one *Peanuts* collector put it: "Every comic collector, while they collect comic art, . . . all read the comics, and collecting *Peanuts* is one of their grails to get. They may never get it—I just wish that I could get a[nother] *Peanuts* strip if I could afford it. . . . It's basically how I think most comic collectors feel."

While actors in the comic art market come mostly from the ranks of preexisting comic fandom, not all fans collect original art. The market then comprises a set of particularly entrepreneurial fans who were often the first to find comic art worthy of collection; who consistently stake their reputation on advancing and promoting comic art; and who practice great role fluidity, intermittently acquiring, promoting, and dealing their art. Or, as Walter Benjamin succinctly put it in his own examination of the modern phenomenon of collecting: "[P]erhaps the most deeply hidden motive of the person who collects can be described in this way: he takes up the struggle against dispersion."[21] In his *Rules of Art*, Pierre Bourdieu singles out the importance of what he calls "the creator of the creator," a role occupied by influential critics composing artistic lineages (aesthetic value) or dealers crafting new product lines (economic value).[22] In comic art, however, much of this work was conducted by entrepreneurial fans working in a distinctly Benjaminian mode, removing objects from their functional relations, imbuing them with a deep sense of history, and placing them in a unique, ordered relation, unapparent to the uninitiated. One collector described to me his efforts to acquire comic art by directly contacting and soliciting the artists themselves, many of whom, the collector explained, expressed surprise that anyone was interested in their work. The same collector frequently referred to his collection in redemptive terms, claiming that he had acquired his pieces "for posterity." Similarly, another collector described the efforts of another fan and artist who had approached Schulz and convinced the artist to sell many of his works through an intermediary. And yet another collector described to me his efforts not only to collect comic art but to work with several other collectors to establish an official archive for neglected works. In all these cases, collectors have taken the initiative to legitimate an art form, a sequence that seems backward with respect to most other art markets, where markers of value are established before collectors risk large-scale investment. Fans, without access to stores of aesthetic, economic, or social value, built the market of comic art based on the only currency at their disposal, namely individual devotion or personal value, already primed through preexisting fandom.

Describing his first encounter with Schulz originals and the subsequent maxing out of his credit cards to acquire several of these pieces, one collector called the event a "purely affective encounter": a fair enough definition of what I have thus far called "personal value." Collectors of comic art, in this regard, share much in common with the collectors extensively studied in the exemplary work of Russell Belk and his circle of collaborators. Belk, in a monumental 1989 study, traced the myriad social processes conducted by collectors to move mundane or everyday objects, via a set of ritual acts such as gift giving, customization, and collecting itself, into the realm of the sacred.[23] Early collectors of comic art certainly can be understood as sacralizing what had previously been cast as the imperfect waste of an industrial process, though one that entailed the practice of skills, like drawing, usually recognized as artistic. In a later piece, Belk also suggested that sacralized objects become a constituent part of a collector's identity itself, forever attached to one's sense of what the theorist called an "extended self."[24] While I would not presume to know the psychological motivations behind collecting comic art, I would argue that Belk's notion of the extended self speaks to the larger notion of personal value and collectors' tendency to frame attachment to Schulz's work through past experience or through a sense of long-standing obligation. Moreover, I contend that personal value, like Belk's extended self, is a social concept, which, while harder to translate, equivalate, or exchange through other forms of value, is squarely a shared phenomenon because of the shared intimacy of mass communication, which speaks both broadly and to individual readers, and because of the camaraderie and small world of the collectors for comic art itself, in which collectors gauge and assess their mutual devotion.

This process of sacralization was initiated arguably by Schulz, who frequently parted with his own drawings but only by giving them away as gifts. Following a typical practice of previous generations of comic artists, Schulz and his contemporaries often gave strips away in response to enthusiastic fan letters or upon meeting fans. Over the course of *Peanuts'* nearly fifty years of publication, Schulz drafted approximately eighteen thousand strips, seven thousand of which are permanently housed at Schulz's official library and research facility, leaving a little more than half of his output in the wild.[25] Many or most of these unaccounted-for strips were loosed to the market first as gifts from Schulz; one dealer speculated that 90 percent of Schulz strips sold are previously gifted strips. In fact, most *Peanuts* strips auctioned or sold display the telltale hallmark of Schulz's own "best wishes" or some similar salutation in the margins. One of my informants recounted receiving a gifted Schulz original through mail correspondence with the artist, while another obtained a piece through a brief visit to Schulz's studio before the artist's retirement. A vast tradition of anthropological theory positions gift exchange in opposition to modern commodity markets, contrasting the financial economy of so-called complex, modern societies with the informal nature of gift exchange. While the market for Schulz art is no longer one of gift exchange, the residue of this sacralizing practice shades collectors' feelings toward Schulz and toward his drawings.

In describing their acquisitions, comic art collectors often use terminology that underscores the personal value they place on the objects. More than any other reason, collectors invoke the term "nostalgia" to describe their attachment to Schulz's work and comic art generally. In my conversations with them, many collectors described their devotion to Schulz as beginning in their past and continuing into the present through a symbolic association with their own childhood. One collector put it most succinctly, saying: "I think [collectors] . . . just want something with the characters that they remember and have grown up with.

It's a very nostalgia-based hobby." Of course, the collector's use of the term "nostalgia" is complicated, reflecting the complexity of the concept as discussed in critical media studies and examinations of so-called popular memory. As with most attempts to reach back to the past, one's quest is met with an imperfect copy; ironically, comic art collectors miss the mark, but by securing the original and not the reproduction, as is typical of other nostalgia-driven markets. This puts Schulz collection in the same conversation with media scholars' observation that nostalgia usually entails not a slavish reconstruction of the past but a purposeful evocation, more often than not suited and reshaped to the needs of the present.[26] Specifically, Henry Jenkins and Lynn Spigel, in their work on fans' nostalgic attachment to another comic character, Batman, argue that individual nostalgia and shared popular memory operate in a clearly different mode of recalling from that of academic history; while the latter is fixed, impersonal, and objective, the former is fluid, informal, and emotional.[27] Jenkins and Spigel further discuss the techniques of popular memory such as reordering narratives, recategorizing details, and, most importantly, using popular culture as a wedge to articulate a relation between personal and public histories, operating in analogous fashion to personal value, which is similarly personally felt and publicly shared.

In his novel *The Mysterious Flame of Queen Loana*, Umberto Eco examines this same paradoxical connection between private and public through the figure of comic art and the strange case of Yambo Bodoni, a used book dealer who suffers a peculiar form of memory loss after suffering a stroke.[28] In the aftermath of the attack, Yambo retains only his so-called semantic memory, the knowledge of dates, facts, narratives, and quotations all gathered from books, but loses his autobiographical memory, anything from his personal life and experience. Yambo, however, begins to regain flashes of his own past upon encountering a Mickey Mouse comic strip that he immediately recognizes and remembers. Yambo's wife reasons that remembering and memorializing such a frivolous text, as opposed to the important details of historical and literary texts, must indicate an idiosyncratic, personal investment and, thus, a kernel of autobiographical memory. Drawing on this revelation, Yambo spends the majority of the remainder of the book digging through popular and material culture (particularly comic strips) from his youth, which ironically and almost tangentially returns small doses of his private, personal past. For example, by pursuing images of *Flash Gordon*'s Dale Arden and *Terry and the Pirates*'s Dragon Lady, Yambo is able to reapproximate his own erotic awakening. I argue that a similar equation of private and public is at play in the market preference for the iconic in comic art. While highlighting the strange mix of shared intimacy adds very little to our understanding of mass culture, which is designed to be publicly distributed but individually felt, I contend that using this notion as a foundation for valuing art objects, a concept that we have called "personal value," is a recent phenomenon.

The distinct, personal value that fuels comic art markets also influences the practice of acquiring and holding onto objects, particularly *Peanuts* art. In the subculture of comic art, collectors often refer to particularly valued pieces as grails or grail pages, referencing the Arthurian myth of the impossible quest for the Holy Grail. This term positions the acquisition of the artwork as the culmination of a long, divinely inspired search and as an apotheosis of some profound, transcendent value, becoming another example of Belk's processes of sacralization. One collector invoked the epic plot that structured his acquisition of Schulz pieces as he recalled: "I'd been reading *Peanuts* since I could read at all, and so once I started buying original art the idea of having a *Peanuts* original naturally followed. It didn't happen for a long time, though." After being brought to market and after being exchanged, pieces of Schulz art only rarely reappear in subsequent transactions. One dealer at a major auction house described this situation as a state of "virtually no turnover at all." Expanding upon this observation, he further claimed that "the thing about Schulz['s strips] is that they're out there because he gave away so many to people . . . so it seems like every auction we have anywhere from two to ten [strips] and I'm trying to think of the last time I saw one that we've sold before—I can't think of one off the top of my head. Based on that, once people buy them and pay market prices, it seems like they're buying them because they love them and we don't see them come back up." Collectors often echo the sentiment expressing their disinterest in parting with Schulz art. One informant described his list of what he called "the last to go," the ten or twelve objects of art among his collection that he would never sell, a short list that included several Schulz works. Another collector flatly stated: "You don't see many resales once a piece changes hands. They tend to stay with someone. I think that it goes to the nostalgia point. It's a personal connection."

In considering individual works by Schulz, both dealers and collectors, with very few exceptions and caveats, share general notions concerning which strips are more desirable and, therefore, worth more. As in traditional art markets, the relative condition of a piece affects the value placed on it, and certain time periods of the artist's output are ranked above others. In the case of Schulz, connoisseurs widely agree that his best work was produced in the first two decades of the strip, the 1950s and 1960s. Collectors and dealers also overwhelmingly look to subject matter, specifically the presence of characters depicted and recurring themes, to assess the value of strips. All other elements being equal, collectors regard a strip featuring Charlie Brown and especially Snoopy as inherently more valuable. Throughout the fifty years of *Peanuts*, Schulz returned again and again to perennial gags and story lines to create a sense of artistic continuity, to facilitate rapid work through simple variation, and to reuse proven and popular concepts. Collectors cite these perennial strips—Linus's devotion to the Great Pumpkin, Lucy pulling the football away from Charlie Brown, Snoopy versus the Red Baron—as the most significant and most valuable. Both collectors and dealers use the term "iconic," once again invoking the sacred, to describe this preference. One dealer described this as a preference for the "immediately identifiable," or, as another collector put it, the preference for "characters and episodes that resonate in the popular perception."

Valuing the iconic in perennial strips, however, creates two puzzling contradictions. Despite the fact that original strips are all unique and one-of-a-kind, the perennial subject matter both in terms of the images (which have been used in myriad other objects and licensed products) and in terms of the art objects themselves (for example, Schulz produced many Red Baron–themed strips) are *not* the most rare, inverting the traditional art association of scarcity and worth. Moreover, the very notion of an intersubjective set of indicators of worth seems necessarily at odds with the dominance of personal value active in the market; how could attachment to the art be both broadly shared and deeply felt?

As mentioned above, all art markets are hybrid constructions dedicated to mediating the contradictory status of objects on a scale from commoditized to sacred. But because the market for Schulz and comic art relies on personal value, collectors and dealers are particularly sensitive to the art versus commerce dilemma and conduct extensive boundary work in conversation to diminish the influence of economic value. In this tendency, they embody what Belk has described as the unique antimaterialist materialism of collectors who frame their acquisitions as acts of sacrifice and passion.[29] While most collectors outline the overall economic contours of the market, often citing the influence of classical concepts such as demand, scarcity, and speculation, all the collectors I spoke with emphatically separate their involvement from these profane aspects; as one collector forcefully put it, "I don't do it for the money." Another collector echoed this sentiment, stating: "Everything I buy, I buy for a personal reason and not because I see it as a commodity." Occasionally, this opposition to the economic aspects of the trade in comic art even manifested in resentment toward hypothetical speculators. As one collector put it: "Unfortunately, with the increase in value in these originals comes the specter of the outside investor who wants a piece of the action and lacks the connection to the source material. These well-heeled individuals unfortunately drive the value and prices higher and higher." In other words, speculators collect in the wrong way, not because they mistake artistic worth with dollar cost—the typical complaint against the stereotypical philistine or nouveau riche—but because they lack the appropriate personal relationship with the art.

Despite occasional collector resistance, the market for Schulz and comic art has rationalized along with its growth. Price points have increasingly stabilized, as there are fewer and fewer "finds"—undervalued pieces not yet attached to the market. Auction sales have consolidated mostly under two or three firms, which boast the highest dollar sales, in many cases absorbing the business of entrepreneurial dealers. And collectors increasingly use these auction houses, or equally impersonal or more formalized purchasing mechanisms, to secure their art, relying less on personal contacts or nascent fan networks. Yet, like all hybrid markets, the market for comic art could never become entirely formalized, evidenced for example in the continued preference for face-to-face contact in deal making and exchanges to facilitate trust and confidence. Moreover, despite rising prices, the community of Schulz collectors remains a small world. One dealer who regularly organizes auctions for *Peanuts* originals cites a group of no more than ten to fifteen individuals who now make up the bulk of purchasers. Similarly, a collector remarked to me that comic art as a field is currently serviced by a relatively small number of dealers, again numbering around ten to fifteen. Because comic art draws not from art connoisseurs but from comic fans, it is already a niche within a niche, further complicating the core function of markets: settling price uncertainty, or what one collector called the problem of "real price."

This combination of personal value and price uncertainty places considerable risk on collectors but also encourages great ingenuity and camaraderie among collectors, as evidenced in the widespread practice of trading. As a communitas, longtime collectors often acquire new objects not through buying and selling in overheated markets but through trading with fellow collectors in deals self-monitored for fairness and guided not by profit maximization but by personal satisfaction and a simple "I just like it more" standard, or even through trading up, exchanging several pieces of art for a more desirable one. In conversation, one collector recalled trading a cover from Marvel Comics' *The Avengers* by Rich Buckler for a DC Comics cover of *Lois Lane* by Bob Oksner, which may have entailed, by the collector's own admission, a slight loss in economic value based on the greater popularity of the former characters. However, the collector reported that both parties in the exchange felt like they got the best of the deal by simply getting what they liked better; the collector called the Oksner cover "a piece that is going to be hanging in my house for a long time." Many other collectors described this practice of maximizing personal value, of finding exchange partners, and of switching ownership based solely on finding the objects that personally mean more to the collector. Such transactions are only possible precisely because, in the market for comic art, personal value looms so large.

However, comic art collectors also enflame price uncertainty by their very appeals to personal value in determining objects' worth. Personal value depends on past attachment; it lacks the semiobjective status of aesthetic, economic, and social value—values that are, by definition, emergent only in populations. As with other collectibles, comic artworks that are imbued with personal value may be generational in their appeal, resulting in a distinct churn in the comic art market. As one dealer describing Schulz's art put it: "[People] who grew up with *Peanuts* will always love to have them. But then you'll start getting kids that grew up with *Ren and Stimpy* or *The Simpsons*; *Peanuts* isn't in the paper the way that it used to be." Another collector also cast doubt on the long-term worth of comic art, explaining, "I'm sure that some of the work will remain to be seen as classics and will have ongoing value, but I'm sure that at least some of them [artists] that the first generation like and enjoyed may not have transitioned to the next generation." Thus, valuing the valueless on the basis of resolutely personal value carries a tremendous amount of risk in that the transience of the popular and the revisions of popular memory might catch up once again. It was exactly this kind of transience that was so often on Schulz's own mind when he considered his own legacy. In several interviews, the artist posited that real art is that which could appeal deeply across time and space, and expressed the feeling that his own work fell short of this mark, saying: "[S]trips aren't made to last; they're made to be funny in the paper, [then] thrown away." It remains to be seen if this new market for Schulz's work will be able to translate personal devotion into something more lasting that even Schulz himself could not apprehend.

NOTES

1. Stan Isaacs, "Comic Strips Aren't Art," in *Charles M. Schulz: Conversations*, ed. M. Thomas Inge (Jackson: University Press of Mississippi, 2000), 88.

2. Frank Pauer, "A Conversation with Charles Schulz," in *Charles M. Schulz: Conversations*, ed. M. Thomas Inge (Jackson: University Press of Mississippi, 2000), 152.

3. Gary Groth, "Schulz at 3 O'Clock in the Morning," in *Charles M. Schulz: Conversations*, ed. M. Thomas Inge (Jackson: University Press of Mississippi, 2000), 199.

4. All prices taken from Heritage Auctions, at http://www.ha.com.

5. Richard A. Peterson and Roger M. Kern, "Changing Highbrow Taste: From Snob to Omnivore," *American Sociological Review* 61, no. 5 (October 1996): 900–907.

6. Igor Kopytoff, "The Cultural Biography of Things: Commoditization as Process," in *The Social Life of Things: Commodities in Cultural Perspective*, ed. Arjun Appadurai (Cambridge: Cambridge University Press, 1986), 64–91.

7. Richard Caves, *Creative Industries: Contracts between Art and Commerce* (Cambridge, MA: Harvard University Press, 2000).

8. Kopytoff, "The Cultural Biography of Things," 82–83.

9. Ramon Lobato and Julian Thomas, *The Informal Media Economy* (Cambridge: Polity, 2015).

10. Olav Velthuis, *Talking Prices: Symbolic Meanings of Prices on the Market for Contemporary Art* (Princeton, NJ: Princeton University Press, 2007).

11. Paul Ardene, "The Art Market in the 1980s," *International Journal of Political Economy* 25, no. 2 (1995): 111.

12. Jud Hurd, "Cartoonist Profiles: Charles Schulz," in *Charles M. Schulz: Conversations*, ed. M. Thomas Inge (Jackson: University Press of Mississippi, 2000), 101.

13. George Dickie, *Art and the Aesthetic: An Institutional Analysis* (Ithaca, NY: Cornell University Press 1974); and Howard Becker, *Art Worlds* (Berkeley: University of California Press, 1982).

14. Gary Alan Fine, "Crafting Authenticity: The Validation of Identity in Self-Taught Art," *Theory and Society* 32, no. 2 (2003): 153–80.

15. Michal M. McCall, "Art without a Market: Creating Artistic Value in a Provincial Art World," *Symbolic Interaction* 1, no. 1 (1977): 32–43.

16. Heather M. FitzGibbon, "From Prints to Posters: The Production of Artistic Value in a Popular Art World," *Symbolic Interaction* 10, no. 1 (1987): 111–28.

17. Raymonde Moulin, "The Museum and the Marketplace: The Constitution of Value in Contemporary Art," *International Journal of Political Economy* 25, no. 2 (1995): 38.

18. For example, see the efforts made to return the artwork of canonical comic artist Jack Kirby detailed in Tom Heintjes, "The Negotiations," *Comics Journal* (1986): 105.

19. I have kept the interviewees anonymous.

20. Chandra Mukerji, "Artwork: Collection and Contemporary Culture," *American Journal of Sociology* 84, no. 2 (1978): 348–65.

21. Walter Benjamin, *The Arcades Project*, trans. Rolf Tiedemann (Cambridge, MA: Belknap Press of Harvard University Press, 1999), 211.

22. Pierre Bourdieu, *The Rules of Art: Genesis and Structure of a Literary Field* (Stanford, CA: Stanford University Press, 1996), 169.

23. Russell Belk, Melanie Wallendorf, and John F. Sherry Jr., "The Sacred and the Profane in Consumer Behavior: Theodicy and the Odyssey," *Journal of Consumer Research* 16, no. 1 (1989): 1–38.

24. Russell W. Belk, "Possessions and the Extended Self," *Journal of Consumer Research* 15, no. 2 (1988): 139–68.

25. "Original *Peanuts* Comic Strip Collection," Charles M. Schulz Museum, at http://schulzmuseum.org/collections/#/peanuts-cartoon-strip-collection.

26. See, for example, George Lipsitz, *Time Passages: Collective Memory and American Popular Culture* (Minneapolis: University of Minnesota Press, 1990).

27. Henry Jenkins and Lynn Spigel, "Same Bat Channel, Different Bat Times: Mass Culture and Popular Memory," in *Many More Lives of the Batman*, ed. Roberta Pearson, William Uricchio, and Will Brooker (London: British Film Institute, 2015).

28. Umberto Eco, *The Mysterious Flame of Queen Loana*, trans. Geoffrey Brock (Orlando: Harcourt, 2004).

29. Russell W. Belk, "The Double Nature of Collecting: Materialism and Anti-Materialism," *Etnofoor* 11, no. 1 (1998): 7–20.

-12-

CHARLIE BROWN CAFÉS AND THE MARKETING OF *PEANUTS* IN ASIA

IAN GORDON

American entertainment media has a global spread that rivals, if not surpasses, the geopolitical, military, and economic, might of the United States. Alongside products like Coca-Cola, McDonald's, Apple, and Microsoft, figures like Mickey Mouse, Spider-Man, and Batman have a global audience. Sometimes, though, American cultural figures like these do not translate into other cultures in quite the same fashion as they are disseminated and received in the United States. One such case is Charlie Brown, Snoopy, and the rest of the *Peanuts* gang.

Charlie Brown and *Peanuts* have a presence in East and Southeast Asia that draws on the strip's American origins but plays out in a slightly different fashion. One significant difference is that in these parts of Asia the *Peanuts* gang is mostly known from the series of animated television films that commenced with *A Charlie Brown Christmas* in 1965 and first aired on CBS on December 9 that year. The *Peanuts* comic strip has not had as wide circulation in Asia, and so the relationship and knowledge that Asian audiences bring to the characters are somewhat different from in the United States. Nonetheless, Charlie Brown, Snoopy, and the whole *Peanuts* gang have been extensively marketed and licensed throughout East and Southeast Asia. In this chapter I will examine how the Hong Kong–based RM Enterprises expanded the *Peanuts* brand in East and Southeast Asia, and I will explain the popularity of Snoopy and the other *Peanuts* characters in terms of their "cuteness," the aesthetic appeal of which derives from Japanese culture and its influence in Asia.

The Charlie Brown Cafés in Asia are an example of the way that comics-based characters have long lent themselves to marketing, a phenomenon that British academic Matthew Freeman has called "narrative-fronted promotional content."[1] Communications scholar Jonathan Gray suggests a way of understanding this dynamic that extends beyond characters being licensed as products for marketing. His notion of paratexts, for instance coffee mugs and T-shirts that use characters' images, offers a way of seeing characters such as Charlie Brown and Snoopy not simply as comic strip characters that are licensed but also as figures in a dynamic relationship between industry, texts, and audiences.[2] Audiences bring a set of situational interpretative acts to these characters as they appear in an array of different forms from comics to coffee mugs. The cafés are an instance, then, of new forms of paratexts in a global marketplace where translations and symbiosis with local popular culture circulate and recirculate the characters in new ways.

Since 2010, the Schulz family in conjunction with the brand management company Iconix have owned the licensing rights to *Peanuts*, which they purchased for $175 million from E. W. Scripps, the company that controlled the syndicate that owned the *Peanuts* comic strip, United Media. According to the US trade journal *Advertising Age*, Charles Schulz earned $1 billion from the strip and its licensing over the course of his life, and his heirs took in some $35 million a year in the early 2010s. At the time, Iconix expected to earn $75 million annually in licensing revenue and hoped to use *Peanuts* to build their other brands. In 2010, *Peanuts* had "150 licensees in the U.S., 250 in Europe, 200 in Japan, 200 in the rest of Asia, 70 in Latin America and 20 in Australia."[3]

Snoopy has a large presence in Japan. Sony Creative Products runs a Snoopy web page for Japan that links to a vast assortment of Snoopy goods and services such as downloadable wallpaper for computer screens. A 2014–2015 exhibition titled Snoopy Japanesque, commemorated on a website, displayed a range of Japanese-influenced Snoopy figurines. A chain of Snoopy Town stores operated by the Kideirando Corporation has branches in Tokyo, Yokohama, Osaka, and Sapporo.[4] In April 2014, a Snoopy-themed tea house opened in Yufu, in Ōita Prefecture.[5] Universal Studio's theme park in Osaka also has a large Snoopy-themed area whose popularity has been so great that it led to an expanded Wonderland section with the addition of a Hello Kitty area. In this theme park, Snoopy acts a conduit for various aspects of American culture, being both a site for Halloween trick-or-treating and serving as a central jester motif in a Mardi Gras parade.[6] The link with Hello Kitty in the Osaka Universal Studios park is indicative of some of the ways Snoopy and the rest of the *Peanuts* gang are marketed by RM Enterprises elsewhere in Asia.

Established in Hong Kong in 1984, RM Enterprises is a licensing firm that represents several American and British character-based products such as Popeye, Peter Rabbit, Fido Dido, and *Peanuts*. They also represent Japanese characters like San-X, Kimmidoll, Rilakkuma, and Shinzi Katoh Design. *Peanuts* is an important part of RM's operations, and they have licensed it extensively throughout East and Southeast Asia, in ways that differ significantly from the licensing of the brand in America. Operated by husband-and-wife team Raymond and Connie Mok, RM Enterprises took the brand to fresh markets often in innovative ways. One such way was through licensing Charlie Brown Cafés and a series of Snoopy attractions. These marketing campaigns extended the appeal of *Peanuts* in Asia not simply by widening the geographic reach of the characters but by positioning Charlie Brown, Snoopy, and the gang within an aesthetic of "cuteness" that derives in part from Japanese notions of *kawaii*.

THE SNOOPY ATTRACTIONS

In September 2000, Snoopy World opened in the New Town Plaza shopping mall in Sha Tin District, Hong Kong. Although some distance from central Hong Kong, the area is well serviced by public transportation and also attracts a good number of shoppers from the nearby Chinese city of Shenzhen, which is under an hour away by train. The attraction occupies forty thousand square feet in a rooftop area that had previously housed tennis courts. It includes an American-style school bus, a playground, a small boat-ride section, and a Snoopy wedding service. Admission is free, but the wedding service must be booked and is a paid service. The attraction had over three million visitors in the first two years of its existence and remains popular today, with large crowds present when I visited in October 2013. Another Snoopy attraction opened in Shunde, China, in 2004, but it seems to have closed. In October 2013, a new Snoopy Garden opened at the Huarun Living Mall in Qinghe District, Beijing. Charles Schulz's widow, Jean, attended the opening. These attractions are not so much amusement parks with rides as large *Peanuts*-themed playgrounds.[7] RM Licensing also licensed a series of Snoopy-themed stores in China, Taiwan, and Hong Kong, mostly selling women's and children's clothing.[8] These ventures may have differed slightly in form and content from similar licensing operations in the United States, but theme park attractions and clothing licensees are fairly standard marketing operations for comics and cartooning characters like Snoopy and Charlie Brown. However, RM Enterprises ventured beyond these familiar bounds by opening a series of Charlie Brown Cafés.

THE CHARLIE BROWN CAFÉS

The Charlie Brown name must seem a natural for the food industry, since there are several restaurants operating under that name or some version thereof. In New Jersey, Charlie Brown's is a chain of fourteen steakhouses. There is a Charlie Brown's Bar and Grill in Denver. In Rochester, New York, Charley Brown's is family-run restaurant that opened in 1969. In Glasgow, Scotland, there is a Charlie Brown coffee shop. And for many years on Young Street in Sydney, Australia, a wine bar operated under the Charlie Brown name. None of these businesses are connected to the *Peanuts* brand. At Sonoma State University in Rohnert Park, California, one of the student cafés is called Charlie Brown's Café. The campus is a little more than ten miles from the Charles Schulz Museum in the cartoonist's former studio in Santa Rosa, and the café is indeed named for the more familiar Charlie Brown from the comic strip. This café, its branding, and its menu seems to have served as inspiration for the various cafés that RM Enterprises licensed in East Asia. The first of these opened under the name Snoopy Place in 1998 in Singapore's Plaza Singapura, a mall at the beginning of the iconic shopping street, Orchard Road. It occupied a large space on the fifth floor of the mall and served American cuisine such as hamburgers, pizzas, and hot dogs. The café closed in 2004 when the mall underwent a renovation. A similarly styled café opened in Korea in 2000 but closed two years later. These setbacks did not discourage RM Enterprises, and in 2006 they opened a Charlie Brown Café in the Tsim Sha Tsui area of Kowloon in Hong Kong. This café prospered and became the model for a series of cafés opened in Malaysia, China, Singapore, Thailand, and Korea.

These cafés have attracted much attention from patrons, many of whom have written extensively in blogs about their experiences and their opinions about the food and ambiance. In researching this chapter, I visited four cafés, on the island of Penang (Malaysia), Hong Kong, Beijing, and Singapore. The Charlie Brown Café in Penang opened in April 2011 in the new Straits Quay Mall, which is part of a marina development. The old area of Penang, the city of George Town, is a UN World Heritage

Site, but the Straits Quay Mall is somewhat distant from George Town and Penang's other tourist and shopping destination, Gurney Drive. When I visited the café on a Saturday in July 2013, there were only three customers in the large establishment, and the mall itself was not at all busy compared to the crowds I noted in George Town and Gurney Drive. Nonetheless, many food bloggers had weighed in with observations about the café.

Cheryl Tan, writing in her blog, the Princess Diaries, wrote an account of her visit in April 2011 shortly after the café opened.[9] After hearing grumbles on the web, she decided to review the café herself. A fan of *Peanuts* since her father bought her a videotape of *A Boy Named Charlie Brown* when she was a girl, she was surprised to hear people in the café ask who Charlie Brown was. She was sure that everyone knew Snoopy. Her review mostly consists of photos from the café accompanied by descriptions of the characters. Indeed, the café features a series of panels with basic details about the characters. She rated the café 4.5/5 because of its ambiance and a "quite nice caffe latte." For Ms. Tan, the experience of the café was about the connection to the characters, which of course is the whole point, but this did not translate into more than a single visit. Another April 2011 visitor, Darren, thought that the food had improved since the café's earlier soft launch, which from his account sounds like a disaster. He rated the drinks and food as overpriced and was most impressed by the ambience.[10]

Other bloggers had similar experiences, bringing their love for the characters to the café but leaving disappointed by the food. In August 2011, Sam Ong, a young professional, went to the Penang branch with friends. His review of the food was damning, with the pizza rated average and the seafood pasta as poor. The details of his blog suggested that the clams in the pasta were not fresh and may indeed have been spoiled. The service was average. But, again, he rated the ambience of the café highly with a 5/5.[11] Another blogger, Eunice Chew, a high school student, took her younger brother to the café in December 2012 and because she wanted to take photographs bought a hot chocolate and a latte.[12] Again, her fascination with the café was with the characters and merchandise, but she only spent money on two drinks. This fascination with the characters is repeated in Pennie Yen Sun's blog of February 2012, which consists entirely of photos of the café with no mention of the quality of the food.[13]

The sentiment of TripAdvisor's various reviews is much the same, with fans of *Peanuts* appreciating the ambience but commenting that the food and service is bad.[14] Another Charlie Brown Café opened in December 2011 in Kuala Lumpur, the capital of Malaysia. Situated in the KLCC (Kuala Lumpur City Centre), a large shopping mall below the Petronas Towers with direct access to a subway station, the café enjoyed a high-profile location in a mall that is constantly packed with shoppers. According to food blogger Sean, who visited in the opening month: "Based on desserts, the café needs tons of work in the food department; still, its fun surroundings make it worth a visit."[15] The café was closed by December 2012.[16] The Penang café closed sometime in mid-2014.

I visited the Hong Kong café on a Sunday in October 2013. The café, located near the Tsim Sha Tsui subway station in Kowloon, was reasonably full at the time. The customers were a mix of parents with children, teenagers, and young adults. Hong Kong acquaintances told me that people went there for the "cutesiness." Since the café is on the second floor and has window seats, it's a good place for people watching. A review on the Asia restaurant review site Open Rice suggested much the same: "This is a café with cutie decoration of Snoopy all around. The food and drink was a little bit expensive. For a Snoopy lover, it should be worthy for it. I had a latte $23 [approximately US$3.00] and one crunchy hazelnut cake $29 for the tea time. The taste of coffee was very weak. Instead of the beautiful 'lattee flower,' there was a chocolate powder snoopy on the top. It was cute! The crunchy hazelnut cake was rather sweet. It was better for sharing. Most people sit there for long time for discussion or chatting."[17] Some of my former students visited the café on a field trip to Hong Kong in late 2011. One of them had this to say when she passed on some of her photos: "Thoughts on the café—food wasn't particularly memorable, but I generally like theme cafés so it was cute."[18] A writer on the Hong Kong–based Rappler site used the word "cute" three times in describing the café.[19] And a visitor to the Singapore café in 2011 said: "It's just a cute café but so so food. I won't return."[20] A visitor to a Charlie Brown Café in Beijing added to the chorus thinking the concept "cute."[21] Likewise, a video review on the Chinese micro network Weixin of a Charlie Brown Café in Shenyang, the capital of northern Liaoning Province, referred to it as "cute."[22] An American resident of Korea also described the many Charlie Brown Cafés in Seoul as "cute locations."[23]

The key response of so many visitors was that the food simply did not live up to the cute ambience of the cafés. My own experience of the cafés was that the food was average but not terrible. The best café I visited was in the Zhongguan Square Shopping Center in Beijing in March 2014.

Tucked in a space behind an escalator bank, it took my Chinese colleague three tries to get directions and for us to locate it. This café sits next to a men's clothing store. It has very little *Peanuts* merchandise and is low on the cute factor, but it does have a range of items for children to play with. I visited on a Monday morning and the crowd was sparse, but as best as I could tell the café has adapted to its location, and from the post-it notes section where people leave messages it seems like a haven for weary shoppers with children in tow.

But it is the cute factor that dominates the Charlie Brown Café experience. Perhaps an overreliance on the *Peanuts* characters to drive traffic to the cafés caused insufficient attention to food and service on the part of café proprietors. Certainly a good many of the Charlie Brown Cafés around Southeast Asia, Korea, and China have closed, but others are still opening—the most recent being in Bangkok. Predictably, the response to the café in Bangkok is that it is "cute."[24] This love of cuteness in many ways stems from the success of the Japanese cultural industry in exporting that aesthetic to the rest of Asia.

THE CUTE AESTHETIC

How did this cute aesthetic spread from Japan through much of the rest of East and Southeast Asia? Nissim Kadosh Otmazgin reports that Japan's "export of popular culture merchandise and related royalties, income, and services coming from products such as recorded sound and image (music, anime, movies, video games), books, magazines, paintings, and art and handicrafts has more than tripled from US$8.37 billion in 1996 to nearly US$25.4 billion in 2006." He notes that this growth comes in the context of the Japanese government offering broad support for cultural industries and targeting cultural exports.[25] These are impressive figures, but the breakdown of direct Japanese cultural exports to both China and a group of four Southeast Asian nations (Indonesia, Malaysia, the Philippines, and Thailand) would at first seem to make this global expansion of Japanese cultural exports a not completely convincing explanation for the conquest of cuteness. Sugiura Tsutomu, from whom Otmazgin derives his figures, shows that Japan's exports to the group of four Southeast Asian nations only increased from US$61.3 million in 1994 to $73.2 million in 2004, an increase of a factor of 1.2. Exports from Japan to China, though, increased by a factor of 3.6 during this time, from US$40 million to $144.5 million. Drawing on a report by Edward Gresser, Tsutomu also offers a broader explanation for Japan's success in global culture, attributing it to a proliferation of economic cooperation and cultural and educational exchanges between East Asian countries, with regional trade now accounting for 55 percent of the exports of countries in the region.[26] These figures shed light on the circulation of goods and services in East Asia, but it is necessary to also understand the place of cuteness—or a particular type of cuteness, *kawaii*—in Japanese culture, how *kawaii* became a commodity, and how that commodity became part of a shared culture in East Asia, as markets and popular culture became regionalized. Only then can we place the marketing of *Peanuts* in Asia within the context of its reception under a rubric of "cute."

THE ORIGIN OF *KAWAII*

Sianne Ngai has tied the rise of *kawaii* figures in Japan post–World War II to that nation's defeat in war and the feelings brought on by that defeat; *kawaii* captured a certain feeling of helplessness. As Kanako Shiokawa tells it, the word *kawaii* evolved over time in Japan from an original meaning associated with pity and empathy and those who engendered such responses, to capturing a certain "charm" in such helplessness.[27] The word became associated with perceived feminine qualities during the shogunate period.[28] Shiokawa argues that *kawaii* lacks a firm meaning and is anything that is "charming, likable, plush, fluffy, endearing, acceptable, desirable, or some combination of the above. However, the term is also strangely nondescript, for it lacks specific external features that are required in adjectives such as *utsukushii* (beautiful) or *minikui* (ugly). Personal taste is the determining factor for things and persons being described as *kawaii*." In a sense, *kawaii* is best described by what it is not: threatening.[29] Japanese manga in the 1960s and 1970s contributed to shaping notions of *kawaii* as essentially a quality associated with girls, and in the 1970s *kawaii* stationery expanded the aesthetic to a more highly commodified cultural form that spread to styles of pop music, clothing, stuffed animal toys, and cell phone cases.[30] An important part of this phenomenon was the development of J-pop, a highly packaged form of pop music featuring cute boys and girls performing in musical groups. J-pop is not so much about the music as about the personalities, who are carefully crafted and presented to the public through a range of activities including taking star turns in commercials. J-pop took Asia by storm in the 1990s and early 2000s, with several music companies releasing compilation albums but only in non-Japanese markets such as Hong Kong, Singapore, Thailand, Indonesia, and Malaysia.[31] The epitome of *kawaii*, the Hello Kitty brand, dates from 1974, and that character's rise roughly charts the rise of *kawaii* style first in Japan, then extending throughout East Asia, and finally across the globe. So successful has *kawaii* been in East Asian cultures that Korean cultural producers have been able to adopt its styles and formats and release a wave of K-pop that replicates much of J-pop's earlier success.

PEANUTS AND KAWAII

RM Enterprises began opening Snoopy cafés and later Charlie Brown Cafés in East and Southeast Asia in the late 1990s, at a time when Japan's *kawaii* style was sweeping the region. Snoopy's popularity in Japan, and what Japanese audiences wanted from the character, offered a model for ways to market the character across the rest of East Asia. The decision to open cafés might seem questionable given the eventual failure of so many of them, but as a strategy for providing a base for the brand to market plush toys and associated knickknacks, it made good sense. Since 1990, the consumption of coffee in East and Southeast Asia has been on the rise. A report from the London-based International Coffee Organization shows that consumption has increased from "8.4 million 60kg bags in 1990 to 19.5 million bags in 2012." To be sure, this was mostly in powdered form, but there is also an expanding market for what might be called prestige coffee like the Starbucks brand.[32] Indeed, these sorts of coffeehouse chains offer something more than simply serving coffee to drink, just as J-pop offered more than music. As Stefano Ponte put it: "Coffee bar chains sell ambience and a social positioning more than just 'good' coffee."[33] Throughout East and Southeast Asia, the numerous coffee chains of this nature have expanded dramatically. Reasons for this vary, but in part coffee drinking in such places represents the attainment of status. For instance, an international marketing textbook cites the Singaporean academic Francis Yim: "Coffeehouses are a sign that Singaporeans have achieved the status of a developed nation and we are breaking new ground in the area of becoming a cultured society."[34]

RM Enterprises then attempted to tie the *Peanuts* brand to two distinct trends in East and Southeast Asia: the growing desire for *kawaii* figures whether of Japanese origin or not, and the desire to visit a brand-name coffee establishment. What Charlie Brown and Snoopy were selling was not so much coffee and cakes but the *Peanuts* experience. Because *kawaii* has no firm characteristics other than not being threatening, the *Peanuts* gang, which is composed of children, Snoopy, and Woodstock, could appeal to the *kawaii* cultural zeitgeist. The *Peanuts* experience is a world where adults are nonexistent, or at most an annoying distraction, signified in the animated features through comical trumpet noises to represent adult speech. In an article about McDonald's, Singapore sociologist Chua Beng Huat notes that the process of ingesting McDonald's is an act of willing modernity through consumption choice, but in the Singapore context it is not an investment in Americanness. He argues that McDonald's inserted itself into the Singapore scene.[35] In much the same way, RM Enterprises has tried to insert the *Peanuts* gang into the East and Southeast Asian scene by situating the characters within a seemingly pan-Asian aesthetic of *kawaii*. Despite the failure of many of the cafés to build a successful business, Charlie Brown and Snoopy have not suffered unduly as brands.

LI & FUNG: GLOBAL BRANDS

In 2012, Li & Fung, a Hong Kong–based international sourcing firm, acquired RM Enterprises. Li & Fung provides services for a variety of global brands and retailers. The core of the business is supplying customers with goods to sell. Li & Fung's role stretches from design to sourcing the materials and manufactures needed to actually make the products. The company also runs a logistics business. The *New York Times* reported that Li & Fung is the world's largest sourcing and logistics company. Primarily they operate in the garment industry, but their reach extends beyond that sector to other products.[36] The company also operates a separate retail division that owns the Asian operation of Toys "R" Us, including stores in China, Singapore, Taiwan, Malaysia, Thailand, Macau, and the Philippines.

In 2005, Li & Fung entered the brand management business. Between 2005 and 2014 they acquired ten firms that concentrated on licensing characters, including RM Enterprises. They also acquired eight firms that offered brand-name goods in accessories such as shoes and handbags and in children's fashion. The firm moved into the home textile and accessory business and signed long-term licenses for Spyder skiwear and Juicy Couture casual wear. In May 2014, Li & Fung spun this business off as a separate company, Global Brands, listing the new firm on the Hong Kong stock exchange. Global Brands has a deal in place with the world's leading brand management company, Iconix, to handle their portfolio of fashion and lifestyle brands in Southeast Asia, Korea, and Europe. Some of the major brands the company holds licenses for are Quiksilver, Under Armour, Disney, and Calvin Klein, and they have done brand management for Mercedes-Benz, Jeep, and Coca-Cola, expanding these names into new product fields.[37]

The tie-up between Iconix and Global Brand brought together the major stakeholders in licensing Charlie Brown and Snoopy in Asia. There are many licensing channels in Asia that these two giants will avail themselves of, and whether they will turn their attention to fixing the problems with the Charlie Brown Cafés is uncertain. If their strategy is for these cafés to act as a focus for the brand, then two key problems need to be addressed. First, the quality of the food is uneven, and this may be damaging the brand. The weight of negative comments on blogs and travel sites is directed at the food, and although this has not yet spilled over into criticism of the brand, such negative associations may have some lasting impact in Asia. Another problem seems to be the location of some of the cafés. Both the café in Penang and the café in Beijing that I visited were not in readily accessible areas. Many of the Charlie Brown Cafés in Korea that have since closed were also not in prime locations. The café in Hong Kong, which is the flagship Charlie Brown Café and the longest lasting, is well located, close to public transport and in an area with abundant pedestrian traffic. The Singapore café has recently moved from what was a semi-outdoor café with good access to pedestrian traffic but nonetheless exposed to the tropical weather, to an indoor site in a youth-oriented mall. But the recently opened Shanghai and Bangkok cafés seem to be in satellite areas. The cafés have extended the *Peanuts* brand into a new geographic region, but at the cost of some of the brand's luster. Nonetheless, by providing opportunities for *Peanuts*' audiences in Asia to interact with the characters through a *kawaii* aesthetic, the characters' owners have successfully engaged a global market.

NOTES

1. Matthew Freeman, "Advertising the Yellow Brick Road: Historicizing the Industrial Emergence of Transmedia Storytelling," *International Journal of Communication* 8 (2014): 2377.

2. Jonathan Gray, *Show Sold Separately: Promos, Spoilers, and Other Media Paratexts* (New York: New York University Press, 2010). See also Ian Gordon, "Refiguring Media: Tee Shirts as a Site of Audience Engagement with Superheroes," *Information Society* 32, no. 5 (2016).

3. Beth Snyder Bulik, "It's a Great Franchise, Charlie Brown," *Advertising Age*, May 3, 2010, 14.

4. See http://www.snoopy.co.jp/sukusuku/blog/2015/05/5–2.html; and http://sj.snoopy.co.jp/schedule.html; http://town.snoopy.co.jp/company.

5. Fran Wrigley, "Good Grief! It's a Snoopy-Themed Japanese Tea House!," *Rocket News*, April 9, 2014, at http://en.rocketnews24.com/2014/04/09/good-grief-its-a-snoopy-themed-japanese-tea-house.

6. Jean Schulz, "Visiting Universal Studios Japan," Charles M. Schulz Museum, October 30, 2013, at https://schulzmuseum.org/universal-studios-japan/.

7. "Snoopy's World," RM Licensing, at http://www.rmlicensing.com/eng/snoopy/snoopyworld.htm; "World's Biggest Snoopy-Themed Park to Be Built in Guangdong," Xinhua, January 15, 2003, at http://www.china.org.cn/english/culture/53603.htm; Sandy Li, "Snoopy Vies for Place in Shanghai Theme Park," *South China Morning Post*, January 27, 2003, B4; and Jean Schulz, "Visiting Snoopy Garden in Beijing," Charles M. Schulz Museum, October 9, 2013, at https://schulzmuseum.org/visiting-snoopy-garden-beijing/.

8. "Snoopy Land, Taipei, Taiwan," RM Licensing, at http://web.archive.org/web/20060412004339/http://www.rmlicensing.com/ENG/snoopy/snoopyland.htm; "Snoopy Ladies Fashion Store, Shanghai, China," RM Licensing, at http://web.archive.org/web/20100719115344/http://www.rmlicensing.com/ENG/snoopy/shop/ladies_fashion_china/html/snoopyladies.htm; and "Snoopy Children Apparel Store, China," RM Licensing, at http://web.archive.org/web/20100719100504/http://www.rmlicensing.com/ENG/snoopy/shop/store_children_apparel/html/snoopy_children_apparel_store_china.htm.

9. Cheryl Tan, "Charlie Brown Cafe Penang Straits Quay: Let's Party with the *Peanuts* Gang," the Princess Diaries, at http://www.princesscheryl.com/2011/04/charlie-brown-cafe-straits-quay-penang.html.

10. Darren, "Revisiting Charlie Brown Cafe @ Straits Quay, Penang," Eaterland, April 24, 2011, at http://eaterland.blogspot.sg/2011/04/revisiting-charlie-brown-cafe-straits.html.

11. Sam Ong, "1st Charlie Brown Cafe Malaysia @ Straits Quay, Tanjong Tokong, Penang (Halal)," Eat Out with Sam, August 9, 2011, at http://eatoutsam.blogspot.sg/2011/08/charlie-brown-cafe-malaysia-straits.html.

12. Eunice Chew, "Charlie Brown Café: Straits Quay, Penang," Love the Life, at http://lurvethelife.blogspot.sg/2012/12/charlie-brown-cafe-straits-quay-penang.html#.UkFXoH_9VyK.

13. Pennie Yen Sun, "Charlie Brown Café, Straits Quay Penang," My Life, My Style, at http://pennieyensun.blogspot.sg/2012/02/charlie-brown-cafe-straits-quay-penang .html.

14. "Charlie Brown Cafe," TripAdvisor, at http://www.tripadvisor.com.sg/Restaurant_ Review-g660694-d2146251-Reviews-Charlie_Brown_Cafe-Penang_Island_Penang.html.

15. Sean, "Charlie Brown Cafe @ KLCC," Eat Drink KL, December 23, 2011, at http:// eatdrinkkl.blogspot.sg/2011/12/charlie-brown-cafe-klcc.html.

16. Kim Choo, "Charlie Brown Cafe, Penang," December 9, 2012, at http://choolicious .blogspot.sg/2012/12/charlie-brown-cafe-penang.html.

17. "Charlie Brown Cafe," Open Rice, post by MinnaMcmug, October 10, 2010, at http://www.openrice.com/english/restaurant/commentdetail.htm?commentid=212274 6&tc=sr2&con=rvw.

18. Mak Wei Shan, personal correspondence with the author, October 15, 2013.

19. Michael G. Yu, "Snoopy Fever in Hong Kong," Rappler, May 21, 2013, at http:// www.rappler.com/life-and-style/travel/29628-good-grief-peanuts-fever-in-hong-kong.

20. Chiu Yen Phua, "Honeymoon Dessert," December 1, 2011, at http://phuachiuyen .blogspot.sg/2011/12/honeymoon-dessert.html.

21. "Charlie Brown Cafe," Foursquare, post by An Xiao, February 24, 2011, at https:// foursquare.com/v/charlie-brown-cafe/4b7fd62af964a5200f4030e3.

22. Weixin micro channel video, at http://mp.weixin.qq.com/mp/appmsg/show?__bi z=MjM5Mzc2NzE3NA==&appmsgid=10000034&itemidx=1&sign=7944b15ad5d84oddef 1f6e1d178b2242&uin=MTA5NTgyMTQ4Mw%3D%3D&key=234b3ec6051a4a54a40738ad 242d88a00626dc76fd49b9e59bbfca82141174957f6cfb4abc554d55a8d01db3e95dbb24&de vicetype=iPhone+OS7.0.4&version=15000311&lang=zh_CN.

23. Elle, "Charlie Brown Theme Cafe's in Korea + Incheon Airport Location Visit!," Cute in Korea, November 12, 2012, at http://cuteinkorea.com/charlie-brown -theme-cafes-in-korea-incheon-airport-location-visit/.

24. "Charlie Brown Cafe, Thailand," Facebook, comments on April 16, 2015, at https:// www.facebook.com/CharlieBrownCafeThai#_=_; and "Charlie Brown Cafe at Mega Bangna," TripAdvisor, at http://www.tripadvisor.com/Restaurant_Review-g644049- d7367276-Reviews-Charlie_Brown_Cafe_at_Mega_Bangna-Bang_Phli_Samut_Prakan_ Province.html#REVIEWS.

25. Nissim Kadosh Otmazgin, *Regionalizing Culture: The Political Economy of Japanese Popular Culture in Asia* (Honolulu: University of Hawai'i Press, 2014), 51–52, 81–87.

26. Sugiura Tsutomu, "Japan's Creative Industries: Culture as a Source of Soft Power in the Industrial Sector," in *Soft Power Superpowers: Cultural and National Assets of Japan and the United States*, ed. Watanabe Yasushi and David L. McConnell (New York: M. E. Sharpe, 2008), 128–53; and Edward Gresser, "The Emerging Asian Union? China Trade, Asian Investment, and a New Competitive Challenge," Progressive Policy Institute, Policy Report, May 2004, at http://web.archive.org/web/http://www.ppionline.org/ documents/china_trade_0504.pdf.

27. Sianne Ngai, "The Cuteness of the Avant-Garde," *Critical Inquiry* 31, no. 4 (Summer 2005): 819.

28. Kanako Shiokawa, "Cute but Deadly: Women and Violence in Japanese Comics," in *Themes and Issues in Asian Cartooning: Cute, Cheap, Mad, and Sexy*, ed. John A. Lent (Bowling Green, OH: Bowling Green State University Popular Press, 1999), 95.

29. Ibid., 93–94.

30. Ibid., 100–102; and Otmazgin, *Regionalizing Culture*, 134.

31. Otmazgin, *Regionalizing Culture*, 110.

32. International Coffee Organization, "Coffee Consumption in East and Southeast Asia, 1990–2012," February 27, 2014, at http://www.ico.org/news/icc-112-4e-consumption-asia.pdf.

33. Stefano Ponte, "The 'Latte Revolution'? Regulation, Markets and Consumption in the Global Coffee Chain," *World Development* 30, no. 7 (2002): 1099.

34. Masaaki Kotabe and Kristiaan Helsen, *Global Marketing Management* (New York: John Wiley, 2001), 642.

35. Chua Beng Huat, "Singaporeans Ingesting McDonald's," in *Life Is Not Complete without Shopping: Consumption Culture in Singapore* (Singapore: National University of Singapore Press, 2003), 121–38.

36. Ian Urbina and Keith Bradsher, "Linking Factories to the Malls, Middleman Pushes Low Costs," *New York Times*, August 8, 2013.

37. "Our History," Global Brands Group, at http://www.globalbrandsgroup.com/about/history.

-13-

CHIPS OFF THE OL' BLOCKHEAD

Evidence of Influence in *Peanuts* Parodies

GENE KANNENBERG JR.

In the January 4, 2000, installment of the syndicated comics panel *Speed Bump* by Dave Coverly, a man sits before a booth labeled "Psychiatric Care 5¢—The Doctor Is Retired." The man thinks to himself, "Now that's depressing . . ." Of course, newspaper readers were expected to recognize that Coverly's strip served as an homage to the achievement of Charles Schulz and his comic strip, *Peanuts*. Lucy Van Pelt's psychiatrist's booth has become both a cultural symbol and an iconic emblem of the strip, and in Coverly's panel it stands as a synecdoche for *Peanuts* itself. The outpouring of editorials and testimonials that appeared on the news of Charles Schulz's retirement and subsequent passing, like Coverly's, marked only the latest manifestation of the regard in which Schulz and *Peanuts* have been held in American (and even international) culture. *Peanuts* became arguably the most successful American comic strip in the form's century-long history, measured in newspaper subscriptions; book publications; adaptations for film, television, and the stage; and, of course, merchandizing and advertising. Not surprisingly, given the strip's enormous popularity and longevity, cartoonists have long expressed their appreciation for Schulz and their influence from *Peanuts* through the comics form itself. Parodies utilizing the strip's characters and themes have appeared in print for decades, from *Mad* magazine in the 1950s and 1960s to Art Spiegelman and Françoise Mouly's avant-garde comics anthology *Raw* in the 1980s and 1990s, and beyond.

These comics-form homages generally follow one of two paths, either using the *Peanuts* characters (or slightly altered versions thereof) to comment on themes and cultural situations outside the strip's typical purview, or to acknowledge *Peanuts* or Schulz outright as objects of influence.

At times, the two forms conflate; for example, some examples discuss Charles Schulz while depicting him as Charlie Brown, as in the satirical "Dry Roasted Peanuts" by Gary Kell, published in the comics anthology *Comix Compendium* in 1992—years before Schulz's retirement was even anticipated. Schulz (drawn to resemble Charlie Brown) goes to hell for overmarketing his characters, as informed by the Devil (drawn as Lucy sitting inside a booth reading "Gates of Hell 5¢").[1] Such examples, which would number in the hundreds if not thousands over nearly fifty years, speak to Schulz's achievement in creating characters and situations that have the ability to address a wide variety of themes, even if occasionally the parodies are not entirely respectful.

This essay discusses a small sampling of these examples in order to illustrate the influence Schulz and *Peanuts* have had on generations of cartoonists by focusing on the mechanism of parody itself as it operates in the comics form. In doing so, I hope to show how the original *Peanuts* distills cultural experience in ways that allow for—and even facilitate—reinterpretation.

I must begin by stating that my use of the word "parody" in this chapter's title is somewhat misleading. The examples I shall discuss usually do not parody *Peanuts* itself; rather, they use the form of the *Peanuts* strip to comment on other texts, be they literary or cultural. Indeed, an even more straightforward parody of *Peanuts*, like the "Peanuts 2000" installment of Peter Kuper's *New York Minute*, still draws upon outside referents from our own society. Subtitled "You can see it everywhere, the times they are a-changin'," the strip illustrates four scenarios: Lucy's temper becomes litigious; Schroeder's piano boasts a bust not of Beethoven but of Marilyn Manson; a rabid Snoopy stars in "When Pets Attack!"; and Charlie Brown responds to the laughter of other children by thinking "We'll see if they laugh at my Dad's *gun*."[2] The incongruity of *Peanuts* characters in such contexts is momentarily humorous, yet it quickly morphs into a reflection on the everyday events we hear about in the news. At its most typical, *Peanuts* never dealt with issues as directly as do such appropriations. The juxtaposition of the humorous with the graphic, the patina of nostalgic innocence with the underlying baseness of contemporary society, gives examples like this their interpretive space, their emotional weight. *Peanuts*, and the associations readers bring to it, is used by parodists as one-half of a dual-focused narrative system.

My interest in comics parody in this chapter hinges on the form's double-coded nature, appropriating different works either to create a comically incongruous structure or for comic dramatic effect. Here I follow Margaret A. Rose's 1993 *Parody: Ancient, Modern, and Post-Modern.* In essence, the parodist decodes an existing text and reencodes it, transforming it for the amusement of an audience. This audience is generally presupposed to be familiar with the source text, although, as Rose notes, the audience "may come to know [the source text] through its evocation in the parody itself, and to understand the discrepancy between it and the parody text through the latter."[3]

There can, of course, be more than one base text in a parody, which complicates the issue in interesting ways. Witness, for example, "Good Ol' Gregor Brown" by R. Sikoryak, published in the influential anthology *Raw* in 1990, which uses two source texts: *Peanuts* and Kafka's "Metamorphosis."[4] The hypothetical—and actual—audience for this strip can be expected to have at least a passing familiarity with both *Peanuts* and the Kafka story. Its primary base text is in fact "Metamorphosis," with *Peanuts* being a second interpretive system used to adapt the story. This is an act of not just adaptation, not just retelling, but of translation in terms of both form and idiom. Sikoryak's achievement here also includes adapting situations to each other, marrying Kafka's narrative incidents to Schulz's daily strip form as well as to its rhythms and typical situations. We note that the individual strips that make up "Gregor Brown" themselves function in the same ways as do "real" *Peanuts* strips: the situations and even character types are the same, the rhythm of the presentation is the same, and the mechanics of the joke or payoff at the end of each strip is the same. Sikoryak not only uses the *Peanuts* characters to retell Kafka's story, he utilizes the day-to-day strip continuity to break down the narrative into smaller, punch-line-punctuated units.

The humor here stems, of course, from incongruity: this adaptation is not only in comics form but in the so-ordinary and commonplace idiom of Charlie Brown and company's daily newspaper episodes. Yet Sikoryak's comic itself, I would argue, becomes even more humorous as we read it and recognize the suitability of Sikoryak's chosen idiom. Both Kafka's prose and Schulz's strip are known for their combination of the ordinary and the bizarre, of faith and existential dread. Recall that in one 1970s-era *Peanuts* sequence, Charlie Brown hallucinates that the sun has turned into a giant baseball, and his own head becomes marked with a rash resembling baseball stitches. Using the *Peanuts* cast to adapt Kafka's story ultimately seems perfectly fitting—a conclusion that can itself bring a smile to a reader's face just as readily as does Sikoryak's stylistic mimicry of Lucy/Grete's exclamation, "Gregor, you blockhead!!"

Sikoryak's example demonstrates one of the strengths of comic art—its own inherently dual-coded communicative system. Given Schulz's oft-stated reluctance to see his creation as Great Art, I am sure he would have cringed a bit at the application of the term *visual literature* to describe comic art—but Sikoryak's parody allows us to see its applicability. Eric Vos has defined visual literature as "[t]he use of visual means of representation in a literary context."[5] For Vos, visual literature exists not as a "hybrid" form between literature and visual art but rather as a system in which verbal and visual symbols retain their traditional denotative functions while affecting each other in complex, form-determined ways. For the purposes of this chapter, I am interested primarily in how our reading of both *Peanuts* strips and their various parodies is informed by their appearance—by the ways in which we read and understand what we see on the page. About visual literature, Vos states:

> [O]ne and the same semiotic procedure underlies the integration of the verbal and the visual. In both cases, that is, we are dealing with not a unilateral referential relationship from sign to referent that we could call iconicity, but with a bi- or even trilateral relationship from the sign to some concept that in turn refers back to a characteristic of the sign in question and leads us toward contemplating conventions of verbal and literary communication.[6]

In clarifying his idea that there is "one and the same semiotic procedure underl[ying] the integration of the verbal and the visual," Vos continues:

> [E]xemplification and complex reference are totally unconcerned with boundaries between media and art forms. As exemplifying symbols, verbal and visual signs function in exactly the same way. This and only this is what allows us to speak of semiotic integration of the verbal and the visual.[7]

The semiotic basis of the statement is open to challenge; verbal signs, as units of a system of language, clearly follow systems of grammatical and syntactical rules that images do not. But visual literature's

Fig. 13.1: R. Sikoryak, "Good Ol' Gregor Brown" (detail), *Raw* 2, no. 2 (1990): 178.1–9. The first tier recalls the initial title panel of a typical *Peanuts* Sunday episode, while each subsequent tier reads as a daily *Peanuts* strip, complete with gag ending. ©1990 R. Sikoryak.

enterprise—to use visual means of representation narratively—asks readers to reconsider the binary opposition between word and image by blurring distinctions between the two. And what we find in comic parodies, broadly defined, is indeed a weave of signifying systems at play. Specifically, when we see a non-Schulz *Peanuts* comic story, we read that story with expectations raised by the appearance of the images and situations that are presented. When we see a "Lucy" holding a football, we expect that a "Charlie Brown" will fail in his task, spectacularly, due to "Lucy's" treachery. There is, loosely speaking, an interpretative system assumed and encoded by the cartoonist/parodist whenever received images are used in comics parody.

Another way of examining the integration of systems into a single form of communication may be seen in Robert E. Horn's *Visual Language*.

Fig. 13.2: Charles Schulz, *Peanuts*, June 15, 1973. PEANUTS © 1973 Peanuts Worldwide LLC. Dist. by UNIVERSAL UCLICK. Reprinted with permission. All rights reserved.

Horn makes the claim that visual language—that is, communication that combines words and images into a single system—has a specific grammar of its own, above and beyond that of the words (of whatever language) that are contained within. Comics, for Horn, in fact represents one type of visual language, and he notes that the most common conventions of the comics form (panel shapes and arrangements, word balloon appearance, and graphic shorthands such as speed lines) are themselves integral parts of semantics of visual language.[8] Horn follows the work of Evelyn Goldsmith in basing his grammar on the concept of visual "unities"—that is, on dealing with recognizable constructs, whether representational or simply those that adhere to the Gestalt principles of group identity.[9]

While Horn's systematic overview of visual language's morphology, syntax, pragmatics, and rhetoric lies beyond the scope of this brief chapter, it is important to note that Horn stresses the importance of "semantic fusion and tight integration—not mere juxtaposition—to convey meaning" in visual language; readers can only be expected to infer systematic relationships among juxtaposed visual elements when they share a common context to aid in perception.[10]

Ultimately, Horn's grammar seems to work on the level of a metaphor. His book does enumerate several representational schema that explore a potential range of applications possible using visual language, but even this same book, itself written using visual language, uses techniques that extend the borders that its argument attempts to define. I am yet to be convinced that even comics, a subset of visual language, can be described by a recognizable and all-encompassing structural grammar; conventions come and go, and even apparently common visual tropes can mean very different things to readers from different cultural backgrounds. Horn's attempt to create a concrete grammar for visual communication may be an impossible goal, but the path he delineates nevertheless is well worth considering.

I do see a benefit in addressing the concept of a visual grammar on a more metaphorical level. If a grammar consists of established rules and patterns of communication, we can see, at least, parallels arising within the traditions of individual daily comic strips. Readers are expected to understand the traditional systems of visual symbolic interaction across different instances from a series; such pictorial interactions become, in Horn's words, instances of tight integration wherein readers interpret the individual images as parts of larger symbolic systems. I, of course, use *Peanuts* as my exemplar here. If a *Peanuts* strip depicts Charlie Brown standing on his pitcher's mound, either he will be knocked over or Lucy will disappoint him; if Schroeder plays his piano while Lucy rests against it, the topic of love is at hand—whereas if Snoopy is nearby, the stage is set for a graphic interpretation of the power of music.

From the structure of the visual elements in a particular *Peanuts* strip, a reader familiar with the strip approaches the new iteration with certain expectations. Part of the fun—the humor—in reading these strips is seeing how the conventions will be used this time, what will be done to reinforce or even slightly expand our notions of possibility with these characters. Such is the nature of serial storytelling.

This acquired grammar—this prior knowledge of the strip's characters, situations, and themes—is an interpretive element presupposed by the creators of so-called parodies. It is assumed not only that readers will recognize these characters as (imperfect) copies of Schulz's own, but also that they will recognize and have certain expectations of the situations presented. In effect, these parodies assume that their audience has already internalized at least one interpretive code, a mode of speech—*Peanuts* proper—and then can add additional codes to it, in order to draw out extended meanings above and beyond the narrative incidents.

Peanuts parody examples all rely upon our prior conceptual knowledge of *Peanuts* for their message—whatever it is—to function. The visual motifs of the comic strips serve as the context in which the parody takes place—even in comics, this parodic element finds its expression in the words just as much as, if not more than, in the images. In this sense, we find that the dual coding of comics' blend of words and pictures in itself is not inherently parodic; however, by its very nature, comics can be adapted quite easily to such a use.

A final example of a *Peanuts* parody serves as a tour-de-force meditation on Schulz's career using his own tools. In "Abstract Thought Is a

The news that Charles (Sparky) Schulz, the 77-year-old creator of "Peanuts," was retiring his almost 50-year-old strip to fight cancer was recognized as a genuine Millennial Event. The end of the most popular comic strip ever was greeted by an outpouring of grief and affection not seen since Paris buried Victor Hugo.

Fig. 13.3: Art Spiegelman, "Abstract Thought Is a Warm Puppy" (detail), *New Yorker*, February 14, 2000.

Warm Puppy," Art Spiegelman presents an extended meditation on the significance of *Peanuts* and of Schulz.[11] The significance and resonance of this *New Yorker* comics essay was made all the more poignant by its publication only days before Schulz's passing. Spiegelman mimics Schulz's line—his drawings, when he wishes them to, do resemble Schulz's own, although not to the extent of Sikoryak's earlier example. More importantly, however, Spiegelman manages to replicate the fluidity and adaptability of Schulz's story types, both their narrative strategies and their visual structure. The various styles and structures used in constructing his argument demonstrate graphically the narrative schemes at Schulz's disposal as a cartoonist.

The first panel of the comics essay is a painted image, which, while not executed in Schulz's style, captures two of the strip's most well-known visual symbols of frustration—the football and the kite in the tree—juxtaposing them with the essay's first word, "Sigh." This word is lettered in an approximation of Schulz's own lettering style (as is much of the text in the accompanying essay, including any dialogue text) and includes Schulz's characteristic diacritical marks.[12] Spiegelman's comparison, in this first panel, of the public reaction to Schulz's retirement to Paris's mourning of Victor Hugo might seem at first to be an attempt to create a comic juxtaposition of high and low, but the somber image that Spiegelman uses here mitigates any apparently conflicting tones. And the arguments he develops as the essay continues, even though couched in Schulz's own "lightweight" visual metaphors and syntax, serve to reinforce the gravity of the initial panel.

Apart from this first panel on the first page and the other painted panel on the third and final page, Spiegelman constructs his essay as a series of *Peanuts* strips, both Sunday and daily versions. In figure 13.4, Spiegelman changes his "strip format" to a two-panel box format,

Fig. 13.4: Art Spiegelman, "Abstract Thought Is a Warm Puppy" (detail), *New Yorker*, February 14, 2000.

mimicking the example reproduced in the adjoining painting. This box format was one of the selling points of the strip to newspaper editors in its early years; the strip's initially unaltered four-square approach to storytelling allowed it to be presented either as a strip or as a square, thus giving editors leeway in designing their comics pages.

In Spiegelman's visual essay we can think of each "strip" as a paragraph or unit of meaning that structures the essay, as each strip-form contains a developed idea in Spiegelman's argument. These "dailies" (the black-and-white four-panel strips) are all based on the strip's original four-panel version. In each of the individual "strips," Spiegelman follows the rhythms and punch lines of the original strips, as did Sikoryak in the Kafka example. He similarly incorporates the initial tier of panels of the color "Sunday strips" into his argument, using these large display panels as places to contain a large amount of text. In the actual Sunday *Peanuts* strips, Schulz needed to make sure that the first two panels were optional, as newspapers could choose whether or not to include these panels in their published versions. Spiegelman violates this rule here in service to his essay, but visually the examples recall their exemplars.

The final tier of panels on the essay's third page replicates *Peanuts'* annual football kicking scene, except Lucy is replaced by the Grim Reaper and the football by "the bucket," mixing visual metaphors. Ironically in

Fig. 13.5: Charles Schulz, *Peanuts*, October 2, 1950. PEANUTS © 1950 Peanuts Worldwide LLC. Dist. by UNIVERSAL UCLICK. Reprinted with permission. All rights reserved.

Spiegelman's example, Death does not allow Charlie Brown to kick the bucket, a commentary on how *Peanuts* has developed, if not an actual immortality, at least an endurance that transcends even the end of the strip's original run.

Spiegelman's question in the final panel—"How did 'Peanuts' consistently depict genuine pain and loss and still keep everything so warm and fuzzy?"—is one he has worked to answer indirectly throughout the three-page essay. As each strip-paragraph concludes, Spiegelman punctuates his various anecdotes or observations in a way identical to how Schulz ended his strips, using what I've called the grammar of the *Peanuts* strip form: Snoopy usurping a situation to his own fantasy ends; a wry observation from a *very* young character; embarrassed frustration; despondently resting one's head against a tree; a parting thought from Snoopy; a brick-wall discussion; a sublime recognition of one's own insignificance; and, of course, that frustrated football kick. The attitude in *Peanuts* may be warm and fuzzy, but it acknowledges more than most "serious" comic strips the presence of disappointment and pain in our everyday lives—not just in comically charged situations but even in our most mundane acts.

In the years immediately following Schulz's death in 2000, there was a flood of parody tributes along the lines of Spiegelman's graphic essay. The often emotionally reticent Chris Ware, for example, meditated on his own passionate attachment to *Peanuts* in a 2003 tribute.[13] The narration describes his own similarities as a child with Charlie Brown: the kind of kid who ate lunch alone, who rarely received Valentines. But one silent panel on the lower tier of the "Sunday" strip articulates more clearly than the textual narration what *Peanuts* meant to the younger Ware, as we see the cartoonist as a child sharing an imaginary lunch with Charlie Brown. Together, both of them appear less lonely, more wholly connected to the world, than either would have been alone.

Fig. 13.6: Curtis Franklin and Chris Haley, "Lil' Folks," Let's Be Friends Again, July 14, 2009.

Ware's comic serves as more than simply a sentimental tribute, however. Where Spiegelman's adoption of Schulz's style serves in part to contrast his own "natural" style with that of the commercial comic strip he had only recently learned to fully appreciate, Ware—who came of age when Schulz's fame and influence were at their height—makes clear in his comic how much his own style has been indebted to Schulz from the start. In so articulating this genealogy, he also indirectly claims for the alternative comics tradition to which he is affiliated—both his own *Jimmy Corrigan: The Smartest Kid on Earth* (2000) but also the rising graphic novel more generally—a genealogy that traces back not to the commercial comic book but to newspaper as epitomized by *Peanuts*.

In the past decade, however, we have seen a rise of *Peanuts* parodies that return to the pre-mourning phase epitomized by Sikoryak's "Good Ol' Gregor Brown." But whereas Sikoryak's 1990 comic was published in *Raw* magazine, the epitome of comics' high print culture ambitions in the years leading up to the rise of the graphic novel, these new parodies are most often published and circulated in new media formats. Produced by cartoonists much younger than Spiegelman (born in 1948, two years before the start of *Peanuts*) or Ware (born in 1967), the most recent *Peanuts* parodies take their deepest inspiration from the logic of new media itself: the composite, the mash-up, and the remix.

In 2011, for example, Charles Forsman shared a comic "mashing up 2 of my all-time favorites: Spielberg and Benchley's *Jaws* drawn like Schulz's *Peanuts*."[14] The series of strips reveals in its overlay of two very different texts something we might not previously have fully appreciated in either of the sources of the parody. For example, Charlie Brown as Chief Brody allows us to see more clearly the haplessness and isolation of Brody in *Jaws* and the courage and resilience of Charlie Brown in *Peanuts*, as he faces down social ostracism and grave personal danger. In the end, such discoveries feel here almost incidental to the pleasure of the mash-up itself—and the rewards of witnessing a young cartoonist showing off his considerable range and skills at the turntables of pop culture. The *Jaws/Peanuts* mash-up, in fact, was an explicit attempt to recapture the alchemy Forsman had put on display a few months earlier with a very popular *Raiders of the Lost Ark* and *Popeye* mash-up.

A more economical but arguably more effective *Peanuts* parody appeared in 2009 in the webcomic *Let's Be Friends Again* by Curtis Franklin and Chris Haley.[15] Here, the very first installment of *Peanuts* from 1950 is reimagined as featuring characters from the Marvel Comics universe: Norman Osborn, Sentry, and, of course, good ol' Spider-Man.

The first strip famously featured Shermy and Patty—the stars of the strip in its earliest weeks but soon exiled by the rising stardom of Charlie Brown, Lucy, and Snoopy—watching Charlie Brown as he slowly walks by, with Shermy finally articulating his hatred for Charlie Brown as soon as he has passed. In the parody version of the strip, the cartoonists allow us to see the deep genome that two very different comics share. While comics historians have acknowledged the affinities between the Marvel Comics of the 1960s and earlier comic book genres (especially the romance genre that Jack Kirby helped pioneer in the late 1940s), this strip allows us to more fully see the influence of Schulz's articulate postwar angst and existential dread. After reading this parody, it is impossible to ever read a panel featuring a hangdog Peter Parker without also superimposing Charlie Brown's shadow behind him.

That same year, a comic on DeviantArt by Ninjaink entitled "That Yellow Shirted Such-And-Such" became an internet sensation.[16] The comic was a mash-up parody of *Peanuts* with Frank Miller's ultraviolent neo-noir *Sin City*. Here, hulking pitcher Charlie Brown faces down his nemesis, the "thumbsucker" Linus, who is taunting him from the batter's

Fig. 13.7: Ninjaink, "That Yellow Shirted Such-And-Such," DeviantArt, March 2009.

box while Charlie Brown's thoughts turn to his sister, Sally, dancing las- civiously for Linus. While the majority of *Peanuts* parodies attempt with varying degrees of success to imitate Schulz's style, Ninjaink instead translates *Peanuts* into Frank Miller's slashing blacks-and-whites, and similarly translates the subtle philosophy and nuanced self-doubt of Charlie Brown into the kill-or-be-killed Manicheanism of Miller's world view. The humor here comes in part from seeing our beloved characters behave so uncharacteristically, but the more lasting humor lies in the parody's highlighting of the banality of Frank Miller's characterizations and recycled Mickey Spillane prose.

One last example from the most recent decade is worth pausing over. In 2013, a Tumblr site appeared titled "This Charming Charlie," featuring mash-ups of *Peanuts* strips with lyrics by the 1980s alternative rock band the Smiths.[17] The Smiths' lyrics are famously operatic in their articula- tions of despair, ennui, and unrequited lust; placed in conjunction with panels from *Peanuts*, the parody worked by allowing the often restrained despair of the pint-sized midwestern philosophers to be transformed into the equivalent of a primal scream. While Morrissey, the Smiths' singer and lyricist, expressed support for the mash-up, Universal Uclick, which controls rights to the comic strips, sent a cease-and-desist order to the site's creator, Lauren LoPrete. LoPrete's lawyers, in turn, claimed that the parodies were covered by the fair use exemption under the copyright code (the Tumblr remains up today). This case serves as a reminder that parody in the Internet age raises new possibilities for mash-ups and remixes unimaginable a generation earlier—but also new challenges and concerns for both parodists and copyright holders alike.

In his essay "What's So Funny about the Comics?," M. Thomas Inge notes that "[c]omedy implies an attitude towards life, an attitude that trusts in a man's potential for redemption and salvation, as in Dante's *Divine Comedy*"; later, in discussing satire, he notes that "[t]o satirize life and institutions is to believe in a better mode of conduct which people fail to live up to, and humor may serve as a gentle but sometimes bitter or angry corrective."[18] Inge compares Charlie Brown to the American comedy stock character type of the "timid soul or the little man trapped in the complexities of modern existence, as represented by Thurber's Walter Mitty, Charlie Chaplin's tramp, or Woody Allen's on-screen character."[19] In his comics essay, Spiegelman portrays a wide variety of *Peanuts*' enduring themes: one small person against a larger, incomprehensible world, seen here in Schulz's own demeanor in conversation; gently satirical responses to unbecoming conduct—the admiration of Spiegelman's young son Dashiel for Lucy; and a belief in redemption even in the face of apparently contrary evidence—Spiegelman's own reevaluation of Schulz and his contributions. These and other themes permeate Spiegelman's essay, themes that are articulated via the medium of comics and storytelling—or, more accurately, Schulz's own method of storytelling.

Elsewhere in *Comics as Culture*, Inge has these words on Great Art—and not coincidentally, on Charles Schulz and *Peanuts*: "A truly significant piece of art, be it visual, plastic, verbal, or musical, is one that draws from the cumulative traditions that have preceded it, at the same time that it reshapes the traditional form in such a way that it gains new life and relevance for the future." *Peanuts*, for Inge, demonstrates the comic strip's "versatility in dealing with the social, psychological, and philosophical tensions of the modern world."[20] I believe that in the *Peanuts* parodies we have examined here, we see the flowering of that versatility, the results of *Peanuts*' relevance for the present and the future. Both in its themes and its approaches to storytelling, Charles Schulz's comic strip gave us new ways to look at the world around us; cartoonists who use his tools and acknowledge their importance allow us to consider anew Schulz's contributions to our storytelling culture.

NOTES

I wrote the initial version of this chapter at the kind invitation of my mentor and friend M. Thomas Inge for the Charles Schultz tribute panel he organized at the Modern Language Association Convention in December 2000. The panel was sponsored by the American Humor Studies Association, and their journal *Studies in American Humor* later published a slightly revised version of that presentation. This new version has been revised and expanded, and I would like gratefully to acknowledge Jared Gardner's editorial guidance and assistance, above and beyond the call of duty.

1. Gary Kell, "Dry Roasted Peanuts," in *Comix Compendium*, ed. Ich Neuman (Toronto: Mangajin, 1992), 96. The last panel of this strip recalls the work of another famous cartoonist, Winsor McCay (1867–1934), by revealing the adventure to be, in Schulz's wife's words, "another bad dream" (panel 8); Schulz is drawn lying next to a bed that looks like the bed used by the main character of McCay's *Little Nemo in Slumberland*, while his wife's comments echo the sentiments expressed in McCay's *Dreams of the Rarebit Fiend*.

2. Peter Kuper, *New York Minute*: "Peanuts 2000," *Daily News* (New York), June 6, 1999, 48.

3. Margaret A. Rose, *Parody: Ancient, Modern, and Post-Modern* (Cambridge: Cambridge University Press, 1993), 39.

4. R. Sikoryak, "Good Ol' Gregor Brown," *Raw* 2, no. 2 (1990): 178–79.

5. Eric Vos, "Visual Literature and Semiotic Conventions," in *The Pictured Word: Word and Image Interactions 2*, ed. Martin Reusser, Claus Cluver, Leo Hoek, and Lauren Weingarden (Amsterdam: Rodopi, 1998), 135.

6. Ibid., 141.

7. Ibid., 144.

8. Robert E. Horn, *Visual Language: Global Communication for the 21st Century* (n.p.: MacroVu Press, 1999), 135–42.

9. Ibid., 69–76.

10. Ibid., 111

11. Art Spiegelman, "Abstract Thought Is a Warm Puppy," *New Yorker*, February 14, 2000, 61–63.

12. The term "diacritical marks" is a bit inaccurate—but only a bit; as graphic symbols, they do influence the reading of the words they surround. As a side note, Italian comics scholar Alvise Mattozzi remarked at the International Comics and Animation Festival in 1999 that, among his friends in Italy, the word "sigh" had become an expression unto itself due to its ubiquity in even translated *Peanuts* strips; people would sometimes say the word "sigh" when they found themselves in situations in which a *Peanuts* character would be likely to utter a sigh.

13. Chris Ware, "Charlie Brown, Snoopy, Linus, Lucy . . .," in *Top Shelf Asks the Big Questions*, ed. Brett Warnock and Robert Goodin (Marietta, GA: Top Shelf, 2003), 282.

14. Charles Forsman, "Show Me the Way to Go Home!," Snake Oil, August 4, 2011, at http://snakeoilcomics.blogspot.com/2011/08/show-me-way-to-go-home.html.

15. Curtis Franklin and Chris Haley, "Lil' Folks," Let's Be Friends Again, July 14, 2009, at http://www.letsbefriendsagain.com/2009/07/14/lil-folks/.

16. Ninjaink, "That Yellow Shirted Such-And-Such," DeviantArt, March 2009, at http://ninjaink.deviantart.com/art/Schulz-City-That-Yellow-S-1-115191442.

17. Lauren LoPrete, "This Charming Charlie," Tumblr, at http://thischarmingcharlie .tumblr.com.

18. M. Thomas Inge, Comics as Culture (Jackson: University Press of Mississippi, 1990), 11, 12.

19. Ibid., 15.

20. Ibid., 101.

CONTRIBUTORS

LEONIE BRIALEY is a cartoonist and writer. She recently completed a PhD on autobiographical comics and sincerity at the University of Melbourne.

M. J. CLARKE is an assistant professor in television, film and media studies at California State University, Los Angeles. He has written extensively on television, video games, and comic book art in articles appearing in *Television and New Media, Games and Culture*, and the *Journal of Graphic Novels and Comics*. In 2013, his book *Transmedia Television: New Trends in Network Serial Production* was published by Bloomsbury.

ROY T. COOK is CLA Scholar of the College and professor of philosophy at the University of Minnesota Twin Cities. He is also a resident fellow and member of the governing board of the Minnesota Center for the Philosophy of Science. He has published widely on the philosophy of mathematics, the philosophy of logic, and the aesthetics of popular art (especially comics).

JOSEPH J. DAROWSKI has a PhD from Michigan State University and teaches English at Brigham Young University. He is a member of the editorial review board of the *Journal of Popular Culture* and the editor of *The Ages of Superheroes* essay collections, which include volumes on Superman, Wonder Woman, the X-Men, the Avengers, Iron Man, the Hulk, and the Justice League.

JARED GARDNER is a professor of English at the Ohio State University. He is the author of three monographs, including *Projections: Comics and the Future of Twenty-First-Century Storytelling*, and he is editor of *Inks: The Journal of the Comics Studies Society*.

IAN GORDON is a professor of American history at the National University of Singapore. His books include *Comic Strips and Consumer Culture*, *Superman: The Persistence of an American Icon*, and *Kid Comic Strips: A Genre across Four Countries*. He has coedited two collections of scholarly writings on comics: *Comics and Ideology* (2001) and *Film and Comic Books* (2007). He is an international contributing editor to the *Journal of American History* and on the editorial board of several journals including the *Journal of Graphic Novels and Comics, Popular Communication, Studies in Comics*, and *ImageText*.

GENE KANNENBERG JR. is a former chair of both the International Comic Arts Festival (now Forum) and the Comic Art and Comics Area of the Popular Culture Association. He works at the Melville J. Herskovits Library of African Studies at Northwestern University, and he cartoons at http://comicsmachine.tumblr.com.

CHRISTOPHER P. LEHMAN is a professor of ethnic studies at St. Cloud State University. His book *The Colored Cartoon: Black Representation in American Animated Short Films, 1907–1954* was named a "*Choice* Outstanding Academic Title," and he was awarded a summer visiting fellowship to the W. E. B. Du Bois Institute at Harvard University.

ANNE C. McCARTHY is an assistant professor of English at Penn State University, where she teaches courses in romantic and Victorian literature and literary theory. She has published essays on Tennyson, Coleridge, and Shelley, as well as on romantic aesthetics in popular culture. Her first book, *Awful Parenthesis: Suspension and the Sublime in Romantic and Victorian Poetry*, will be published by the University of Toronto Press.

BEN NOVOTNY OWEN is a PhD candidate in English at the Ohio State University, studying film, graphic narrative, and twentieth-century American literature and art. He has published on race and early sound cinema in *Screen* and has an essay on comics form and the politics of history in the recent collection *The Comics of Joe Sacco: Journalism in a Visual World*. He is currently working on a dissertation about the interrelation of cartoon aesthetics and modernism in the United States during the period 1915–1965.

LARA SAGUISAG is an assistant professor of English at the College of Staten Island, City University of New York. Her forthcoming book, *Incorrigibles and Innocents: Constructions of Childhood and Citizenship in Progressive Era Comics Strips*, examines representations of childhood in late nineteenth- and early twentieth-century comic strips. Her essays on comics, children's literature, and childhood have appeared in various anthologies as well as *Children's Literature Association Quarterly*, the *Lion and the Unicorn*, and the *International Journal of Comic Art*. She has also published eight books for children, the most recent of which are *Animal Games* (Anvil 2007) and *Kara at Play* (Adarna 2016).

BEN SAUNDERS is a professor in the Department of English at the University of Oregon, where he teaches English Renaissance studies and comics studies. He is the author of two books, *Desiring Donne: Poetry, Sexuality, Interpretation* (Harvard University Press, 2006) and *Do the Gods Wear Capes? Spirituality, Fantasy, and Superheroes* (Continuum Press, 2011), and coeditor of two critical anthologies, *Rock over the Edge: Transformations in Popular Music Culture* (Duke University Press, 2002), with Roger Beebe and Denise Fulbrook, and *Comic Book Apocalypse: The Graphic Worlds of Jack Kirby* (IDW, 2015), with Charles Hatfield. He has also published numerous critical essays on a range of topics, from the plays of Shakespeare to the drumming of Keith Moon, and has served as curator for several high-profile exhibitions of comic strip and comic book art. In 2012 he founded the country's first undergraduate minor in comics and cartoon studies at the University of Oregon.

JEFFREY O. SEGRAVE is a professor of health and exercise sciences at Skidmore College, Saratoga Springs, New York, where he has also served as department chair, director of athletics, and dean of special programs. In 2005, he was awarded the David H. Potter Endowed Chair at Skidmore College. He currently serves as codirector of Project Vis, an Andrew W. Mellon–funded program to advance visual literacy at Skidmore. His main area of scholarly interest lies in the sociocultural analysis of sport; hence, he embraces an interdisciplinary approach that seeks to study sport at the intersections of history, sociology, and literature. He has coedited three anthologies on sport and published fifteen book chapters and more than sixty articles in a wide variety of scholarly journals.

MICHAEL TISSERAND is the author of *Krazy: George Herriman, a Life in Black and White* (HarperCollins). His other books include *The Kingdom of Zydeco*, which won the ASCAP–Deems Taylor Award for music writing, and the Hurricane Katrina memoir *Sugarcane Academy*. He lives in New Orleans and on the Internet at www.michaeltisserandauthor.com.

INDEX